GRACE LIVINGSTON HILL

Aunt Crete's Emancipation
The Girl From Montana
The Story of a Whim

Three complete and unabridged novels in one volume

Grace Livingston Hill is one of the most popular authors of all time because of her unique style of combining elements of the Christian faith with tasteful and exciting romance.

Find out why generations of readers of all ages have been entertained and inspired by the fiction of Grace Livingston Hill.

Grace Livingston Hill . . . fiction that fills the heart as well as the spirit!

Barbour Books
164 Mill Street
Westwood, New Jersey 07675

Three Complete Novels In One Arrangement
Copyright ©1988
by Barbour and Company, Inc.
All Rights Reserved
Printed In the United States of America

ISBN 1-55748-014-1

AUNT CRETE'S EMANCIPATION

Chapter 1
A Telegram and a Flight

"Who's at the front door?" asked Luella's mother, coming in from the kitchen with a dish towel in her hand. "I thought I heard the doorbell."

"Luella's gone to the door," said her sister from her vantage point at the crack of the sitting room door. "It looks to me like a telegraph boy."

"It couldn't be, Crete," said Luella's mother impatiently, coming to see for herself. "Who would telegraph now that Hannah's dead?"

Lucretia was short and dumpy, with the comfortable, patient look of the maiden aunt that knows she is indispensable because she will meekly take all the burdens that no one else wants to bear. Her sister could easily look over her head into the hall, and her gaze was penetrative and alert.

"I'm sure I don't know, Carrie," said Lucretia apprehensively, "but I'm all of a tremble. Telegrams are dreadful things."

"Nonsense, Crete, you always act like such a baby. Hurry up, Luella. Don't stop to read it. Your aunt Crete will have a fit. Wasn't there anything to pay? Who is it for?"

Luella, a rather stout young woman in stylish attire, with her mother's keen features unsoftened by sentiment, advanced, irreverently tearing open her mother's telegram and reading it as she came. It was one of the family grievances that Luella was stout like her aunt instead of tall and slender like her mother. The aunt always felt secretly that they somehow blamed her for being of that type. "It makes one so hard to fit," Luella's mother remarked frequently, and adding with a disparaging glance at her sister's dumpy form, "So impossible!"

At such times the aunt always wrinkled up her pleasant little forehead into a V upside down, and trotted off to her kitchen, or her buttonholes, or whatever was the present task, sighing helplessly. She tried to be the best that she could always; but one couldn't help one's figure, especially when one was partly dependent on one's family for support, and dressmakers and tailors took so much money. It was bad enough to have one stout figure to fit in the family without two; and the aunt always felt called upon to have as little dressmaking done as possible, in order that Luella's figure might be improved from the slender treasury. "Clothes do make a big difference," she reflected. And sometimes when she was all

1

alone in the twilight, and there was really nothing that her alert conscience could possibly put her hand to doing for the moment, she amused herself by thinking what kind of dress she would buy, and who should make it, if she should suddenly attain a fortune. But this was a harmless amusement, inasmuch as she never let it make her discontented with her lot, or ruffle her placid brow for an instant.

But just now she was "all of a tremble," and the V in her forehead was rapidly becoming a double V. She watched Luella's dismayed face with growing alarm.

"For goodness' sake alive!" said Luella, flinging herself into the most comfortable rocker, and throwing her mother's telegram on the table. "That's not to be tolerated! Something 'll have to be done. We'll have to go to the shore at once, Mother. I should die of mortification to have a country cousin come around just now. What would the Grandons think if they saw him? I can't afford to ruin all my chances for a cousin I've never seen. Mother, you simply must do something. I won't stand it!"

"What in the world are you talking about, Luella?" said her mother impatiently. "Why didn't you read the telegram aloud, or why didn't you give it to me at once? Where are my glasses?"

The aunt waited meekly while her sister found her glasses, and read the telegram.

"Well, I declare! That is provoking to have him turn up just now of all times. Something must be done, of course. We can't have a gawky westerner around in the way. And, as you say, we've never seen him. It can't make much difference to him whether he sees us or not. We can hurry off, and be conveniently out of the way. It's probably only a duty visit he's paying, anyway. Hannah's been dead ten years, and I always heard the child was more like his father than his mother. Besides, Hannah married and went away to live when I was only a little girl. I really don't think Donald has much claim on us. What a long telegram! It must have cost a lot. Was it paid for? It shows he knows nothing of the world, or he would have put it in a few words. Well, we'll have to get away at once."

She crumpled the telegram into a ball, and flung it to the table again; but it fell wide of its mark, and dropped to the floor instead. The aunt patiently stooped and picked it up, smoothing out the crushed yellow paper.

"Hannah's boy!" she said gently, and she touched the yellow paper as if it had been something sacred.

Am taking a trip east, and shall make you a little visit if convenient. Will be with you sometime on Thursday.

DONALD GRANT

She sat down suddenly in the nearest chair. Somehow the relief from anxiety had made her knees weak. "Hannah's boy!" she murmured again, and laid her hand caressingly over the telegram, smoothing down a torn place in the edge of the paper.

Luella and her mother were discussing plans. They had decided that they must leave on the early train the next morning, before there was any chance of the western visitor's arriving.

"Goodness! Look at Aunt Crete," said Luella, laughing. "She looks as if she has seen a ghost. Her lips are all white."

"Crete, you oughtn't to be such a fool. As if a telegram would hurt you! There's nobody left to be worried about like that. Why don't you use your reason a little?"

"Hannah's boy is really coming!" beamed Aunt Crete, ignoring their scorn of herself.

"Upon my word! Aunt Crete, you look as if it were something to be glad about, instead of a downright calamity."

"Glad, of course I'm glad, Luella. Wouldn't you be glad to see your oldest sister's child? Hannah was always very dear to me. I can see her now the way she looked when she went away, so tall and slim and pretty —"

"Not if she'd been dead for a century or so, and I'd never seen the child, and he was a gawky, embarrassing creature who would spoil the prospects of the people I was supposed to love," retorted Luella. "Aunt Crete, don't you care the least bit for my happiness? Do you want it all spoiled?"

"Why, of course not, dearie," beamed Aunt Crete, "but I don't see how it will spoil your happiness. I should think you'd want to see him yourself."

"Aunt Crete! The idea! He's nothing to me. You know he's lived away out in the wild west all his life. He probably never had much schooling, and doesn't know how to dress or behave in polite society. I heard he went away off up in the Klondike somewhere, and worked in a mine. You can imagine just what a wild, ignorant creature he will be. If Clarence Grandon should see him, he might imagine my family were all like that, and then where would I be?"

"Yes, Crete, I'm surprised at you. You've been so anxious all along for Luella to shine in society, and now you talk just as if you didn't care in the least what happened," put in Luella's mother.

"But what can you do?" asked Aunt Crete. "You can't tell him not to come — your own sister's child!"

"Oh, how silly you are, Crete!" said her sister. "No, of course we can't very well tell him not to come, as he hasn't given us a chance; for this telegram is evidently sent on the way. It is dated Chicago, and he hasn't given us a trace of an address. He doesn't live in Chicago. He's very likely almost here, and may arrive any time tomorrow. Now you know we've simply got to go to the shore next week, for the rooms are all engaged at the hotel, and paid for, and we might as well hurry up and get off tonight or early in the morning, and escape him. Luella would die of mortification if she had to visit with that fellow and give up her trip to the shore. As you weren't going anyway, you can receive him. It will keep him quietly at home, for he won't expect an old woman to go out with him, and show him the sights, so nobody will notice him much, and there won't be a lot of talk. If he looks very ridiculous, and that prying Mrs. Brown next door speaks of it, you might explain he's the son of an old school friend who went out west to live years ago —"

"Oh Carrie!" exclaimed Aunt Crete, "that wouldn't be true; and, besides, he can't be so very bad as that. And even if he is, I shall love him — for he's Hannah's boy."

"Love him all you want to," sniffed her sister, "but for pity's sake don't let the neighbors know what relation he is."

"That's just like you, Aunt Crete," said Luella in a hurt tone. "You've known me and pretended to love me all your life. I'm almost like your own child, and yet you take up with this unknown nephew, and say you'll love him in spite of all the trouble he's making me."

Aunt Crete doubled the V in her forehead, and wiped away the beads of perspiration. Somehow it always seemed that she was in the wrong. Would she be understood in heaven? she wondered.

Luella and her mother went on planning. They advised what Aunt Crete was to do after they left.

"There's the raspberries and blackberries not done up yet, Crete, but I guess you can manage alone. You always do the biggest part of the canning, anyway. I'm awfully sorry about your sewing, Crete. I meant to fit your two thin dresses before we went away, but the dressmaker made Luella's things so much more elaborate than I expected that we really haven't had a minute's time, what with all the lace insertion she left for us to sew on. Perhaps you better run down to Miss Mason, and see if she has time to fit them, if you think you can't wait till we get back. You'll hardly be going out much while we're gone, you know."

"Oh, I'll be all right," said Aunt Crete happily. "I guess I can fix up my gray lawn for while Donald's here."

"Donald! Nonsense! It won't matter what you wear while he's here. He'll never know a calico from a silk. Now look here, Crete, you've got to be awfully careful, or you'll let out when we went off. There's no use in his finding out we didn't want to see him. You wouldn't want to hurt his feelings, you know. Your own sister's child!"

"No, of course not," agreed Aunt Crete, though there was a troubled look in her eyes. She never liked prevarication; and, when she was left with some polite fabrication to excuse her relatives out of something they wanted to shirk, she nearly always got it twisted so that it was either an out-and-out lie, which horrified her, or else let the whole thing "out of the bag," as Luella said.

But there was little time for discussion; for Luella and her mother had a great deal of packing to do, and Aunt Crete had the dinner to get and the house to set in order, surreptitiously, for the expected guest.

They hurried away the next morning in a whirl of bags and suitcases and parasols and umbrellas. They had baggage enough for a year in Europe, although they expected to stay only two or three weeks at the shore at most. Aunt Crete helped them into the station cab, ran back to the house for Luella's new raincoat, back again for the veil and her sister's gloves, and still a third time to bring the new book, which had been set aside for reading on the journey. Then at last they were gone, and with one brief sigh of satisfaction Aunt Crete permitted herself to reflect that she was actually left alone to receive a dear guest all her own.

Never in all her maiden existence had she had this pleasure before. She might use the best china, and have three kinds of pie at once, yes, and plum cake if she chose. Boys like pie and cake. Donald would be a big, nice boy.

What did it matter to her if he was awkward and from the west? He was in a large sense her own. Hannah was gone, and there was no one else to take a closer place. Who but his mother's sister should have the right to mother him for a while? He would be her own as Luella never had been, because there was always Luella's mother to take the first place. Besides, Luella had been a disappointing baby. Even in her infancy she had developed an independence that scorned kissing and cuddling. Luella always had too many selfish interests on hand to have time for breathing out love and baby graces to admiring subjects. Her frown was always quicker than her smile. But somehow Aunt Crete felt that it would be different with this boy, and her heart swelled within her as she hurried into the house to make ready for his coming.

The front hall was littered with rose leaves. Luella had shaken a bunch of roses to get rid of the loose leaves, and had found they were all loose leaves; therefore she flung them down upon the floor. She had meant to wear them with her new pongee traveling suit. It looked well to wear roses on a journey, for it suggested a possible admirer. But the roses had not held out, and now Aunt Crete must sweep them up.

A glance into the parlor showed peanut shells scattered over the floor and on the table. A few of Luella's friends had come in for a few minutes the evening before, and they had indulged in peanuts, finishing up by throwing the shells at one another amid shouts of hilarious laughter. Aunt Crete went for the broom and dustpan. If he came early, the hall and parlor must be in order first.

Luella and her mother had little time to waste, for the tickets were barely bought and the trunks checked before the train thundered up. It was a through vestibuled train; and, as Luella struggled up the steps of one car with her heavy suitcase, a tall young man with dark, handsome eyes and a distinguished manner swung himself down the steps of the next car.

"Hello, Luella!" called a voice from a pony cart by the platform. "You're not going away today, are you? Thought you said you weren't going till next week."

"Circumstances made it necessary," called Luella from the top step of the car while the porter held up the suitcase for her to take. "I'm running away from a backwoods cousin that's coming to visit. I'll write and tell you all about it. Good-bye. Sorry I can't be at your house tomorrow night, but it couldn't be helped."

Then Luella turned another gaze upon the handsome stranger, who was standing on the platform just below her, looking about interestedly. She thought he had looked at her more than casually; and, as she settled herself in the seat, she glanced down at her pongee traveling suit consciously, feeling that he could but have thought she looked well.

He was still standing on the platform as the train moved out, and Luella could see the girl in the pony cart turn her attention to him. She half wished she were sitting in the pony cart too. It would be interesting to find out who he was. Luella preened herself, and settled her large hat in front of the strip of mirrow between the windows, and then looked around the car that she might see who were her fellow passengers.

"Well, I'm glad we're off," said her mother nervously. "I was afraid as could be your cousin might come in on that early through train before we got started. It would have been trying if he'd come just as we were getting away. I don't know how we could have explained it."

"Yes," said Luella. "I'm glad we're safely off. He'll never suspect now."

It was just at that moment that the grocery boy arrived at the back door with a crate of red raspberries.

"Land alive!" said Miss Crete disappointedly. "I hoped those wouldn't come till tomorrow." She bustled about, taking the boxes out of the crate so that the boy might take it back; and before she was done the doorbell rang.

"Land alive!" said Miss Crete again as she wiped her hands on the kitchen towel and hurried to the front door, taking off her apron as she went. "I do hope he hasn't come yet. I haven't cleared off that breakfast table; and, if he should happen to come out, there's three plates standing."

But the thought had come too late. The dining room door was stretched wide open, and the table in full view. The front door was guarded only by the wire screen. The visitor had been able to take full notes, if he so desired.

Chapter 2
The Backwoods Cousin

Miss Lucretia opened the screen, and noticed the fine appearance of the young man standing there. He was not shabby enough for an agent. Someone had made a mistake, she supposed. She waited pleasantly for him to tell his errand.

"Is this where Mrs. Carrie Burton lives?" he asked, removing his hat courteously.

And, when she answered, "Yes," his whole face broke into dancing eagerness.

"Is this my Aunt Carrie? I wonder"; and he held out a tentative, appealing hand for welcome. "I'm Donald Grant."

"Oh!" said Miss Lucretia delightedly, "Oh!" and she took his hand in both her own. "No, I ain't your Aunt Carrie, I'm your Aunt Crete; but I'm just as glad to see you. I didn't think you'd be so big and handsome. Your Aunt Carrie isn't home. They've just — why — that is — they are — they had planned to be at the shore for three weeks, and they'll be real sorry when they know —" This last sentence was added with extra zeal, for Aunt Crete exulted in the fact that Carrie and Luella would indeed be sorry if they could look into their home for one instant and see the guest from whom they had run away. She felt sure that if they had known how fine-looking a young man he was, they would have stayed and been proud of him.

"I'm sorry they are away," said the young man, stooping to kiss Aunt Crete's plump, comfortable cheek, "but I'm mighty glad you're at home, Aunt Crete," he said with genuine pleasure. "I'm going to like you for all I'm worth to make up for the absence of my aunt and cousin. You say they have gone to the shore. When will they be at home? Is their stay there almost up?"

"Why, no," said Aunt Crete, flushing uncomfortably. "They haven't been gone long. And they've engaged their rooms there for three weeks at a big hotel. Luella, she's always been bound to go to one of those big places where rich people go, the Traymore. It's advertised in all the papers. I expect you've seen it sometimes. It's one of the most expensive places at the shore. I've almost a notion to write and tell them to come

8

home, for I'm sure they'll be sorry when they hear about you, but you see it's this way. There's a young man been paying Luella some attention, and he's going down there soon; I don't know but he's there already, and his mother and sister are spending the whole season there, so Luella had her heart set on going down and boarding at the same hotel.''

"Ah, I see," said the nephew. "Well, it wouldn't do to spoil my cousin's good time. Perhaps we can run down to the shore for a few days ourselves after we get acquainted. Say, Aunt Crete, am I too late for a bite of breakfast? I was so tired of the stuff they had on the dining car I thought I'd save up my appetite till I got here, for I was sure you'd have a bite of bread and butter, anyway.''

"Bless your dear heart, yes," said Aunt Crete, delighted to have the subject turned; for she had a terrible fear she would yet tell a lie about the departure of her sister and niece, and a lie was a calamity not always easily avoided in a position like hers. "You just sit down here, you dear boy, and wait about two minutes till I set the coffeepot over the fire and cut some more bread. It isn't a mite of trouble, for I hadn't cleared off the breakfast table yet. In fact, I hadn't rightly finished my own breakfast, I was so busy getting to rights. The grocery boy came, and — well I never can eat much when folks are going — I mean when I'm alone,'' she finished triumphantly.

She hurried out into the dining room to get the table cleared off, but Donald followed her. She tried to scuttle the plates together and remove all traces of the number of guests at the meal just past, but she could not be sure whether he noticed the table or not.

"May I help you?" asked the young man, grabbing Luella's plate and cup, and following her into the kitchen. "It's so good to get into a real home again with somebody who belongs to me. You know Father is in Mexico, and I've been in the university for the last four years.''

"The university!" Aunt Crete's eyes shone. "Do you have universities out west? My! Won't Luella be astonished? I guess she thinks out west is all woods.''

Donald's eyes danced.

"We have a few good schools out there," he said quietly.

While they were eating the breakfast that Aunt Crete prepared in an incredibly short space of time, Donald asked a great many questions. What did his aunt and cousin look like? Was Aunt Carrie like her, or like his mother? And Luella, had she been to college? And what did she look like?

Aunt Crete told him mournfully that Luella was more like herself than like her mother. "And it seems sometimes as if she blamed me for it," said the patient aunt. "It makes it hard, her being a sort of society girl, and wanting to look so fine. Dumpy figures like mine don't dress up pretty, you know. No, Luella never went to college. She didn't take much to books. She liked having a good time with young folks better. She's been wanting to go down to the shore and be at a real big hotel for three summers now, but Carrie never felt able to afford it before. We've been saving up all winter for Luella to have this treat, and I do hope she'll have a good time. It's real hard on her, having to stay right home all the time when all her girl friends go off to the shore. But you see she's got in with some real wealthy people who stay at expensive places, and she isn't satisfied to go to a common boarding-house. It must be nice to have money and go to a big hotel. I've never been in one myself, but Luella has, and she's told all about it. I should think it would be grand to live that way awhile with not a thing to do."

"They ought to have taken you along, Aunt Crete," said the young man. "I do hope I didn't keep you at home to entertain me."

"Oh, no, bless your heart," said the aunt, "I wasn't going. I never go anywhere. Why, what kind of a figure would I cut there? It would spoil all Luella's good time to have me around, I'm so short-waisted. She always wants me to wear a coat when I go anywhere with her, so people won't see how short-waisted I am."

"Nonsense," said Donald. "I think you are lovely, Aunt Crete. You've got such pretty white hair, all wavy like Mother's; and you've got a fine face. Luella ought to be proud to have you."

Aunt Crete blushed over the compliment, and choking tears of joy throbbed for a minute in her throat.

"Now hear the boy!" she exclaimed. "Donald, do have another cup of coffee."

After breakfast Aunt Crete showed her guest to his room, and then hurried down to get the stack of dishes out of the way before he came down again. But he appeared in the kitchen door in a few minutes.

"Give me a dish and some berries," he demanded. "I'm going to help you."

And despite all her protests he helped her with such vigor that by twelve o'clock twenty-one jars of crimson berries stood in a shining row on the kitchen table, and Aunt Crete was dishing up a savory dinner for two, with her face shining as brightly as if she had done nothing but play the whole morning.

"We did well, didn't we?" said Donald as he ate his dinner. "I haven't had such a good time since I went camping in the Klondike. Now after we get these dishes washed you are going to take a nice long nap. You look tired and warm."

Aunt Crete protested that she was not tired, but Donald insisted. "I want you to get nice and rested up, because tomorrow we're going shopping. By the way, I've brought you a present." He sprang up from the table, and went to his suitcase to get it.

Aunt Crete's heart beat with anticipation as he handed her a little white box. What if it should be a breastpin? How she would like that! She had worn her mother's, a braid of hair under a glass, with a gold band under it, ever since she was grown up, and sometimes she felt as if it was a little old-fashioned. Luella openly scoffed at it, and laughed at her for wearing it, but no one ever suggested getting her a new one, and, if she had ventured to buy one for herself, she knew they would have thought her extravagant.

She opened the box with excited fingers, and there inside was a little leather case. Donald touched a spring, and it flew open and disclosed a lovely star made all of seed pearls, reposing on white velvet. It was a breastpin indeed, and one fit for a queen. Fortunately Aunt Crete did not know enough about jewelry to realize what it cost, or her breath might have been taken away. As it was, she was stunned for the moment. Such a beautiful pin, and for her! She could scarcely believe it. She gazed and gazed, and then, laying the box on the table, rose up and took Donald's face in her two toil-worn hands, and kissed him.

"I'm glad you like it," he said with a pleased smile. "I wasn't quite sure what to get, but the salesman told me these were always nice. Now let's get at these dishes."

In a daze of happiness Aunt Crete washed the dishes while Donald wiped them, and then despite her protest he made her go upstairs and lie down.

When had she ever taken a nap in the daytime before? Not since she was a little girl and fell from the second-story window. The family had rushed around her frightened, and put her to bed in the daytime, and for one whole day she had been waited upon and cared for tenderly. Then she had been able to get up, and the hard, careless, toilsome world had rushed on again for her. But the memory of that blessed day of rest, touched by gentleness, had lingered forever a bright spot in her memory. She had always been the one that did the hard things in her family, even when she was quite young.

Aunt Crete lay cautiously down upon her neatly made bed after she had attired herself in her best gown, a rusty black and white silk made over from one Luella had grown tired of, and clasped her hands blissfully on her breast, resting with her eyes wide open and a light of joy upon her face. She hardly felt it right to relax entirely, lest Donald might call her, but finally the unaccustomed position in the middle of the day sent her off into a real doze, and just about that time the telephone bell rang.

The telephone was in the sitting room downstairs. It had been put in at the time when the telephone company was putting them in free to introduce them in that suburb. It was ordinarily a source of great interest to the whole family, though it seldom rang except for Luella. Luella and her mother were exceedingly proud of its possession.

Donald was in the sitting room reading. He looked up from his paper, hesitated a moment, and then took down the receiver. Perhaps his aunt was asleep already, and he could attend to this without waking her.

"Hello; is this 53 M?"

Donald glanced at the number on the telephone, and answered, "Yes."

"Here you are, Atlantic. Here is Midvale," went on the voice of the operator at central.

"Hello! Is that you, Aunt Crete? This is Luella," came another girl's strident voice in hasty impatience. "What in the world were you so long about answering the phone for? I've been waiting here an age. Now, listen, Aunt Crete. For heaven's sake don't you tell that crazy cousin of ours where to find us, or like as not he'll take a notion to run down here to see us, and I should simply die of mortification if he did. This is a very swell hotel, and it would be fierce to have a backwoods relation appear on the scene. Now be sure you keep quiet. I'll never forgive you if you don't. And say, Aunt Crete, won't you please sew on the rest of that Val edging down the ruffles of the waist and on the skirt of my new lavender organdie, and do it up, and send it by mail? I forgot all about it. It's on the bed in the spare room, and the edging is started. You sew it on the way it is begun. You'll see. Now don't you go to sewing it on in the old way because it is quicker; for it doesn't look a bit pretty, and you've nothing much else to do, now we're gone, anyway. And say, Aunt Crete, would you mind going down to Peter's today, and telling Jennie I forgot all about getting those aprons to finish for the fair, and tell her you'll finish them for her? Do it today, because she has to send the box off by the end of the week. And Mother says you better clean the cellar right away, and she wondered if you'd feel equal to whitewashing it. I should think you'd like to do that, it's so cool this warm weather to be down cellar. And, Oh, yes, if you get lonesome and want something to do, I forgot to tell you I left those three flannel shirtwaists all cut out ready to be made in the upper bureau drawer of the spare room. Now don't read your eyes out the way you did the last time we went off and left you, and have to wear dark glasses for a week, because I have lots of things planned to do when I get home. I'm going to have Helena Bates for a week, and there'll be several lunches and picnics doing. Oh, say, Aunt Crete, Mother says, if there's any more pie cherries to be had, you better put up some, and be sure and stone them all. I just hate them with the seeds in. And I guess that's all, only don't forget you promised to have all those buttonholes worked for me in those underclothes I'm making, before I get back. Are you all right? Let me see. There was something else. Oh, yes, Mother says you don't need to get out the best china and make a great fuss as if you had grand company; he's only a country boy, you know. Say, Aunt Crete. Are you there? Why don't you answer? Aunt Crete! Hello! For pity's sake, what is the matter with this phone? Hello, central! Oh, dear! I suppose she's gone away. That's the way Aunt Crete always does!''

Donald, a strange, amused expression upon his face, stood listening and hesitating. He did not know exactly what to do. Without any intention at all he had listened to a conversation not intended for his ears. Should he answer and tell who he was? No, for that would but embarrass Luella. Neither would it do to call Aunt Crete now, for they would be sure to find out he had heard. Perhaps it was better to keep entirely still. There seemed to be nothing serious at stake. Ruffles and shirtwaists and gingham aprons for a guild and whitewashing the cellar! Nobody would die if none of them were done, and his blood boiled over the tone in which the invisible cousin at the other end of the wire had ordered Aunt Crete about. He could read the whole life story of the patient self-sacrifice on the one hand and imposition on the other. He felt strongly impelled to do something in the matter. A rebuke of some sort should be administered. How could it best be done?

Meantime Luella was fuming with the telephone girl, and the girl was declaring that she could get no answer from Midvale anymore. Donald stood wickedly enjoying their discomfiture, and was at last rewarded by hearing Luella say: "Well, I guess I've said all I want to say, anyway; so you needn't ring them up again. I've got to go out boating now." The receiver at the shore clicked into place, and the connection was cut off.

Then the young man hung up the receiver at the Midvale end of the line, and sat down to think. Bit by bit he pieced together the story until he had very nearly made out the true state of affairs. So they were ashamed of him, and were trying to get away. Could it be possible that they had been the people that got on the train as he got off? Was that girl with the loud voice and the pongee suit his cousin? The voice over the telephone seemed like the one that had called to the girl in the pony cart. And had his eyes deceived him, or were there three plates on the breakfast table that morning? Poor Aunt Crete! He would give her the best time he knew how, and perhaps it was also set for him to give his cousin a lesson.

Chapter 3
A Wonderful Day

Aunt Crete woke up at last from an uncomfortable dream. She thought Carrie and Luella had come back, and were about to snatch Donald away from her and bear him off to the shore.

She arose in haste and smoothed her hair, astonished at the freshness of her own face in the glass. She was afraid she had overslept and lost some of the precious time with Donald. There was so much to ask him, and he was so good to look at. She hurried down and was received warmly. Donald's meditations had culminated in a plan.

"Sit down, Aunt Crete; are you sure you are rested? Then I want to talk. Suppose we run down to the shore and surprise the folks. How soon could you be ready?"

"Oh, dear heart! I couldn't do that!" exclaimed Aunt Crete, her face nevertheless alight with pleasure at the very thought.

"Why not? What's to hinder?"

"Oh, I never go. I always stay at home and attend to things."

"But that's no reason. Why couldn't things attend to themselves."

"Why I couldn't leave the house alone."

"Now, what in the world could possibly happen to the house that you could prevent by staying in it? Be reasonable, dear Aunt. You know the house won't run away while you are gone, and, if it does, I'll get you another one. You don't mean to tell me you never go off on a vacation. Then it's high time you went, and you'll have to stay longer to make up for lost time. Besides, I want your company. I've never seen the eastern coast, and expect to enjoy it hugely, but I need somebody to enjoy it with me. I can't half take things in alone. I want somebody my very own to go with me. That's what I came here for. I had thought of inviting you all to go down for a little trip, but, as the others are down there, why, we can join them."

Aunt Crete's face clouded. What would Luella say at having them appear on her horizon? The young man was all right, apparently, but there was no telling how angry Luella might be if her aunt came. She knew that Luella preferred to keep her in the background.

"I really couldn't go, dear," she said wistfully. "I'd like it with all my

14

heart. And it would be specially nice to go with you, for I never had anybody to go round with me, not since your mother was a girl and used to take me with her wherever she went. I missed her dreadfully after she was married and went west. She was always so good to me.''

The young man's face softened, and he reached his hand impulsively across the table, and grasped the toil-worn hand of his aunt.

"Well, you shall have somebody to go round with you now, Auntie; that is, if you'll let me. I'm not going to take 'No' for an answer. You just must go. We'll have a vacation all by ourselves, and do just as we please, and we'll bring up at the hotel where Aunt Carrie and Luella are, and surprise them.''

"But, child, I can't!" said Aunt Crete in dismay, seeing his determination. "Why, I haven't any clothes suitable to wear away from home. We were all so busy getting Luella fixed out that there wasn't any time left for mine, and it didn't really matter about me anyway. I never go anywhere.''

"But you're going now, Aunt Lucretia," said he, "and it does matter, you see. Clothes are easily bought. We'll go shopping after breakfast tomorrow morning.''

"But I really can't afford it, Donald," said his aunt with an air of finality. "You know I'm not rich. If Carrie weren't good enough to give me a home here, I shouldn't know how to make two ends meet.''

"Never mind that, Aunt Crete; this is my layout, and I'm paying for it. We'll go shopping tomorrow morning. I've got some money in my pocket I'm just aching to spend. The fact is, Aunt Crete, I struck gold up there in the Klondike, and I've got more money than I know what to do with.''

"Oh!" said Aunt Crete with awe in her voice at the thought of having more money than one knew what to do with. Then shyly, "But —"

"But what, Aunt Lucretia?" asked Donald as she hesitated and flushed till the double V came into her forehead in the old helpless, worried way.

"Why, there's lots of canning and housecleaning that has got to be done, and I don't really think Carrie would like it to have me leave it all, and run away on a pleasure excursion.''

Righteous indignation filled the heart of the nephew. "Well, I should like to know why she wouldn't like it!" he exclaimed impulsively. "Has she any better right to have a vacation than you? I'm sure you've earned it. You blessed little woman, you're going to have a vacation now, in spite of yourself. Just put your conscience away in pink cotton till we get back — though I don't know whether I shall let you come back to stay. I may spirit you off with me somewhere if I don't like the looks of my cousin. I'll take all the responsibility of this trip. If Aunt Carrie doesn't like it, she may visit her wrath on me, and I'll tell her just what I think of her. Anyhow, to the shore you are going right speedily; that is, if you want to go. If there's some other place you'd rather go besides to the Traymore, speak the word, and there we'll go. I want you to have a good time.''

Aunt Crete gasped with joy. The thought of the ocean, the real ocean, was wonderful. She had dreamed of it many times, but never had seen it, because she was always the one who could just as well stay at home as not. She never got run down or nervous or cross, and was ordered to go away for her health, and she never insisted upon going when the rest went. Her heart was bounding as it had not bounded since the morning of the last Sunday-school picnic she had attended when she was a girl.

"Indeed, dear boy, I do want to go with all my heart if I really ought. I have always wanted to see the ocean, and I can't imagine any place I'd rather go than the Traymore, Luella's talked so much about it.''

"All right. Then it's settled that we go. How soon can we get ready? We'll go shopping tomorrow morning bright and early, and get a trunkful of new clothes. It's always nice to have new things when you go off; you feel like another person, and don't have to be sewing on buttons all the time,'' laughed Donald, as if he was enjoying the whole thing as much as his aunt. "I meant to have a good time getting presents for the whole family, but, as they aren't here, I'm going to get them all for you. You're not to say a word. Have you got a trunk?''

"Trunk? No, child. I haven't ever had any need for a trunk. The time I went to Uncle Hiram's funeral I took Carrie's old haircloth one, but I don't know 's that's fit to travel again. Carrie's got her flannels packed away in camphor in it now, and I shouldn't like to disturb it.''

"Then we'll get a trunk.''

"Oh, no,'' protested Aunt Crete, "that would be a foolish expense. There's some pasteboard boxes upstairs. I can make out with them in a shawl strap. I shan't need much for a few days.''

"Enlarge your scale of things, Aunt Crete. You're going to stay more than a few days. You're going to stay till you're tired, and just want to come back. As we're going to a 'swell' hotel'' — Donald reflected that Aunt Crete could not understand his reference to Luella's description of the Traymore — "we can't think of shawl straps and boxes. You shall have a big trunk. I saw an advertisement of one that has drawers and a hat-box in it, like a bureau. We'll see if we can find one to suit.''

"It sounds just like the fairy tales I used to read to Luella when she was a little girl,'' beamed Aunt Crete. "It doesn't seem as if it was I. I can't make it true.''

"Now let's write down a list of things you need," said the eager planner, "we'll have to hurry up things, and get off this week if possible. I've been reading the paper, and they say there's coming a hot wave. I need to get you to the shore before it arrives, if possible. Come, what shall I put down first? What have you always thought you'd like, Aunt Crete? Don't you need some silk dresses?"

"Oh, dear heart! Hear him! Silk dresses aren't for me. Of course I've always had a sort of hankering after one, but nothing looks very well on me. Carrie says my figure is dumpy. I guess, if you're a mind to, you can get me a lace collar. It'll please me as well as anything. Luella saw some for a quarter that were real pretty. She bought one for herself. I think it would do to wear with my new pin, and all my collars are pretty much worn out."

"Now look here, Aunt Crete! Can't I make you understand? I mean business, and no collars for a quarter are going to do. You can have a few cheap ones for morning if you want them, but we'll buy some real lace ones to wear with the pin. And you shall have the silk dress, two or three of them, and a lot of other things. What kind do you want?"

"Oh, my dear boy! You just take my breath away. I with two or three silk dresses! The idea! Carrie would think me extravagant, and Luella wouldn't like it a bit. She always tells me I'm too gay for my years."

Donald set his lips, and wished he could have speech for a few minutes with the absent Luella. He felt that he would like to express his contempt for her treatment of their aunt.

"I've always thought I'd like a gray silk," mused Aunt Crete with a dreamy look in her eyes, "but I just know Luella would think it was too dressy for me. I suppose black would be better. I can't deny I'd like black silk, too."

"We'll have both," said Donald decidedly. "I saw a woman in a silver-gray silk once. She had white hair like yours, and the effect was beautiful. Then you'll need some other things. White dresses, I guess. That's what my chum's grandmother used to wear when I went there visiting in the summer."

"White for me!" exclaimed the aunt. "Oh, Luella would be real angry at me getting white. She says it's too conspicuous for old women to dress in light colors."

"Never mind Luella. We're doing this, and whatever we want goes. If Luella doesn't like it, she needn't look at it."

Aunt Crete was all in a flutter that night. She could hardly sleep. She did not often go to town. Luella did all the shopping. Sometimes she suggested going, but Carrie always said it was a needless expense, and, besides, Luella knew how to buy at a better bargain. It was a great delight to go with Donald. Her face shone, and all the weariness of the day's work, and all the toilsome yesterdays, disappeared from her brow.

She looked over her meager wardrobe, most of it cast-offs from Carrie's or Luella's half-worn clothing, and wrote down in a cramped hand a few absolute necessities. The next morning they had an early breakfast, and started at once on their shopping expedition. Aunt Crete felt like a little child being taken to the circus. The idea of getting a lot of new clothes all for herself seemed too serious a business to be true. She was dazed when she thought of it, and so, when Donald asked what they should look at first, she showed plainly that she would be little help in getting herself fitted out. She was far too happy to bring her mind down to practical things, and, besides, she could not adjust herself to the vast scale of expenditure Donald had set.

"Here are some collars," said Donald. "We might as well begin on these."

Aunt Crete examined them with enthusiasm, and finally picked out two at twenty-five cents apiece.

"Are those the best you have?" questioned Donald.

"Oh, no," said the saleswoman, quick to identify the purchaser that did not stop at price, "did you want real or imitation?"

"Real, by all means," he answered promptly.

"Oh, Donald," breathed Aunt Crete in a warning whisper, "real lace comes dreadful high. I've heard Luella say so. Besides, I shouldn't have anything to wear it with, nor any place to go fixed up like that."

"Have you forgotten you're going to the Traymore in a few days?" he asked her with a twinkle in his eye. "And what about the gray silk? Won't it go with that? If not, we'll get something better."

Assisted by the saleswoman, they selected two beautiful collars of real lace, and half a dozen plain ones for everyday wear.

"Couldn't you go with us?" asked Donald of the saleswoman as the purchase was concluded. "My aunt wishes to get a good many things, and neither she nor I is much used to shopping. We'd like to have your advice."

"I'm sorry; I'd like to, but I'm not allowed to leave this counter," said the woman with a kindly smile. "I'm head of this department, and they can't get along without me this morning. But they have buyers in the office just for that purpose. You go up to the desk over on the east side just beyond the rotunda, and ask for a buyer to go around with you. Get Miss Brower if you can, and tell her the head of the lace department told you to call for her. She'll tell you just what to get," and she smiled again at Aunt Crete's kindly, beaming face.

They went to the desk, and found Miss Brower, who, when she heard the message, took them smilingly under her wing. She knew that meant a good sale had been made, and there would be something in it for her. Besides, she had a kindly disposition, and did not turn up a haughty nose at Aunt Crete's dumpy little figure.

"Now, just what do you want first?" she asked brightly.

"Everything," said Donald helplessly. "We've only bought a lace collar so far, and now we want all the rest of the things to go with it. The only things we've decided on so far are two silk dresses, a black one and a silver-gray. How do we go about it to get them? Do they have them ready-made?"

"Nothing that would be quite suitable, I'm afraid, in silks. But we'll go and see what there is in stock," said the assistant with skillful eye, taking in Aunt Crete's smiling, helpless face, lovely white hair, dumpy, ill-fitted figure, and all. "There might be a gray voile that would suit her. In fact, I saw one this morning, very simple and elegant, lined with gray silk, and trimmed with lace dyed to match. It is a beauty, and just reduced this morning to thirty dollars from sixty. I believe it will fit her."

Aunt Crete gasped at the price, and looked at Donald; but he seemed pleased, and said: "That sounds good. Let's go and see it. We'll have a gray — what was it you called it — voile? Remember that name, Aunt Crete. You're going to have a gray voile. But we want the silk too. Do they make things here? We want to go away in a few days, and would like to take them with us."

"Oh, yes, they'll make anything to order; and this time of year we're not so busy. I guess you could get a 'hurry-up' order on it, and have it done in a couple of days; or it could be forwarded to you if it was not quite finished when you left."

They stepped into the elevator, and in a moment were ushered into the presence of the rare and the imported. Aunt Crete stood in a maze of delight and wonder. All this was on exhibition just for her benefit, and she was Alice in Wonderland for the hour. Donald stood back with his arms folded, and watched her with satifaction. One thing alone was wanted to complete it. He would have liked to have Luella up in the gallery somewhere watching also. But that he held in anticipation. Luella should be made to understand that she had done wrong in underrating this sweet, patient soul.

The gray voile was entirely satisfactory to the two shoppers. Donald recognized it as the thing many women of his acquaintance wore at the receptions he had attended in university circles. Aunt Crete fingered it wistfully, and had her inward doubts whether anything so frail and lovely, like a delicate veil, would wear; but, looking at Donald's happy face, she decided not to mention it. The dress was more beautiful than anything she had ever dreamed of possessing. "But it won't fit me," she sighed as she and Miss Brower were on the way to the trying-on room where the garment was to be fitted to her. "I'm so dumpy, you know, and Luella always says it's no use to get me anything ready-made."

"Oh, the fitter will make it fit," said Miss Brower convincingly; and then, with a glance at the ample waist, whose old-fashioned lines lay meekly awry as if they were used to being put on that way and were beyond even discouragement: "Why don't you wear one of those stiffened waists? There's a new one on sale, has soft bones all around, and is real comfortable. It would make your dresses set a great deal better. If you like, I'll go get one, and you can be fitted over it. You don't like anything very tight, do you?"

"No," said Aunt Crete in a deprecatory tone, "I never could bear anything real tight. That's what puts Luella out so about me. But, if you say there's a waist that's comfortable, I should be so obliged if you'd get it. I'd be willing to pay any price not to look so dumpy."

She felt that if it took the last cent she possessed, and made all her relatives angry with her, she must have something to fit her once.

Miss Brower, thus commissioned, went away, and returned very soon with the magical waist that was to transform Miss Lucretia's "figger." If Donald could have seen his aunt's face when she was finally arrayed in the soft folds of the gray voile and was being pinned up and pinned down and pinned in and pinned out, he would have been fully repaid. Aunt Crete's ecstasy was marred only by the fact that Luella could not see her grandeur. Actually being fitted in a department store to a real imported dress! Could mortal attain higher in this mundane sphere?

When the fitting was pronounced done and Aunt Crete was about to don her discouraged shirtwaist once more, Miss Brower appeared in the doorway with a coat and skirt suit over her arm, made of fine soft black taffeta.

"Just put this on and let the gentleman see how he likes it," she said. She had been out to talk over matters with Donald and have an understanding as to what was wanted. She had advised the taffeta coat and skirt for traveling, with an extra cloth coat for cool days. Aunt Crete, with the new dignity that consciousness of her improved figure gave her, rustled out to her nephew looking like a new woman, her face beaming.

That was a wonderful day. Aunt Crete retired again for the black taffeta to be altered a little, and yet again for a black and white dotted swiss, and a white linen suit, and a handsome black crepe de chine, and then to have the measure taken for the silver-gray silk, which the head dressmaker promised could be hurried through. They bought a black chiffon waist and some filmy, dreamy white shirt-waists, simple and plain in design, and exquisite lace simply applied, fine handmade tucks, and finer material. Miss Brower advised white linen and white lawn for morning wear at the seashore, and gave Aunt Crete confidence, telling how she had a customer, "a woman about as old as you, with just such lovely white hair," who but yesterday purchased a set of white dresses for morning wear at the seashore. This silenced the thoughts of her sister's horror at "White for you, Crete! What are you thinking of?" Never mind, she was going to have one good time, even if she had to put all her lovely finery away in a trunk afterwards, and never bring it out again, or — dreary thought — were made to cut it over for Luella sometime. Well, it might come to that, but at least she would enjoy it while it was hers.

Two white linen skirts, a handsome black cloth coat, several pairs of silk gloves, black and white, some undergarments dainty enough for a bride, a whole dozen pairs of stockings! How Aunt Crete rejoiced in those! She had been wearing stockings whose feet were cut out of old stocking legs for fifteen years. She couldn't remember when she had had a whole new pair of stockings all her own. And then two new bonnets.

All these things were acquired little by little. It was while they were in the millinery department, and Miss Brower had just set a charming black lace bonnet made on a foundation of white roses on the white hair, that Donald decided she was one of the most beautiful old ladies he had ever seen. The drapery was a fine black lace scarf, which swept around the roses and tied loosely on the breast, and it gave the quiet little woman a queenly air. She was getting used to seeing her own face in strange adornments, but it startled her to see that she really looked handsome in this bonnet. She stood before the transformation in the mirror almost in awe, and never heard what Miss Brower was saying:

"That's just the thing for best, and there's a lovely lace wrap in the cloak department she ought to have to go with it. It would be charming."

"Get it," said Donald with respectful brevity. He was astonished himself at the difference mere clothes made. Aunt Crete was fairly impressive in her new bonnet. And the lace wrap proved indeed to be the very mate to the bonnet, hiding the comfortable figure, and making her look "just like other people," as she breathlessly expressed it after one glance at herself in the lace wrap.

They bought a plain black bonnet, a sweet little gray one, a fine silk umbrella, a lot of pretty belts and handkerchiefs, some shoes and rubbers, a handbag of cut steel, for which Luella would have bartered her conscience — what there was left of it; and then they smiled good-bye at Miss Brower, and left her for a little while, and went to lunch.

Such a lunch! Soup and fish and spring lamb and fresh peas and new potatoes and two kinds of ice cream in little hard sugar cases that looked like baked snowballs. Aunt Crete's hand trembled as she took the first spoonful. The wonders of the day had been so great that she was fairly worn out, and two little bright red spots of excitement had appeared in her cheeks, but she was happy! Happier than she remembered ever to have been in her life before. Her dear old conscience had a moment of sighing that Luella could not have been there to have enjoyed it too, and then her heart bounded in wicked gleefulness that Luella was not there to stop her nice time.

They went into a great hall in the same store, and sat among the palms and coolness made by electric fans, while a wonderful organ played exquisite music, and Aunt Crete felt she certainly was in heaven without the trouble of dying; and she never dreamed, dear soul, that she had been dying all her life that others might live, and that it is to such that the reward is promised.

They went back to Miss Brower later; and behold! the silver-gray silk had been cut out, and was ready to fit. Aunt Crete felt it was fairy work, the whole of it, and she touched the fabric as if it had been made by magic.

Then they went and bought a trunk and a handsome leather satchel, and Donald took a notion that his aunt must have a set of silver combs for her hair such as he saw in the hair of another old lady.

"Now," said Donald reflectively, "we'll go home and get rested, and tomorrow we'll come down and buy any things we've forgotten."

"And I'm sure I don't see what more a body could possibly need," said Aunt Crete, as, tired and absolutely contented, she climbed into the train and sat down in the hot plush seat.

The one bitter drop in the cup of bliss came the next morning — or rather two drops — in the shape of letters. One from Aunt Carrie for Donald was couched in stiffest terms, in which she professed to have just heard of his coming, and to be exceedingly sorry that she was not at home, and was kept from returning only by a sprained ankle, the doctor telling her that she must not put her foot to the ground for two or three weeks yet, or she would have to suffer for it.

The other letter was for Aunt Crete, and was a rehash of the telephone message, with a good sound scolding for having gone away from the telephone before she finished speaking. Luella had written it herself because she felt like venting her temper on someone. The young man that had been so attentive to her in town had promenaded the piazza with another young woman all the evening before. Luella hoped Aunt Crete would put up plenty of gooseberry jam. Aunt Crete put on her double V as she read, and sighed for a full minute before Donald looked up amused from his letter.

"Now, Aunt Crete, you look as if a mountain had rolled down upon you. What's the matter?"

"Oh, I'm just afraid, Donald, that I'm doing wrong going off this way, when Carrie expects me to do all this canning and sewing and cleaning. I'm afraid she'll never forgive me."

"Now, Aunt Crete, don't you love me? Didn't I tell you I'd stand between you and the whole world? Please put that letter up, and come and help me pack your new trunk. Do you want that gray silk put in first, or shall I put the shoes at the bottom? Don't you know you and I are going to have the times of our lives? We're going to run away from every care. Do you suppose your own sister would want you to stay here roasting in the city if she knew you had a nephew just aching to carry you off to the ocean? Come, forget it. Cut it out, Aunt Crete, and let's pack the trunk. I'm longing to be off to smell the briny deep." And laughingly he carried her away, and plunged her into thoughts of her journey, giving her no time the rest of the day to think of anything else.

Chapter 4

Aunt Crete Transformed

They locked the house early one morning when even the dusty bricks had a smell of freshness to them before the hot sun baked them for another day. The closed blinds seemed sullen like a conquered tyrant, and the front door looked reproachfully at Aunt Crete as she turned the key carefully and tried it twice to be sure it was locked. The lonesome look of the house gave the poor old lady a pang as she turned the corner in her softly rustling silk coat and skirt. She felt it had hardly been right to put on a new black silk in the morning, and go off from all the cares of the world, just leave them, boldly ignore them, like any giddy girl, and take a vacation. She regarded herself with awe and a rising self-respect in every window she passed. Somehow the look of dumpiness had passed away mysteriously. It was not her old self that was passing along the street to the station bearing a cut-steel handbag, while Donald carried her new satchel, and her new trunk bumped on a square ahead in the expressman's wagon.

It was a hot morning, and the great city station seemed close and stuffy, but Aunt Crete mingled with the steaming crowd blissfully. To be one with the world, attired irreproachably; to be on her way to a great hotel by the sea, with new clothes, and escorted devotedly by someone who was her very own, this indeed was happiness. Could anyone desire more upon the earth?

Donald put her into a cab at the station, and she beamed happily out at the frightful streets that always made her heart come into her mouth on the rare occasions when she had to cross them. The ride across the city seemed a brief and distinguished experience. It was as if everybody else was walking and they only had the grandeur of a carriage. Then the ferry boat was delightful to the new traveler, with its long, white-ceiled passages, and its smell of wet timbers and tarred ropes. They had a seat close to the front, where they could look out and watch their own progress and see the many puffing monsters laboriously plying back and forth, and the horizon line of many masts, like fine brown lines against the sky. Aunt Crete felt that at last she was out in the world. She could not have felt it more if she had been starting for Europe.

The seashore train, with its bamboo seats and its excited groups of children bearing tin pails and shovels and tennis-rackets, filled her with a fine exhilaration. At last, at last, her soul had escaped the bounds of red brick walls that she had expected would surround her as long as she lived. She drew deep breaths, and beamed upon the whole trainful of people, yelling baby and all. She gazed and gazed at the fast-flying Jersey scenery, grown so monotonous to some of the travelers, and admired every little white and green town at which they paused.

Donald put her into a carriage when they reached the shore. Half an hour off they had begun to smell the sea, and to catch glimpses of low-flying marshes and a misty blueness against the sky. Now every friendly hackman at the station seemed a part of the great day to Aunt Crete. So pretty a carriage, with low steps and gray cushions and a fringe all around the canopy, and a white speckled horse, with long, gentle, white eyelashes. Aunt Crete leaned back self-consciously on the gray cushions, and enjoyed the creak of her silk jacket as she settled into place. She felt as if this was a play that would soon be over; but she would enjoy it to the very end, and then go back to her dishwashing and cellar-cleaning, and being blamed, and bear them all in happy remembrance of what she had had for one blissful vacation.

She did not know that Donald had telephoned ahead for the best apartments in the hotel. She was engaged in watching for the first blue line of the great mysterious ocean; and, when it came into sight, billowing suddenly above the line of boardwalk as they turned a corner, her heart stood still for one moment, and then bounded onward set to the time of wonder.

Two obsequious porters jumped to assist Aunt Crete from the carriage. The hand baggage drifted up the steps as if by magic, and awaited them in the apartments to which they arose in a luxurious elevator. Aunt Crete noticed several old ladies with pink and blue wool knitting, sitting in a row of large rocking chairs, as she glided up to the second floor. It gave her rest on one point, for they all wore white dresses. She had been a little dubious about those white dresses that Donald had insisted upon. But now she might enjoy them unashamed. Oh, what would Luella say?

She glanced around the room, half-fearfully expecting to find Luella waiting there. Somehow, now she was there, she wanted to get used to it and enjoy it all before Luella came. For Luella was an uncertain quantity. Luella might not like it, after all! Dreadful thought! And after Donald had taken so much trouble and spent so much money all to surprise them!

The smiling porter absorbed the goodly tip that Donald handed him, and went his way. Aunt Crete and Donald were left alone. They looked at each other and smiled.

"Let's look around and see where they've put us," said Donald, pushing the swaying curtains aside, and there before them rolled the blue tide of the ocean. Aunt Crete sank into a chair, and was silent for a while; and then she said: "It's just as big as I thought it would be. I was so afraid it wouldn't be. Some folks next door went down to the shore last year, and they said it didn't look big enough to what they'd expected, and I've been afraid ever since."

Donald's eyes filled with a tender light that was beautiful to see. He was enjoying the spending of his money, and it was yielding him a rich reward already.

The apartments that had been assigned to them consisted of a parlor and two large bedrooms with private baths. Donald discovered a few moments later, when he went down to the office to investigate, that Luella and his aunt occupied a single room on the fourth floor back, overlooking the kitchen court. It was not where he would have placed them, had they chosen to await his coming and be taken down to the shore in style. But now that they had run away from him, and were too evidently ashamed of him, perhaps it was as well to let them remain where they were, he reflected.

"Aunt Carrie and Luella have gone out with a party in a carriage for an all-day drive to Pleasure Bay," announced Donald when he came up. "Aunt Carrie's ankle must be better."

"Well, that's real nice!" exclaimed Aunt Crete with a smile, turning from her view of the sea, where she had been ever since he left her. "I'm glad Luella is having a good time, and we shan't miss her a mite. You and I'll have the ocean all to ourselves today."

Donald smiled approvingly. He was not altogether sure he cared to meet that other aunt and cousin at all. He was not sure but he would like to run away from them, and carry Aunt Crete with him.

"Very well," he said, "I'm glad you're not disappointed. We'll do just whatever we want to. Would you like to go in bathing?"

"Oh, my! Could I! I've always thought I'd like to see how it would feel, but I guess I'm too old. Besides, there's my figger. It wouldn't look nice in a bathing suit. Luella wouldn't like it a bit, and I don't want to disgrace her, now I'm here. She always makes a lot of fun of old people going in and sitting right on the edge of the water. I guess it won't do."

"Yes, it will do, if you want to. Didn't I tell you this was my party, and Luella isn't in it? That's ridiculous. I'll take you in myself, Aunt Crete, and we'll have the best time out; and you shan't be scared, either. I can swim like a fish. You shall go in every day. Would you like to begin at once?"

"I should," said Aunt Crete, rising with a look of resolution in her face. She felt that Luella would condemn the amusement for her; so, if she was to dare it, it must be done before her niece appeared.

They went down to the beach, and for a few minutes surveyed the bathers as they came out to the water. Then with joy and daring in her face Aunt Crete went into the little bathhouse with wildly beating heart, arrayed herself in the gay blue flannel garb provided for her use, and came timidly out to meet Donald, tall and smiling in his blue jerseys.

They had a wonderful time. It was almost better than shopping. Donald led her down to the water, and very gently accustomed her to it until he had led her out beyond the roughness, where his strong arms lifted her well above the swells until she felt as if she was a bird. It was marvelous that she was not afraid, but she was not. It was as if she had that morning been transferred back over forty years to her youth again, and was having the good times that she had longed for, such as other girls had — the swings and the rides and the skatings and bicyclings. How many such things she had watched through the years, with her heart palpitating with daring to do it all herself! Her petulant sister and the logy Luella never dreamed that Aunt Crete desired such unauntly indulgences. If they had, they would have taken it out of her, scorched it out with scorn.

The white hair with its natural waves fluffed out beautifully, like a canary's feathers, after the bath, and Aunt Crete was smiling and charming at lunch in one of her fine new white dresses. She had hurried to put it on before Luella appeared, lest they might all be spirited away from her if Luella discovered them. She reflected with a sigh that they would likely fit Luella beautifully, and that that would probably be their final destination, just as Luella's discarded garments came to her.

But there was nothing to mar the lunchtime and the beautiful afternoon, wherein, after a delicious nap to the accompaniment of the music of the waves, she was taken to drive in the fringed carriage again, while a bunch of handsome ladies, old and young, sat on the hotel piazza in more of those abundant rockers, and watched her approvingly. She felt that she was of some importance in their eyes. She had suddenly blossomed out of her insignificance, and was worth looking at. It warmed her heart with humble pleasure. She felt that she had won approval, not through any merit of her own, but through Donald's loving-kindness. It was wonderful what a charm clothes could work.

"Put on your gray silk for dinner," said Donald with malice aforethought in his heart.

"Oh," gasped Aunt Crete, "I think I ought to keep that for parties, don't you?"

"If ever there was a party, it's going to be tonight," said Donald. "It's going to be a surprise-party. You want to see if Aunt Carrie and Luella will know you, you know."

So with trembling fingers Aunt Crete arrayed herself in her gray silk and fine linen, very materially assisted by a quiet maid, whom Donald had ordered sent to the room, and who persuaded Aunt Crete to let her arrange the pretty white hair.

It was surprising to see, when the coiffure was complete, that she looked quite like the other old ladies, who were not old at all, only playing old.

"I don't believe they will know me," whispered Aunt Crete to herself as she stood before the full-length mirror and surveyed the effect. "And I didn't think I could ever look like that!" she murmured after a more prolonged gaze, during which she made the acquaintance of her new self. Then she added half wistfully: "I wish I had known it before. I think perhaps they'd have — liked me — more if I'd looked that way all the time." She sighed half regretfully, as if she were bidding good-bye to this new vision, and went out to Donald, who awaited her. She felt that the picnic part of her vacation was almost over now, for Carrie and Luella would be sure to manage to spoil it someway.

Donald looked up from his paper with a welcome in his eyes. It was the first time she had seen him in evening dress, and she thought him handsome as a king.

"You're a very beautiful woman, Aunt Crete; do you know it?" said Donald with satisfaction. He had felt that the French maid would know how to put just the right touch to Aunt Crete's pretty hair to take away her odd "unused" appearance. Now she was completely in fashion, and she looked every inch a lady. She somehow seemed to have natural intuition for gentle manners. Perhaps her kindly heart dictated them, for surely there can be no better manners than come wrapped up with the Golden Rule, and Aunt Crete had lived by that all her life.

They entered the great dining hall, and made their way among the palms in a blaze of electric light, with the headwaiter bowing obsequiously before them. They had a table to themselves, and Aunt Crete rejoiced in the tiny shaded candles and the hothouse roses in the center, and lifted the handsome napkins and silver forks with awe. Sometimes it seemed as if she were still dreaming.

The party from Pleasure Bay had reached home rather late in the afternoon, after a tedious time in the hot sun at a place full of peanut stands and merry-go-rounds and moving picture shows. Luella had not had a good time. She had been disappointed that none of the young men in the party had paid her special attention. In fact, the special young man for whose sake she had prodded her mother into going had not accompanied them at all. Luella was thoroughly cross.

"Mercy, how you've burned your nose, Luella!" said her mother sharply. "It's so unbecoming. The skin is all peeling off. I do wish you'd wear a veil. You can't afford to lose your complexion, with such a figure as you have."

"Oh, fiddlesticks! I wish you'd let up on that, Ma," snapped Luella. "Didn't you get a letter from Aunt Crete? I wonder what she's thinking about not to send that lavender organdie. I wanted to wear it tonight. There's to be a hop in the ballroom, and that would be just the thing. She ought to have got it done; she's had time enough since I telephoned. I suppose she's gone to reading again. I do wish I'd remembered to lock up the bookcase. She's crazy for novels."

All this time Luella was being buttoned into a pink silk muslin heavily decorated with cheap lace. There were twenty-six tiny elusive buttons, and Luella's mother was tired.

"What on earth makes you so long, Ma?" snarled Luella, twisting her neck to try to see her back. "We'll be so late we won't get served, and I'm hungry as a bear."

They hurried down, arriving at the door just as Aunt Crete and Donald were being settled into their chairs by the smiling headwaiter.

"For goodness' sake! those must be swells," said Luella in a low tone. "Did you see how that waiter bowed and smiled? He never does that to us. I expect he got a big tip. See, they're sitting right next to our table. Goodness, Ma, your hair is all slipped to one side. Put it up quick. No, the other side. Say, he's an awfully handsome young man. I wonder if we can get introduced. I just know he dances gracefully. Say, Mother, I'd like to get him for a partner tonight. I guess those stuck-up Grandons would open their eyes then."

"Hush, Luella, he'll hear you."

They settled into their places unassisted by the dilatory waiter, who came languidly up a moment later to take their order.

Aunt Crete's back was happily toward her relatives, so she ate her dinner in comfort. The palms were all about, and the gentle clink of silver and glass, and refined voices. The soft strains of an orchestra hidden in a balcony of ferns and palms drowned Luella's strident voice when it was raised in discontented strain, and so Aunt Crete failed to recognize the sound. But

Donald had been on the alert. In the first place, he had asked a question or two, and knew about where his relatives usually sat, and had purposely asked to be placed near them. He studied Luella when she came in, and felt pretty sure she was the girl he had seen on the platform of the train the morning he arrived in Midvale; and finally in a break in the music he distinctly caught the name "Luella" from the lips of the sour woman in the purple satin with white question-marks all over it and plasters of white lace.

Aunt Carrie was tall and thin, with a discontented droop to her lips, and premature wrinkles. She wore an affected air of abnormal politeness and disapproval of everything. She was studying the silver-gray silk back in front of her and wondering what there was about that elegant-looking woman with the lovely white waved pompadour and puffs, and that exquisite real lace collar, to remind her of poor sister Lucretia. She always coupled the adjective "poor" with her sister's name when she thought of all her shortcomings.

Luella's discontent was somewhat enlivened by the sight of the young man that had not gone on the drive to Pleasure Bay. He stood in the doorway, searching the room with keen, interested eyes. Could it be that he was looking for her? Luella's heart leaped in a moment's triumph. Yes, he seemed to be looking that way as if he had found the object of his search, and he was surely coming down toward them with a real smile on his face. Luella's face broke into preparatory smiles. She would be very coy, and pretend not to see him, so she began a voluble and animated conversation with her mother about the charming time they had had that day, which might have surprised the worthy woman if she had not been accustomed to her daughter's wiles. She knew it to be a warning of the proximity of someone that Luella wished to charm.

The young man came on straight by the solicitous waiters, who waved him frantically to various tables. Luella cast a rapid side glance, and talked on gayly with drooping head and averted gaze. Her mother looked up, wondering, to see what was the cause of Luella's animation. He was quite near now, and in a moment more he would speak. The girl felt excited thrills creeping up her back, and the color rushed into her cheeks, which were already red enough from the wind and sun of the day.

"Well, well," said the young man's voice in a hearty eagerness Luella had never hoped to hear addressed to herself, "this is too good to be true. Don, old man, where did you drop from? I saw your name in the register, and rushed right into the dining room —"

"Clarence Grandon, as true as I live!" said a pleasant voice behind

Luella. "I thought you were in Europe, bless your heart. This is the best thing that could have happened. Let me introduce my aunt —"

Some seconds before this Luella's thrills had changed to chills. Mortification stole over her face and up to the roots of her hair. Even the back of her neck, where her bathing suit was cut low and square, turned angry looking. The pink muslin had a round neck, and showed a half-circle of whiter neck below the bathing suit square. But Luella had the presence of mind to smile on to her mother in mild pretense that she had but just noticed the advent of the young man behind. An obsequious waiter was bringing an extra chair for Mr. Grandon, and he was to be seated so that he could look toward their table. Perhaps he would recognize her yet, and there might be a chance of introduction to the handsome stranger. Luella dallied with her dinner in fond hope, and her mother aided and abetted her.

The lovely old lady with the silver-gray silk and the real lace collar and beautiful hair had her back squarely toward the table where Luella and her mother sat. They could not see her face. They could only notice how interested both the young men were in her, and how courteous they were to her, and they decided she must be some very great personage indeed. They watched her half enviously, and began to plan some way to scrape an acquaintance with her. One glimpse they had of her face as the headwaiter rushed to draw back her chair when she had finished her dinner. It was a fine, handsome face, younger than they had expected to see, with beautiful sparkling eyes full of mirth and contentment. What was there in the face that reminded them of something? Had they ever met that old lady before?

Luella and her mother brought their dallied dessert to a sudden ending, and followed hard upon the footsteps of the three down the length of the dining hall; but the lady in gray with her two attendants had disappeared already, and disconsolately they lingered about, looking up and down the length of piazzas in vain hope to see them sitting in one of the great rows of rockers, watching the many-tinted waves in the dying evening light, but there was no sign of them anywhere.

As they stood thus leaning over the balcony, a large automobile, gray, with white cushions, like a great gliding dove, slipped silently up to the entrance below them in the well-bred silence that an expensive machine knows how to assume under dignified owners.

Luella twitched her mother's sleeve. "That's Grandon's car," she whispered. "P'raps I'll get asked to go. Let's sit down here and wait."

The mother obediently sat down.

Chapter 5

Luella and Her Mother Are Mystified

They had not long to wait. They heard the elevator door slide softly open, and then the gentle swish of silken skirts. Luella looked around just in time to be recognized by young Mr. Grandon if he had not at that moment been placing a long white broadcloth coat about his mother's shoulders. There were four in the party, and Luella's heart sank. He would not be likely to ask another one. The young man and the gray-silk, thread-lace woman from the other dining table were going with them, it appeared. Young Mr. Grandon helped the gray-silk lady down the steps while the handsome stranger walked by Mrs. Grandon. They did not look around at the people on the piazza at all. Luella bit her lips in vexation.

"For pity's sake, Luella, don't scowl so," whispered her mother; "they might look up yet and see you."

This warning came just in time; for young Mr. Grandon just as he was about to start the car glanced up, and, catching Luella's fixed gaze, gave her a distant bow, which was followed by a courteous lifting of the stranger's hat.

Aunt Crete was seated beside Mrs. Grandon in the back seat and beaming her joy quietly. She was secretly exulting that Luella and Carrie had not been in evidence yet. She felt that her joy was being lengthened by a few minutes more, for she could not get away from the fear that her sister and niece would spoil it all as soon as they appeared upon the scene.

"I thought Aunt Carrie and Luella would be tired after their all-day trip, and we wouldn't disturb them tonight," said Donald in a low tone, looking back to Aunt Crete as the car glided smoothly out from the shelter of the wide piazza.

Aunt Crete smiled happily back to Donald, and raised her eyes with a relieved glance toward the rows of people on the piazza. She had been afraid to look her fill before lest she should see Luella frowning at her somewhere; but evidently they had not got back yet, or perhaps had not finished their dinner.

As Aunt Crete raised her eyes, Luella and her mother looked down into her upturned face enviously, but Aunt Crete's gaze had but just grazed them and fallen upon an old lady of stately mien with white, fluffy hair like

32

her own, and a white crepe de chine gown trimmed with much white lace. In deep satisfaction Aunt Crete reflected that, if Luella had aught to say against her aunt's wearing modest white morning gowns, she would cite this model, who was evidently an old aristocrat if one might judge by her jewels and her general makeup.

"Somewhere I've seen that woman with the gray silk!" exclaimed Luella's mother suddenly as Aunt Crete swept by. "There's something real familiar about the set of her shoulders. Look at the way she raises her hand to her face. My land! I believe she reminds me of your Aunt Crete!"

"Now, Mother!" scorned Luella. "As if Aunt Crete could ever look like that! You must be crazy to see anything in such an elegant lady to remind you of poor old Aunt Crete. Why, Ma, this woman is the real thing! Just see how her hair's put up. Nobody but a French maid could get it like that. Imagine Aunt Crete with a French maid. Oh, I'd die laughing. She's probably washing our country cousin's supper dishes at this very minute. I wonder if her conscience doesn't hurt her about my lavender organdie. Say, Ma, did you notice how graceful that handsome stranger was when he handed the ladies into the car? My, but I'd like to know him. I think Clarence Grandon is just a stuck-up prig."

Her mother looked at her sharply.

"Luella, seems to me you change your mind a good deal. If I don't make any mistake, you came down here so's to be near him. What's made you change your mind? He doesn't seem to go with any other girls."

"No, he just sticks by his mother every living minute," sighed Luella unhappily. "I do wish I had that lavender organdie. I look better in that than anything else I've got. I declare I think Aunt Crete is real mean and selfish not to send it. I'm going in to see if the mail has come; and, if the organdie isn't here, nor any word from Aunt Crete, I'm going to call her up on the telephone again."

Luella vanished into the hotel office, and her mother sat and rocked with puckered brows. She very much desired a place in high society for Luella, but how to attain it was the problem. She had not been born for social climbing, and found it difficult to do.

Meantime the motorcar rolled smoothly over the perfect roads, keeping always that wonderful gleaming sea in sight; and Aunt Crete, serenely happy, beamed and nodded to the pleasant chat of Mrs. Grandon, and was so overpowered by her surroundings that she forgot to be overpowered by the grand Mrs. Grandon. As in a dream she heard the kindly tone, and responded mechanically to the questions about her journey and the weather in the city, and how lovely the sea was tonight; but, as she spoke the few words with her lips, her soul was singing, and the words of its song were these:

> Must I be carried to the skies
>   On flowery beds of ease,
> While others fought to win the prize
>   And sailed through bloody seas?

And it seemed to her as they glided along the palace-lined shore, with the rolling sea on one hand, and the beautiful people in their beautiful raiment at ease and happy on the other hand, that she was picked right up out of the hot little brick house in the narrow street, and put on a wonderfully flowery bed of ease, and was floating right into a heaven of which her precious Donald was a bright, particular angel. She forgot all about Luella and what she might say, and just enjoyed herself.

She even found herself telling the elegant Mrs. Grandon exactly how she made piccalilli, and her heart warmed to the other woman as she saw that she was really interested. She had never supposed, from the way in which Luella spoke of the Grandons, that they would even deign to eat such a common thing as a pickle, let alone knowing anything about it. Aunt Crete's decision was that Mrs. Grandon wasn't stuck-up in the least, but just a nice, common lady like anyone; and, as she went up in the elevator beside her, and said good-night, she felt as if she had known her all her life.

It was not until she had turned out her light and crept into the great hotel bed that it came to her to wonder whether Luella and Carrie could be meant by the ones in the hymn,

> While others fought to win the prize
>   And sailed through bloody seas.

She couldn't help feeling that perhaps she had been selfish in enjoying her day so much when for aught she knew Luella might not be having a good time. For Luella not to have a good time meant blame for her aunt generally. Ever since Luella had been born it had been borne in upon Aunt Crete that there was a moral obligation upon her to make Luella have a good time. And now Aunt Crete was having a good time, the time of her life; and she hugged herself, she was so happy over it, and thought of the dear stars out there in the deep, dark blue of the arching sky, and the cool, dark roll of the white-tipped waves, and was thankful.

Luella and her mother had gloomily watched the dancing through the open windows of the ballroom; but, as they knew no one inside, they did not venture in. Luella kept one eye out for the return of the car, but somehow missed it, and finally retired to the solace of cold cream and the comforts of the fourth floor back, where lingered in the atmosphere a reminder of the dinner past and a hint of the breakfast that was to come.

As the elevator ascended past the second floor, the door of one of the special apartments stood wide, revealing a glimpse of the handsome young stranger standing under the chandelier reading a letter, his face alive with pleasure. Luella sighed enviously, and in her dreams strove vainly to enter into the charmed circle where these favored beings moved, and knew not that of her own free will she had closed the door to that very special apartment, which might have been hers but for her own action.

The next morning Luella was twisting her neck in a vain endeavor to set the string of artificial puffs straight upon the enormous cushion of her hair, till they looked for all the world like a pan of rolls just out of the oven. She had jerked them off four separate times, and pulled the rest of her hair down twice in a vain attempt to get just the desired effect; and her patience, never very great at any time, was well-nigh exhausted. Her mother was fretting because the best pieces of fish and all the hot rolls would be gone before they got down to breakfast, and Luella was snapping back in most undaughterly fashion, when a noticeable tap came on the door. It was not the tap of the chambermaid of the fourth floor back, nor of the elevator boy, who knew how to modulate his knock for every grade of room from the second story, ocean front, up and back. It was a knock of rare condescension, mingled with a call to attention; and it warned these favored occupants of room 410 to sit up and take notice, not that they were worthy of any such consideration as was about to fall upon them.

Luella drove the last hairpin into the puffs, and sprang to the door just as her mother opened it. She felt something was about to happen. Could it be that she was to be invited to ride in that automobile at last, or what?

There in the hall, looking very much out of place, and as if he hoped his condescension would be appreciated, but he doubted it, stood the uniformed functionary who usually confined his activities to the second floor front, where the tips were large and the guests of unquestioned wealth, to say nothing of culture. He held in his hand a shining silver tray on which lay two cards, and he delivered his message in a tone that not only showed the deference he felt for the one who had sent him, but compelled such deference also on the part of those to whom he spoke.

"The lady and gen'leman say, Will the ladies come down to the private pahlah as soon aftah breakfus' as is convenient, room number 2, second floor front?" He bowed to signify that his mission was completed, and that if it did not carry through, it was entirely beyond his sphere to do more.

Luella grasped the cards and smothered an exclamation of delight.

"Second floor front," gasped her mother. "The private parlor! Did you hear, Luella?"

But Luella was standing by the one window, frowning over the cards. One was written and one was engraved, a lady's and a gentleman's cards. "Miss Ward." "Mr. Donald Ward Grant."

"For the land's sake, Ma! Who in life are they? Do you know any Miss Ward? You don't s'pose it's that lovely gray-silk woman. Miss Ward. Donald Ward Grant. Who can they be, and what do you suppose they want? Grant. Donald Grant. Where have I, why —! Oh, horrors, Ma! It can't be that dreadful cousin has followed us up, can it? Donald Grant is his name, of course; yes, Donald Ward Grant. It was the Ward that threw me off. But who is the other? Miss Ward. Ma! You don't —"

"Luella Burton, that's just what it is! It's your Aunt Crete and that dreadful cousin. Crete never did have any sense, if she is my sister. But just let me get ahold of her! If I don't make her writhe. I think I'll find a way to make her understand —"

Luella's expansive bravery beneath the row of biscuit puffs seemed to shrink and cringe as she took in the thought.

"Oh, Ma!" she groaned. "How could she? And here of all places? To come here and mortify me! It is just too dreadful. Ma, it can't be true. Aunt Crete would never dare. And where would she get the money? She hasn't a cent of her own, has she? You didn't go and leave her money, did you?"

"No, only a little change in my old pocketbook; it wouldn't have been enough to come down here on, unless she bought a day excursion. Wait. I did leave five dollars to pay the grocery bill with. But Crete surely wouldn't take that. Still, there's no telling. She always was a kind of a child. Oh, dear! What shall we do?" The mother sat down on the tumbled bed beside the tray of Luella's cheap trunk.

"Well, we must do something, that's certain, if we have to run away again. It would never do to have those two appear here now. Mercy! think of Aunt Crete in her old black and white silk sitting next table to that lovely lady in gray. I should simply sink through the floor."

"We can't run away, Luella," snapped the practical mother. "We've paid for our room two weeks ahead. I didn't want to do that; but you thought if Aunt Crete should get any nonsense into her head about our coming home, we would tell we'd paid for the room, and that would settle it with her. So now it's done, and we can't afford not to abide by it. Besides, what good would that do? We couldn't afford to go anywhere but home, and that would be as bad as it was in the first place. We've got to think it out. If I just had hold of Crete a minute, I'd make her fix it up. She'd have to think of some way out of it herself without any of my help, to pay her for her stupidity in coming. I can't understand how she'd do it."

"I didn't think she'd dare!" glared Luella with no pleasant expression on her face.

"I'll tell you what we'll have to do, Luella," said her mother. "We'll slip down those stairs in the back hall. I went down one day, and they go right out on the piazza that runs in front of the dining room. We'll just slip in the back door, and get our breakfast right away. It's getting pretty late. You better hurry. They've likely come up from town on that very early train, and they'll sit and wait for us. We'll ring for a messenger bellboy, and send down a note that my ankle is so much worse I can't come downstairs, and you can't leave me. We'll say: 'Mrs. Burton and Miss Burton regret that they cannot come down as requested: but Mrs. Burton is confined to her bed by a sprained ankle, and her daughter cannot leave her. Miss Ward will have to come up.' You write it on one of your visiting cards, Luella, and we'll send it down as quick as we get back from breakfast. Hurry up. The only thing about it will be that climb up three flights after breakfast, but it won't do for us to risk the elevator. Crete might recognize us, for the elevator goes right by that second floor front parlor. What I don't understand is how they got in there. It's only rich people can afford that. But, land! Crete's just like a baby; hasn't been out in the world ever; and very likely she never asked how much the rooms were, but just took the best she could lay eyes on. Or more likely it's a mistake, and she's sitting in that little reception room down on the office floor, and thinks it the second floor because she came up such a long flight of steps from the sidewalk. We'll have to tell the bellboy to hunt up the fellow that brought their cards, and take it to the same folks. Come on now, Luella, and go slow when you turn corners. There's no telling but they might be prowling round trying to hunt us; so keep a lookout."

Thus by devious and back ways they descended to a late breakfast, and scuttled up again without being molested.

Luella wrote the note on her card as her mother dictated, and a small boy all brass buttons was despatched with careful directions; and then the two retired behind their ramparts, and waited.

Time went by, until half an hour had elapsed since they came back from breakfast. They had listened anxiously to every footfall in the hall, and part of the time Luella kept the door open a crack with her ear to it. Their nerves were all in a quiver. When the chambermaid arrived, they were fairly feverish to get her out of the way. If Aunt Crete should come while she was in the room, it might get all over the hotel what kind of relatives they had.

Mrs. Burton suggested to the chambermaid that she leave their room till last, as they wanted to write some letters before going out; but the maid declared she must do the room at once or not at all. The elevator slid up and down around the corner in the next hall. They heard a footfall now and then, but none that sounded like Aunt Crete's. They rang again for the office-boy, who declared he had delivered the message in the second floor front, and that the lady and gentleman were both in and said, "All right." He vanished impudently without waiting for Luella's probing questions, and they looked at each other in anxiety and indignation.

"It is too mean, Ma, to lose this whole morning. I wanted to go in bathing," complained Luella, "and now no telling how long I'll have to stick in this dull room. I wish Aunt Crete was in Halifax. Why couldn't I have had some nice relatives like that lovely old gray-silk lady and her son?"

Just then the elevator clanged open and shut, and steps came down the hall. It certainly was not Aunt Crete. Luella flew to the door at the first tap; and there, submerged in a sheaf of American Beauty roses, stood the functionary from the lower floor, with a less pompous manner than he had worn before. The roses had caused his respect for the occupants of the fourth floor back, to rise several degrees.

Luella stood speechless in wonder, looking first at the roses and then at the servant. Such roses had never come into her life before. Could it be — must it be — but a miserable mistake?

Then the servant spoke.

"Miss Ward sends the flowers, an' is sorry the ladies aren't well. She sends her regrets, an' says she can't come to see the ladies 'count of a drive she'd promised to take today, in which she'd hoped to have the ladies' comp'ny. She hopes the ladies are better this even'n."

He was gone, and the mother and daughter faced each other over the roses, bewilderment and awe in their faces.

"*What* did he say, Luella? *Who* sent those roses? Miss *Ward?* Luella, there's some mistake. Aunt Crete couldn't have sent them. She wouldn't *dare!* Besides, where would she get the money? It's perfectly impossible. It can't be Aunt Crete, after all. It must be someone else with the same name. Perhaps Donald has picked up someone here in the hotel; you can't tell; or perhaps it isn't our Donald at all. It's likely there's other Donald Grants in the world. What we ought to have done was to go down at once and find out, and not skulk in a corner. But you're always in such a hurry to do something, Luella. There's no telling at all who this is now. It might be those folks you admired so much, though what on earth they should have sent their cards to us for — and those lovely roses — I'm sure I don't know."

"Now, Ma, you needn't blame me. It was you proposed sending that note down; you know it was, Mother; and of course I had to do what you said. I was so upset, anyway; I didn't know what was what. But now, you see, perhaps you've cut me out of a lovely day. We might have gone on a ride with them."

"Luella," her mother broke in sharply, "if you talk another word like that, I'll take the next train back home. You don't know what you are talking about. It may be Aunt Crete, after all, and a country cousin for all you know; and, if it is, would you have wanted to go driving in the face of the whole hotel, with like as not some old shin-and-bones horse and broken-down carriage?"

Luella was silenced for the time, and the room settled into gloomy meditation.

Chapter 6
An Embarrassing Meeting

Meantime Aunt Crete in the whitest of her white was settling herself comfortably on the gray cushions of the fringed phaeton again, relief and joy mingled in her countenance. It was not that she was glad that Carrie's ankle was so bad, but that she was to have another short reprieve before her pleasure was cut off. Soon enough, she thought, would she be destined to sit in the darkened room and minister to her fussy sister, while Luella took her place in the carriages and automobiles with her handsome young cousin, as young folks should do, of course; but Oh, it was good, good, that a tired old lady, who had worked hard all her life, could yet have had this bit of a glimpse of the brighter side of life before she died.

It would be something to sit and think over as she scraped potatoes for dinner, or picked over blackberries for jam, or patiently sewed on Val lace for Luella. It would be an event to date from, and she could fancy herself mildly saying to Mrs. Judge Waters, when she sat beside her sometime at missionary meeting, if she ever did again, "When my nephew took me down to the shore," and so forth. She never knew just what to talk about when she sat beside Mrs. Judge Waters, but here was a topic worth laying before such a great lady.

Well, it was something to be thankful for, and she resolved she just would not think of poor Carrie and Luella until her beautiful morning was over. Then she would show such patience and gratitude as would fully make up to them for her one more day of pleasure.

It was Donald, of course, who had suggested the roses. When the message came from the fourth floor back, Aunt Crete had turned white about the mouth, and her eyes had taken on a frightened, hunted look, while the double V in her forehead flashed into sight for the first time since they had reached the Atlantic coast. He saw at once in what terror Aunt Crete held her sister and niece, and his indignation arose in true Christian fashion. He resolved to place some nice hot coals on the heads of his unpleasant relatives, and run away with dear Aunt Crete again; hence the roses and the message, and Aunt Crete was fairly childish with pleasure over them when he finally persuaded her that it would be all right to send these in place of going up herself as she had been bidden.

She listened eagerly as Donald gave careful directions for the message, and the stately functionary respectfully repeated the words with his own high-sounding inflection. It made the pink come and go again in Aunt Crete's cheeks, and she felt that Luella and Carrie could not be angry with her after these roses, and especially when everything was being done up in so nice, stylish a manner.

The drive was one long dream of bliss to Aunt Crete. They went miles up the coast, and took lunch at a hotel much grander than the one they had left, so that when they returned in the afternoon Aunt Crete felt much less in awe of the Traymore, her experience in hotels having broadened. They also met some friends of Donald's, a professor from his alma mater, who with his wife was just returning from a trip to Europe.

The bathers were making merry in the waves as they returned, and Aunt Crete's wistful look made Donald ask whether she felt too tired to take another dip, but she declared she was not one bit tired.

She came from her bath with shining eyes and triumphant mien. Whatever happened now, she had been in bathing twice. She felt like quite an experienced bather, and she could dream of that wonderful experience of being lifted high above the swells in Donald's strong young arms.

She obediently took her nap, and surrendered herself to the hands of the maid to have the finishing touches put to her toilet. It was the soft gray voile that she elected to wear tonight, and Donald admired her when she emerged from her room in the dress, looking every inch a lady.

A knock sounded at the door before he had had time to give Aunt Crete a word of his admiration; but his eyes had said enough, and she felt a flow of humble pride in her new self, the self that he had created out of what she had always considered an unusually plain old woman. With the consciousness of her becoming attire upon her she turned with mild curiosity to see who had knocked, and, behold, her sister and niece stood before her!

The day had been passed by them in melancholy speculations and the making and abandoning of many plans of procedure. After careful deliberation they at last concluded that there was nothing to be done but go down and find out who these people really were, and if possible allay the ghost of their fears and set themselves free from their dull little room.

"If it should be Aunt Crete and Donald, we'll just settle them up and send them off at once, won't we, Mother?"

"Certainly," said Mrs. Burton with an angry snap to her eyes. "Trust me to settle with your Aunt Crete if it's really her. But I can't think it is. It isn't like Crete one bit to leave her duty. She's got a lot of work to do, and she never leaves her work till it's done. It must be someone else. What if it should be those folks you admire so much? I've been thinking. We had some New York cousins by the name of Ward. It might be one of them, and Donald might have gone to them first, and they've brought him down here. I can't think he's very much, though. But we'll just hope for the best, anyway, till we find out. If it's Aunt Crete, I shall simply talk to her till she is brought to her senses, and make her understand that she's got to go right home. I'll tell her how she's mortifying you, and spoiling your chances of a good match, perhaps —"

"Oh, Ma!" giggled Luella in admiration.

"I'll tell her she must tell Donald she's got to go right home, that the sea air don't agree with her one bit — it goes to her head or something like that, and then we'll make him feel it wouldn't be gallant in him not to take her home. That's easy enough, if 'tis them."

"But Ma, have you thought about your sprained ankle? How 'll they think you got over it so quick? S'posing it shouldn't be Aunt Crete."

"Well, I'll tell her the swelling's gone down, and all of a sudden something seemed to slip back into place again, and I'm all right."

This was while they were buttoning and hooking each other into their best and most elaborate garments for the peradventure that the people they were to meet might prove to be of patrician class.

They had been somewhat puzzled how to find their possible relatives after they were attired for the advance on the enemy, but consultation with the functionary in the office showed them that, whoever Miss Ward and Donald Grant might be, they surely were at present occupying the apartments on the second floor front.

For one strenuous moment after the elevator had left them before the door of the private parlor they had carefully surveyed each other, fastening a stubborn hook here, putting up a stray rebellious lock there, patting a puff into subordination. Mrs. Burton was arrayed in an elaborate tucked and puffed and belaced lavender muslin whose laborious design had been attained through hours of the long winter evenings past. Luella wore what she considered her most fetching garment, a long, scant, high-waisted robe of fire-red crepe, with nothing to relieve its glare, reflected in staring hues in her already much-burned nose and cheeks. Her hair had been in preparation all the afternoon, and looked as if it was carved in waves and puffs out of black walnut, so closely was it beset with that most noticeable of all invisible devices, an invisible net.

They entered, and stood face to face with the wonderful lady in the gray gown, whose every line and graceful fold spoke of the skill of a foreign tailor. And then, strange to say, it was Aunt Crete who came to herself first.

Perfectly conscious of her comely array, and strong in the strength of her handsome nephew who stood near to protect, she suddenly lost all fear of her fretful sister and bullying niece, and stepped forward with an unconscious grace of welcome that must have been hers all the time, or it never would have come to the front in this crisis.

"Why, here you are at last, Luella! How nice you look in your red crepe! Why Carrie, I'm real glad you've got better so you could come down. How is your ankle? And here is Donald. Carrie, can't you see Hannah's looks in him?"

Amazement and embarrassment struggled in the faces of mother and daughter. They looked at Aunt Crete, and they looked at Donald, and then they looked at Aunt Crete again. It couldn't be, it wasn't, yet it was, the voice of Aunt Crete, kind and forgiving, and always thoughtful for everyone, yet with a new something in it. Or was it rather the lack of something? Yes, that was it, the lack of a certain servile something that neither Luella nor her mother could name, yet which made them feel strangely ill at ease with this new-old Aunt Crete.

They looked at each other bewildered, and then back at Aunt Crete again, tracing line by line the familiar features in their new radiance of happiness, and trying to conjure back the worried V in her forehead, and the slinky sag of her old gowns. Was the world turned upside down? What had happened to Aunt Crete?

"Upon my word, Lucretia Ward, is it really you?" exclaimed her sister, making a wild dash into the conversation, determined to right herself and everything else if possible. She felt like a person suddenly upset in a canoe, and she struggled wildly to get her footing once more if there was any solid footing anywhere, with her sister Crete standing there calmly in an imported gown, her hair done up like a fashion plate, and a millionaire's smile on her pleasant face.

But Luella was growing angry. What did Aunt Crete mean by masquerading round in that fashion and making them ashamed before this handsome young man? and was he really their western cousin? Luella felt that a joke was being played upon her, and she always resented jokes — at least, unless she played them herself.

Then Donald came to the front, for he feared for Aunt Crete's poise. She must not lose her calm dignity and get frightened. There was a sharp ring in the other aunt's voice, and the new cousin looked unpromising.

"And is this my aunt Carrie? And my cousin Luella?" He stepped forward, and shook hands pleasantly.

"I am glad to be able to speak with you at last," he said as he dropped

Luella's hand, "though it's not the first time I've seen you, nor heard your voice, either, you know."

Luella looked up puzzled, and tried to muster her scattered graces, and respond with her ravishing society air, but somehow the ease and grace of the man before her overpowered her. And was he really her cousin? She tried to think what he could mean by having seen and talked with her before. Surely he must be mistaken, or — perhaps he was referring to the glimpse he had of her when Mr. Grandon bowed the evening before. She tossed her head with a kittenish movement, and arched her poorly pencilled eyebrows.

"Oh, how is that?" she asked, wishing he had not been quite so quick to drop her hand. It would have been more impressive to have had him hold it just a second longer.

"Why, I saw you the morning you left your home, as I was getting out of the train. You were just entering, and you called out of the window to a young lady in a pony cart. You wore a light kind of a yellowish suit, didn't you? Yes, I was very sure it was you."

He was studying her face closely, a curious twinkle in his eyes, which might or might not have been complimentary. Luella could not be sure. The color rose in her cheeks and neck and up to her black-walnut hair till the red dress and the red face looked all of a flame. She suddenly remembered what she had called out to the young lady in the pony cart, and she wondered whether he had heard or noticed.

"And then," went on her handsome persecutor, "I had quite a long talk with you over the telephone, you know —"

"What!" gasped Luella. "Was that you? Why, you must be mistaken, I never telephoned to you; that is, I couldn't get anyone on the phone."

"What's all this about, Luella?" questioned her mother sharply, but Donald interposed.

"Sit down, Aunt Carrie. We are so excited over meeting you at last that we are forgetting to be courteous." He shoved forth a comfortable chair for his aunt, and another for the blushing, overwhelmed Luella, and then he took Aunt Crete's hands lovingly, and gently pushed her backward into the most comfortable rocker in the room. "It's just as easy to sit down, dear Aunt," he said, smiling. "And you know you've had a pretty full day, and must not get tired for tonight's concert at the Casino. Now, Aunt Carrie, tell us about your ankle. How did you come to sprain it so badly, and how did it get well so fast? We were quite alarmed about you. Is it really better? I am afraid you are taxing it too much to have come down this evening. Much as we wanted to see you, we could have waited until it was quite safe for you to use it, rather than have you run any risks."

Then it was the mother's turn to blush, and her thin, somewhat colorless face grew crimson with embarrassment.

"Why, I —" she began; "that is, Luella was working over it, rubbing it with liniment, and all of a sudden she gave it a sort of a little pull, and something seemed to give way with a sharp pain, and then it came all right as good as ever. It feels a little weak, but I think by morning it'll be all right. I think some little bone got out of place, and Luella pulled it back in again. My ankles have always been weak, anyway. I suffer a great deal with them in going about my work at home."

"Why, Carrie," said Aunt Crete, leaning forward with troubled reproach in her face, "you never complained about it."

A dull red rolled over Mrs. Burton's thin features again, and receded, leaving her face pinched and haggard-looking. She felt as if she were seeing visions. This couldn't be her own sister, all dressed up so, and yet speaking in the old sympathetic tone.

"Oh, I never complain, of course. It don't do any good."

The conversation was interrupted by another tap on the door. Donald opened it, and received a large express package. While he was giving some orders to the servant, Mrs. Burton leaned forward, and said in a low tone to her sister:

"For goodness' sake, Lucretia Ward, what does all this mean? How ever did you get decked out like that?"

Then Donald's clear voice broke in upon them as the door closed once more, and Luella watched him curiously cutting with eager, boyish haste the cords of the express package.

"Aunt Crete, your cloak has come. Now we'll all see if it's becoming."

"Bless the boy," said Aunt Crete, looking up with delighted eyes. "Cloak; what cloak? I'm sure I've got wraps enough now. There's the cloth coat, and the silk one, and that elegant black lace —"

"No, you haven't. I saw right off what you needed when we went out in the auto last night, and I telephoned to that Miss Brower up in the city this morning, and she's fixed it all up. I hope you'll like it."

With that he pulled the cover off the box, and brought to view a long, full evening cloak of pale pearl-colored broadcloth lined with white silk, and a touch about the neck of black velvet and handsome creamy lace.

He held it up at arm's length admiringly.

"It's all right, Aunt Crete. It looks just like you. I knew that woman would understand. Stand up, and let's see how you look in it, and then after dinner we'll take a little spin around the streets to try you in it."

Aunt Crete, blushing like a pretty girl, stood up, and he folded the soft garment about her in all its elegant richness. She stood just in front of the full-length mirror, and could not deny to herself that it was becoming. But she was getting used to seeing herself look well, and was not so much overpowered with the sight as she was with the tender thought of the boy that had got it for her. She forgot Carrie and Luella, and everything but that Donald had gone to great trouble and expense to please her, and she just turned around, and put her two hands, one on each of his cheeks, standing on her tiptoes to reach him, and kissed him.

He bent and returned the kiss laughingly.

"It's a lot of fun to get you things, Aunt Crete," he said; "you always like them so much."

"It is beautiful, beautiful," she said, looking down and smoothing the cloth tenderly as if it had been his cheek. "It's much too beautiful for me. Donald, you will spoil me."

"Yes, I should think so," sniffed Luella, as if offering an apology in some sort for her childish aunt.

"A little spoiling won't hurt you, dear Aunt," said Donald seriously. "I don't believe you've had your share of spoiling yet, and I mean to give it to you if I can. Doesn't she look pretty in it, Cousin Luella? Come now, Aunt Carrie, I suppose it's time to go down to dinner, or we shan't get through in time for the fun. Are you sure your ankle is quite well? Are you able to go to the Casino tonight? I've tickets for us all. Sousa's orchestra is to be there, and the program is an unusually fine one."

Luella was mortified and angry beyond words, but a chance to go to the Casino, in company with Clarence Grandon and his mother, was not to be lightly thrown away, and she crushed down her mortification, contenting herself with darting an angry glance and a hateful curl of her lip at Aunt Crete as they went out the door together. This, however, was altogether lost on that little woman, for she was watching her nephew's face, and wondering how it came that such joy had fallen to her lot.

There was no chance for the mortified mother and daughter to exchange a word as they went down in the elevator or followed in the wake of their relatives, before whom all porters and office boys and even headwaiters bowed, and jumped to offer assistance. They were having their wish, to be sure, entering the dining hall behind the handsome young man and the elegant, gray-clad, fashionably coiffured old lady, a part of the train, with the full consciousness of "belonging," yet in what a way! Both were having ample opportunity for reflection, for they could see at a glance that no one noticed them, and all attention was for those ahead of them.

Luella bit her lip angrily, and looked in wonder at Aunt Crete, who somehow had lost her dumpiness, and walked as gracefully beside her tall young nephew as if she had been accustomed to walk in the eyes of the world thus for years. The true secret of her grace, if Luella had but known it, was that she was not thinking in the least of herself. Her conscience was at rest now, for the meeting between the cousins was over, and Luella was to have a good time too. Aunt Crete was never the least bit selfish. It seemed to her that her good time was only blooming into yet larger things, after all.

Behind her walked her sister and niece in mortified humiliation. Luella was trying to recall just what she had said about "country cousins" over the telephone, and exactly what she had said to the girl in the pony cart the morning she left home. The memory did not serve to cool her already heated complexion. It was beginning to dawn upon her that she had made a mighty mistake in running away from such a cousin and in such a manner.

All her life, in such a case, Luella had been accustomed to lay the blame of her disappointments upon someone else, and vent, as it were, her spite upon that one. Now, in looking about to find such an object of blame her eyes naturally fell upon the one that had borne the greater part of all blame for her. But, try as she would to pour out blame and scorn from her large, bold eyes upon poor Aunt Crete, somehow the blame seemed to slip off from the sweet gray garments, and leave Aunt Crete as serene as ever, with her eyes turned trustingly toward her dear Donald. Luella was brought to the verge of vexation by this, and could scarcely eat any dinner.

The dessert was just being served when the waiter brought Aunt Crete a dainty note from which a faint perfume of violets stole across the table to the knowing nostrils of Luella.

With the happy abandonment of a child Aunt Crete opened it joyously.

"Who in the world can be writing to me?" she said wonderingly. "You'll have to read it for me, Donald; I've left my glasses up in my room."

Luella made haste to reach out her hand for the note, but Donald had it first, as if he had not seen her impatient hand claiming her right to read Aunt Crete's notes.

"It's from Mrs. Grandon, Auntie," he said.

"Dear Miss Ward," he read, "I am sorry that I am feeling too weary to go to the concert this evening as we had planned, and my son makes such a baby of me that he thinks he cannot leave me alone; but I do hope we can have the pleasure of the company of yourself and your nephew on a little auto trip to-morrow afternoon. My brother has a villa a few miles up the

shore, and he telephoned us this morning to dine with them tonight. When he heard of your being here, he said by all means to bring you with us. My brother knows of your nephew's friendship with Clarence, and is anxious to meet him, as are the rest of his family. I do hope you will feel able to go with us.

"With sincere regrets that I cannot go with you to the Casino this evening,

HELEN GRANDON."

For the moment Luella forgot everything else in her amazement at this letter. Aunt Crete receiving notes from Mrs. Grandon, from whom she and her mother could scarcely get a frigid bow! Aunt Crete invited on automobile trips and dinners in villas! Donald an intimate friend of Clarence Grandon's! Oh, fool and blind! What had she done! Or what had she undone? She studied the handsome, keen face of her cousin as he bent over the letter, and writhed to think of her own words, "I'm running away from a backwoods cousin"! She could hear it shouted from one end of the great dining hall to the other, and her face blazed redder and redder till she thought it would burst. Her mother turned from her in mortified silence, and wondered why Luella couldn't have had a good complexion.

Studied politeness was the part that Donald had set for himself this evening. He began to see that his victims were sufficiently unhappy. He had no wish to see them writhe under further tortures, though when he looked upon Aunt Crete's happy face, and thought how white it had turned at dread of them, he felt he must let the thorns he had planted in their hearts remain long enough to bring forth a true repentance. But he said nothing further to distress them, and they began to wonder whether, after all, he really had seen through their plan of running away from him.

It was all Aunt Crete's fault. She ought to have arranged it in some way to get them quietly home as soon as she found out what kind of cousin it was that had come to see them. It never occurred to Luella that nothing her poor, abused aunt could have said would have convinced her that her cousin was worthy of her homecoming.

As the concert drew near to its close, Luella and her mother began to prepare for a time of reckoning for Aunt Crete. When she was safely in her room what was to hinder them from going to her alone and having it out? The sister's face hardened, and the niece's eyes glittered as she stonily thought of the scornful sentences she would hurl after her aunt.

Donald looked at her menacing face, and read its thoughts. He resolved to protect Aunt Crete, whatever came; so at the door, when he saw a motion on his Aunt Crete's part to pause, he said gently: "Aunt Crete, I guess we'll have to say good-night now, for you've had a hard day of it, and I want you to be bright and fresh for morning. We want to take an early dip in the ocean. The bathing hours are early tomorrow, I see."

He bowed good-night in his pleasantest manner, and the ladies from the fourth floor reluctantly withdrew to the elevator, but fifteen minutes later surreptitiously tapped at the private door of the room they understood to be Aunt Crete's.

Chapter 7
Luella's Humiliation

The door was opened cautiously by the maid, who was doing Aunt Crete's hair, having just finished a most refreshing facial massage given at Donald's express orders.

Aunt Crete looked round upon her visitors with a rested, rosy countenance, which bloomed out under her fluff of soft, white hair, and quite startled her sister with its freshness and youth. Could it be possible that this was really her sister Crete, or had she made a terrible mistake, and entered the wrong apartment?

But a change came suddenly over the ruddy countenance of Aunt Crete as over the face of a child that in the midst of happy play sees a trouble descending upon it. A look almost of terror came over her, and she caught her breath, and waited to see what was coming.

"Why, Carrie, Luella!" she gasped weakly. "I thought you'd gone to bed. Marie's just doing up my hair for night. She's been giving me a face massage. You ought to try one. It makes you feel young again."

"H'm!" said her affronted sister. "I shouldn't care for one."

Marie looked over Luella and her mother, beginning with the painfully elaborate arrangement of hair, and going down to the tips of their boots. Luella's face burned with mortification as she read the withering disapproval in the French woman's countenance.

"Let's sit down till she's done," said Luella, dropping promptly on the foot of Aunt Crete's bed and gazing around in frank surprise over the spaciousness of the apartment.

Thereupon the maid ignored them, and went about her work, brushing out and deftly manipulating the wavy white hair, and chattering pleasantly meanwhile, just as if no one else were in the room. Aunt Crete tried to forget what was before her, or, rather, behind her; but her hands trembled a little as they lay in her lap in the folds of the pretty pink and gray challis kimono she wore; and all of a sudden she remembered the unwhitewashed cellar, and the uncooked jam, and the unmade shirtwaists, and the little hot brick house gazing at her reproachfully from the distant home, and she here in this fine array, forgetting it all and being waited upon by a maid — a lazy truant from her duty.

Did the heart of the maid divine the state of things, or was it only her natural instinct that made her turn to protect the pleasant little woman, in whose service she had always been well paid, against the two women that were so evidently of the common walks of life, and were trying to ape those that in the eyes of the maid were their betters? However it was, Marie prolonged her duties a good half hour, and Luella's impatience waxed furious, so that she lost her fear of the maid gradually, and yawned loudly, declaring that Aunt Crete had surely had enough fussing over for one evening.

They held in their more personal remarks until the door finally closed upon Marie, but burst forth so immediately that she heard the opening sentences through the transom, and thought it wise to step to the young gentleman's door and warn him that his elderly relative of whom he seemed so careful was likely to be disturbed beyond a reasonable hour for retiring. Then she discreetly withdrew, having not only added to her generous income by a good bit of silver, but also having followed out the dictates of her heart, which had taken kindly to the gentle woman of the handsome clothes and few pretensions.

"Well, upon my word! I should think you'd be ashamed, Aunt Crete!" burst forth Luella, arising from the bed in a majesty of wrath. "Sitting there, being waited on like a baby, when you ought to be at home this minute earning your living. What do you think of yourself, anyway, living in this kind of luxury when you haven't a cent in the world of your own, and your own sister, who has supported you for years, up in a little dark fourth-floor room? Such selfishness I never saw in all my life. I wouldn't have believed it of you, though we might have suspected it long ago from the foolish things you were always doing. Aunt Crete, have you any idea how much all this costs?"

She waved her hand tragically over the handsome room, including the trunk standing open, and the gleam of silver-gray silk that peeped through the half-open closet door. Aunt Crete fairly cringed under Luella's scornful eyes.

"And you, nothing in the world but a beggar, a *beggar!* That's what you are — a beggar depending upon *us;* and you swelling around as if you owned the earth, and daring to wear silk dresses and real lace collars and expensive jewelry, and even having a maid, and shaming your own relatives, and getting in ahead of us, who have always been good to you, and taking away our friends, and making us appear like two cents! It's just fierce, Aunt Crete! It's — it's *heathenish!*" Luella paused in her anger for a fitting word, and then took the first one that came.

Aunt Crete winced. She was devoted to the Woman's Missionary Society, and it was terrible to be likened to a heathen. She wished Luella had chosen some other word.

"I should think you'd be so ashamed you couldn't hold your head up before your honest relatives," went on the shameless girl. "Taking money from a stranger — that's what he is, a *stranger* — and you whining round and lowering yourself to let him buy you clothes and things, as if you didn't have proper clothes suited to your age and station. He's a young upstart coming along and daring to buy you any — and such clothes! Do you know you're a laughingstock? What would Mrs. Grandon say if she knew whom she was inviting to her automobile rides and dinners? Think of you in your old purple calico washing the dishes at home, and scrubbing the kitchen, and ask yourself what you would say if Mrs. Grandon should come to call on you, and find you that way. You're a hypocrite, Aunt Crete, an awful hypocrite!"

Luella towered over Aunt Crete, and the little old lady looked into her eyes with a horrible fascination, while her great grief and horror poured down her sweet face in tears of anguish that would not be stayed. Her kindly lips were quivering, and her eyes were wide with the tears.

Luella saw that she was making an impression, and she went on more wildly than before, her fury growing with every word, and not realizing how loud her voice was.

"And it isn't enough that you should do all that, but now you're going to spoil my prospects with Clarence Grandon. You can't keep up this masquerade long, and when they find out what you really are, what will they think of *me?* It'll be all over with me, and it'll be your fault, Aunt Crete, your fault, and you'll never have a happy moment afterwards, thinking of how you spoiled my life."

"Now, Luella," broke in Aunt Crete solemnly through her tears, "you're mistaken about one thing. It won't be my fault there, for it wouldn't have made a bit of difference, poor child. I'm real sorry for you, and I meant to tell you just as soon as we got home, for I couldn't bear to spoil your pleasure while we were here, but that Clarence Grandon belongs to someone else. He isn't for you, Luella, and there must have been some mistake about it. Perhaps he was just being kind to you. For Donald knows him real well, and he says he's engaged to a girl out west, and they're going to be married this fall, and Donald says she's real sweet and —"

But Aunt Crete's quavering voice stopped suddenly in mild affright, for Luella sprang toward her like some mad creature, shaking her finger in her aunt's face, and screaming at the top of her voice:

"It's a lie! I say it's a lie! Aunt Crete, you're a liar; that's what you are with all the rest."

And the high-strung, uncontrolled girl burst into angry sobs.

No one heard the gentle knock that had been twice repeated during the scene, and no one saw the door open until they all suddenly became aware that Donald stood in the room, looking from one face to another in angry surprise.

Donald had not retired at once after bidding Aunt Crete good-night. He found letters and telegrams awaiting his attention, and he had been busy writing a letter of great importance when the maid gave him the hint of Aunt Crete's late callers. Laying down his pen, he stepped quietly across the private parlor that separated his room from his aunt's, and stopped a moment before the door to make sure he heard voices. Then he had knocked, and knocked again, unable to keep from hearing the most of Luella's tirade.

His indignation knew no bounds, and he concluded his time had come to interfere, so he opened the door, and went in.

"What does all this mean?" he asked in a tone that frightened his Aunt Carrie, and made Luella stop her angry sobs in sudden awe.

No one spoke, and Aunt Crete looked a mute appeal through her tears. "What is it, dear Aunt?" he said, stepping over by her side, and placing his arm protectingly round the poor, shrinking little figure, who somehow in her sorrow and helplessness reminded him strongly of his own lost mother. He could not remember at that moment that the other woman, standing hard and cold and angry across the room, was also his mother's sister. She did not look like his mother, nor act like her.

Aunt Crete put her little curled white head in its crisping-pins down on Donald's coat sleeve, and shrank into her pink and gray kimono appealingly as she tried to speak.

"It's just as I told you, Donald, you dear boy," she sobbed out. "I — oughtn't to have come. I knew it, but it wasn't your fault. It was all mine. I ought to have stayed at home, and not dressed up and come off here. I've had a beautiful time, but it wasn't for me, and I oughtn't to have taken it. It's just spoiled Luella's nice time, and she's blaming me, just as I knew she would."

"What does my cousin mean by using that terrible word to you, which I heard as I entered the room?"

Donald's voice was keen and scathing, and his eyes fairly piercing as he asked the question and looked straight at Luella, who answered not a word.

"That wasn't just what she'd have meant, Donald," said Aunt Crete apologetically. "She was most out of her mind with trouble. You see I had to tell her what you told me about that Clarence Grandon being engaged to another girl —"

"Aunt Crete, don't say another word about that!" burst out Luella with flashing eyes and crimson face.

"For mercy's sake, Crete, can't you hold your tongue?" said Luella's mother sharply.

"Go on, Aunt Crete, did my cousin call you a liar for saying that? Yet it was entirely true. If she is not disposed to believe me either, I can call Mr. Grandon in to testify in the matter. He will come if I send for him. But I feel sure, after all, that that will not be necessary. It is probably true, as Aunt Crete says, that you were excited, Luella, and did not mean what you said; and after a good night's sleep you will be prepared to apologize to Aunt Crete, and be sorry enough for worrying her. I am going to ask you to leave Aunt Crete now, and let her rest. She has had a wearying day, and needs to be quiet at once. She is my mother's sister, you know, and I feel as if I must take care of her."

"You seem to forget that I am your mother's sister, too," said Aunt Carrie coldly, as she stood stiff and disapproving beside the door, ready to pass out.

"If I do, Aunt Carrie, forgive me," said Donald courteously. "It is not strange when you remember that you forgot that I was your sister's child, and ran away from me. But never mind, we will put that aside and try to forget it. Good-night, Aunt Carrie. Good-night, Cousin Luella. We will all feel better about it in the morning."

They bowed their diminished heads, and went with shame and confusion to the fourth floor back; and, when the door was closed upon them, they burst into angry talk, each blaming the other, until at last Luella sank in a piteous heap upon the bed, and gave herself over to helpless tears.

"Luella," said her mother in a businesslike tone, "you stop that bawling and sit up here and answer me some questions. Did you or did you not go riding with Mr. Clarence Grandon last winter in his automobile?"

Luella paused in her grief, and nodded assent hopelessly.

"Well, how'd it come about? There's no use sniffing. Tell me exactly."

"Why, it was a rainy day," sobbed out the girl, "and I met him on the street in front of the public library the day I'd been to take back *The Legacy of Earl Crafton,* and that other book by the same author —"

"Never mind what books; tell me what happened," said the exasperated mother.

"Well, if you're going to be cross, I shan't tell you anything," was the final reply; and for a moment nothing was heard in the room but sobs.

However, Luella recovered the thread of her story and went on to relate how in company with a lot of other girls she had met Mr. Grandon the day before at the golf links, where a championship game was being played. She did not explain the various maneuvers by which she had contrived to be introduced to him, nor that he had not seemed to know her at first when she bowed in front of the library building. She had called out, "It's a fine day for ducks, Mr. Grandon; isn't it good the game was yesterday instead of today?" and he had asked her to ride home with him.

That was her version. Her mother by dint of careful questioning finally arrived at the fact that the girl had more than hinted to be taken home, having loudly announced her lack of rubbers and umbrella, though she seldom wore rubbers, and had on a raincoat and an old hat.

"But how about that big box of chocolates he sent you, Luella? That was a very particular attention to show if he was engaged."

"Oh," pouted Luella, "I don't suppose that meant anything either, for I caught him in a philopena on the way home that day. We said the same words at the same time, something like 'It's going to clear off,' and I told him, when we girls did that, the one that spoke first had to give the other a box of chocolates; so the next day he sent them."

"Luella, I never brought you up to do things like that. I don't think that was very nice."

"Oh, now, Ma, don't you preach. I guess you weren't a saint when you were a girl. Besides, I don't think you're very sympathetic." She mopped her swollen eyes.

"Luella, didn't he ever pay you any more attention after that? I kind of thought you thought he liked you, by the way you talked."

"No, he never even looked at me," sobbed the girl, her grief breaking out afresh. "He didn't even know me the next time we met, but stared straight at me till I bowed, and then he gave me a cold little touch of his hat. And down here he hasn't even recognized me once. I suppose that lady mother of his didn't like my looks."

"Look here, Luella; I wish you'd act sensible. This has been pretty expensive trying to run around after the Grandons. Here's the hotel bills, and all that dress making, and now no telling how Aunt Crete will act after we get home. Like as not she'll think she's got to have a maid, and dress in silks and satins. There's one comfort, probably some of her clothes will fix over for you when she gets off her high horse and comes down to everyday living again. But I wish you'd brace up and forget these Grandons. It's no use trying to get up in the world higher than you belong. There's that nice

John Peters who would have been real devoted to you if you'd just let him; and he owns a house of his own already, and has the name of being the best plumber in Midvale.''

Luella sighed.

"He's only a plumber, Ma, and his hands are all red and rough.''

"Well, what's that?'' snapped her practical mother. "He may have his own automobile before long, for all that. Now dry up your eyes, and go to sleep; and in the morning you go down real early, and apologize to your silly Aunt Crete, and make her understand that she's not to disgrace us under any consideration by going bathing while she's here. My land! I expect to see her riding round on one of those saddle ponies on the beach next, or maybe driving that team of goats we saw today, with pink ribbon reins. Come now, Luella, don't you worry. Set out to show your cousin Donald how nice you can be, and maybe some of the silk dresses will come your way. Anyhow, this can't last forever, and John Peters is at home when we get there.''

So Luella, soothed in spirit, went to bed, and arose very early the next morning, descending upon poor Aunt Crete while yet the dreams of sailing alone with Donald on a moonlit sea were mingling with her waking thoughts.

Chapter 8
Aunt Crete's Partnership

Luella did her work quietly, firmly, and thoroughly. She vanished before Marie had thought of coming to her morning duties.

At breakfast-time Donald found a sad, cowed little woman waiting for him to go down to the dining room. He tried to cheer her up by telling her how nice a time they were to have in bathing that morning, for the water was sure to be delightful, but Aunt Crete shook her head sadly, and said she guessed she had better not go in bathing anymore. Then she sighed, and looked wistfully out on the blue waves dancing in the sunshine.

"Don't you feel well, Aunt Crete?" asked Donald anxiously.

"Oh, yes, real well," she answered.

"Did it hurt you to go in yesterday, do you think?"

"No, not a mite," she responded promptly.

"Then why in the name of common sense don't you want to go in to-day? Has Luella been trying to talk some of her nonsense?"

"Well, Luella thinks my figger looks so bad in a bathing suit. She says of course you want to be polite to me, but you don't really know how folks will laugh at me, and make her ashamed of belonging to me."

"Well, I like that!" said Donald. "You just tell Miss Luella we're not running this vacation for her sole benefit. Now, Aunt Crete, you're going in bathing, or else I won't go, and you wouldn't like to deprive me of that pleasure, would you? Well, I thought not. Now come on down to breakfast, and we'll have the best day yet. Don't you let Luella worry you. And, by the way, Aunt Crete, I'm thinking of taking a run up to Cape Cod, and perhaps getting a glimpse of the coast of Maine before I get through. How would you like to go with me?"

"Oh!" gasped Aunt Crete in a daze of delight. "Could I?" Then, mindful of Luella's mocking words the night before: "But I mustn't be an expense to you. I'd just be a burden. You know I haven't a cent of my own in the world, so I couldn't pay my way, and you've done a great deal more than I ought to have let you do."

"Now, Aunt Crete, once for all you must get that idea out of your head. You could never be a burden to me. I want you for a companion. If my mother were here, shouldn't I just love to take her on a journey with

57

me, and spend every cent I had to make her happy? Well, I haven't Mother here; but you are the nearest to Mother I can find, and I somehow feel she'd like me to have you in her place. Will you come? Or is it asking too much to ask you to leave Aunt Carrie and Cousin Luella? They've got each other, and they never really needed you as I do. I've got plenty of money for us to do as we please, and I mean it with all my heart. Will you come and stay with me? I may have to take a flying trip to Europe before the summer's over, and, if I do, it would be dreadfully lonesome to go alone. I think you'd like a trip on the ocean, wouldn't you? and a peep at London, and perhaps Paris and Vienna and old Rome for a few days? And in the fall I'm booked for work in my old university. It's only an assistant professorship yet, but it means a big thing for a young fellow like me, and I want you to come with me and make a cozy little home for me between whiles and a place where I can bring my friends when they get homesick."

He paused and looked down for an answer, and was almost startled by the glory of joy in Aunt Crete's face.

"Oh, Donald, could I do that? Could I be that to you? Do you really think I could be of use enough to you to earn my living?"

He stooped and kissed her forehead reverently to hide the tears that had come unbidden to his eyes. It touched him beyond measure that this sweet life had been so empty of love and so full of drudgery that she should speak thus about so simple a matter. It filled him with indignation against those who had taken the sweetness from her and given her the dregs of life instead.

"Dear Aunt," he said, "you could be of great use to me, and more than earn anything I could do for you many times over, just by being yourself and mothering me; but as for work, there is not to be one stroke done except just what you want to do for amusement. We'll have servants to do all the work, and you shall manage them. I want you for an ornament in my home, and you are going to have a good rest and a continual vacation the rest of your life, if I know anything about it. Now come down to breakfast, so we can go in bathing early, and don't you worry another wrinkle about Luella. You don't belong to her anymore. We'll send her a parasol from New York and a party gown from Paris, and she won't bother her pompadour anymore about you, you may be sure."

In a maze of delight Aunt Crete went down to breakfast, and dawned upon the astonished vision of her sister and niece in all the beauty of her dainty white morning costume. They were fairly startled at the vision she was in white, with her pretty white hair to match it. Luella gasped and held her disapproving breath, but Aunt Crete was too absorbed in the vision of joy that had opened before her to know or care what they thought of her in a white dress.

No girl in the new joy of her first love was ever in a sweeter dream of bliss than was Aunt Crete as she beamed through her breakfast. Luella's looks of scorn and Luella's mother's sour visage had no effect upon her whatever. She smiled happily, and ate her breakfast in peace, for had she not been set free forever from the things that had made her life a burden heretofore, and shown into a large place of new joys where her heart might find rest?

After breakfast Donald made them all walk down the boardwalk to the various shops filled with curios, where he bought everything that Luella looked at, and lavished several gifts also upon her mother, including a small Oriental rug that she admired. They returned to the hotel in a good humor, and Luella began to have visions of luxurious days to come. She felt sure she could keep Aunt Crete down about where she wanted her, and her eyes gloated over the beautiful white dress that she hoped to claim for her own when they all went home and she had convinced Aunt Crete how unsuitable white was for old ladies.

She was quite astonished, after her morning talk with her aunt, to hear Donald say as he looked at his watch, "Come, Aunt Crete, it's time for our bath," and to see Aunt Crete walk smiling off toward the bathhouses, utterly regardless of her wrathful warning glances. It was rather disconcerting to have Aunt Crete become unmanageable right at the beginning this way. But in view of the fact that her hands were filled with pretty trifles bought by her cousin she did not feel like making any protest beyond threatening glances, which the dear soul whose mind was in Europe, and whose heart was in a cozy little home all her own and Donald's, did not see at all.

Aunt Crete was happy. She felt it in every nerve of her body as she stepped into the crisp waves and bounded out to meet them with the elasticity of a girl.

Luella, following a moment later in her flashy bathing suit of scarlet and white, watched her aunt in amazement, and somehow felt that Aunt Crete was drifting away from her, separated by something more than a few yards of blue salt water.

Donald kept up a continual flow of bright conversation during the noon meal, and managed to engage Luella and her mother on the long piazza in looking through the marine glass at a great ship that went lazily floating by, while Aunt Crete was getting ready to go on the ride; and before Luella and her mother were quite aware of what was happening they stood on the piazza watching Aunt Crete in her handsome black crepe de chine, which even boasted a modest train, and her black lace wrap and bonnet, being handed into the Grandon motorcar, while Donald carried her long new gray cloak on his arm. The gray car moved smoothly away out of sight, and Luella and her mother were left staring at the sea with their own bitter reflections.

The automobile party did not return until late that night, for the moon was full and the roads were fine, and Donald saw to it that Aunt Crete was guarded against any intrusion.

It was at breakfast next morning that Donald told them, and Aunt Crete was listening with the rapt smile that a slave might have worn as he listened to the reading of the proclamation of emancipation.

"Aunt Carrie," he began as pleasantly as if he were about to propose that they all go rowing, "Aunt Crete and I have decided to set up a permanent partnership. She has consented to come and mother me. I have accepted a position in my old university, and I am very tired of boarding. I think we shall have a cozy, pleasant home; and we'll be glad to have you and Luella come and visit us sometimes after we get settled and have some good servants so that Aunt Crete will have plenty of time to take you around and show you the sights. In the meantime, it is very likely that I may have to take a brief trip abroad for the university. If so, I shall probably start in about a week, and before that I want to get a glimpse of the New England coast. I have decided to take Aunt Crete, and run away from you today. We leave on the noon train; so there is time for a little frolic yet. Suppose we go down to the boardwalk, and eat an ice-cream cone. I saw some delicious ones last night that made my mouth water, and we haven't had that experience yet. We'll get some rolling chairs so that Aunt Crete won't be too tired for her journey. Come, Aunt Crete, you won't need to go upstairs again, shall you? I told Marie about the packing. It won't be necessary for you to go back until it's time for you to change to your traveling garb."

In a daze of anger and humiliation Luella and her mother climbed into their double rolling chair, and ate their ice-cream cones sullenly, propelled by a large boy; but Aunt Crete had a chair to herself, and was attended by Donald, who kept up a constant stream of delightfully funny conversation about the people and things they passed that made Aunt Crete laugh until the tears came into her happy eyes.

There was no opportunity for Luella and her mother to talk to Aunt Crete alone, even after they returned to the hotel, for Donald kept himself in evidence everywhere, until at last Luella made bold to declare that she didn't see why Donald thought he had a right to come and take Aunt Crete away from them, when they had always taken care of her; and her mother added in an injured tone:

"Yes, you don't seem to realize what a burden it's been all these years, having to support Crete, and her so childish and unreasonable in a great many ways, and not having any idea of the value of money. I've spent a good deal on Crete, take it all in all; and now, when Luella's going out, and has to have clothes and company, it's rather hard to have her leave us in the lurch this way, and me with all the work to do."

"That being the case, Aunt Carrie," said Donald pleasantly, "I should suppose you'd be very glad to have me relieve you of the burden of Aunt Crete's support, for it will be nothing but a pleasure to me to care for her the rest of her life. As for what you have spent for her, just run it over in your mind, and I shall be quite glad to reimburse you. Aunt Crete is really too frail and sweet to have to work any longer. I should think my cousin was almost old enough to be a help to you now, and she looks perfectly strong and able to work."

Luella flashed a vindictive glance at her cousin, and turned haughtily toward the window; then the porter came for the trunks, and the travelers said a hasty good-bye, and flitted.

As Donald shook hands with Luella in parting, he looked merrily into her angry eyes, and said:

"I do hope, Luella, that it hasn't been too much of a trial to have your 'backwoods cousin' spend a few days here. You'll find a box of bonbons up in your room, if the porter did his duty, which may sweeten your bitter thoughts of me; and we hope you'll have a delightful time the remainder of your stay here. Goodbye."

* * *

About three months after Donald had returned from Europe and settled into his western university life Aunt Crete received a letter from her sister. It was brief and to the point, and Aunt Crete could read between the lines. It read:

> *Dear Crete* — Aren't you about sick of that nonsense, and ready to come home? Luella has decided that she can't do better than take John Peters. He has promised to buy an auto next year, if the plumbing business keeps up. I think at least you might come home and help get her things ready, for there's a gread deal of sewing to do, and you know I can't afford to hire it; and Luella's out so much, now she's engaged. Do come soon.
>
> Your sister, CARRIE.

Aunt Crete looked sober, but Donald, looking over her shoulder, read, and then went to his desk for a moment. Coming back, he dropped a check for five hundred dollars into his aunt's lap.

"Send her that from me, Aunt Crete, and another from yourself, if you like, and let her hire the sewing done. They don't want you, and I do."

Aunt Crete had her own bank account now, thanks to her thoughtful nephew, and she smiled back a delighted, "I will," and went off to write the letter, for Aunt Crete was at last emancipated.

THE GIRL
FROM
MONTANA

Chapter 1

The Girl, and a Great Peril

The late afternoon sun was streaming in across the cabin floor as the girl stole around the corner and looked cautiously in at the door.

There was a kind of tremulous courage in her face. She had a duty to perform, and she was resolved to do it without delay. She shaded her eyes with her hand from the glare of the sun, set a firm foot upon the threshold, and, with one wild glance around to see whether all was as she had left it, entered her home and stood for a moment shuddering in the middle of the floor.

A long procession of funerals seemed to come out of the past and meet her eye as she looked about upon the signs of the primitive, unhallowed funeral which had just gone out from there a little while before.

The girl closed her eyes, and pressed their hot, dry lids hard with her cold fingers; but the vision was clearer even than with her eyes open.

She could see the tiny baby sister lying there in the middle of the room, so little and white and pitiful; and her handsome, careless father sitting at the head of the rude home-made coffin, sober for the moment; and her tired, disheartened mother, faded before her time, dry-eyed and haggard, beside him. But that was long ago, almost at the beginning of things for the girl.

There had been other funerals, the little brother who had been drowned while playing in a forbidden stream, and the older brother who had gone off in search of gold or his own way, and had crawled back parched with fever to die in his mother's arms. But those, too, seemed long ago to the girl as she stood in the empty cabin and looked fearfully about her. They seemed almost blotted out by the last three that had crowded so close within the year. The father, who even at his worst had a kind word for her and her mother, had been brought home mortally hurt — an encounter with wild cattle, a fall from his horse in a treacherous place — and had never roused to consciousness again.

At all these funerals there had been a solemn service, conducted by a travelling preacher when one happened to be within reach, and, when there was none, by the trembling, determined, untaught lips of the white-faced mother. The mother had always insisted upon it, especially upon a

1

prayer. It had seemed like a charm to help the departed one into some kind of a pitiful heaven.

And when, a few months after the father, the mother had drooped and grown whiter and whiter, till one day she clutched at her heart and lay down gasping, and said: "Good-by, Bess! Mother's good girl! Don't forget!" and was gone from her life of burden and disappointment forever, the girl had prepared the funeral with the assistance of the one brother left. The girl's voice had uttered the prayer, "Our Father," just as her mother had taught her, because there was no one else to do it; and she was afraid to send the wild young brother off after a preacher, lest he should not return in time.

It was six months now since the sad funeral train had wound its way among sage-brush and greasewood; and the body of the mother had been laid to rest beside her husband. For six months the girl had kept the cabin in order, and held as far as possible the wayward brother to his work and home. But within the last few weeks he had more and more left her alone, for a day, and sometimes more, and had come home in a sad condition and with bold, merry companions who made her life a constant terror. And now, but two short days ago, they had brought home his body lying across his own faithful horse, with two shots through his heart. It was a drunken quarrel, they told her; and all were sorry, but no one seemed responsible.

They had been kind in their rough way, those companions of her brother. They had stayed and done all that was necessary, had dug the grave, and stood about their comrade in good-natured grimness, marching in order about him to give the last look; but, when the sister tried to utter the prayer she knew her mother would have spoken, her throat refused to make a sound, and her tongue cleaved to the roof of her mouth. She had taken sudden refuge in the little shed that was her own room, and there had stayed till the rough companions had taken away the still form of the only one left in the family circle.

In silence the funeral procession wound its way to the spot where the others were buried. They respected her tearless grief, these great, passionate, uncontrolled young men. They held in the rude jokes with which they would have taken the awesomeness from the occasion for themselves, and for the most part kept the way silently and gravely, now and then looking back with admiration to the slim girl with the stony face and unblinking eyes who followed them mechanically. They had felt that some one ought to do something; but no one knew exactly what, and so they walked silently.

Only one, the hardest and boldest, the ringleader of the company, ventured back to ask whether there was anything he could do for her, anything she would like to have done; but she answered him coldly with a "No!" that cut him to the quick. It had been a good deal for him to do, this touch of gentleness he had forced himself into. He turned from her with a wicked gleam of intent in his eyes, but she did not see it.

When the crude ceremony was over, the last clod was heaped upon the pitiful mound, and the relentless words, "dust to dust," had been murmured by one more daring than the rest, they turned and looked at the girl, who had all the time stood upon a mound of earth and watched them, as a statue of Misery might look down upon the world. They could not make her out, this silent, marble girl. They hoped now she would change. It was over. They felt an untold relief themselves from the fact that their reckless comrade was no longer lying cold and still among them. They were done with him. They had paid their last tribute, and wished to forget. He must settle his own account with the hereafter now; they had enough in their own lives without the burden of his.

Then there had swept up into the girl's face one gleam of life that made her beautiful for the instant, and she had bowed to them with a slow, almost haughty, inclination of her head, and spread out her hands like one who would like to bless but dared not, and said clearly, "I thank you — all!" There had been just a slight hesitation before the last word "all," as if she were not quite sure, as her eyes rested upon the ringleader with doubt and dislike; then her lips had hardened as if justice must be done, and she had spoken it, "all!" and, turning, sped away to her cabin alone.

They were taken by surprise, those men who feared nothing in the wild and primitive West, and for a moment they watched her go in silence. Then the words that broke upon the air were not all pleasant to hear; and, if the girl could have known, she would have sped far faster, and her cheeks would have burned a brighter red than they did.

But one, the boldest, the ringleader, said nothing. His brows darkened, and the wicked gleam came and sat in his hard eyes with a green light. He drew a little apart from the rest, and walked on more rapidly. When he came to the place where they had left their horses, he took his and went on toward the cabin with a look that did not invite the others to follow. As their voices died away in the distance, and he drew nearer to the cabin, his eyes gleamed with cunning.

The girl in the cabin worked rapidly. One by one she took the boxes on which the crude coffin of her brother had rested, and threw them far out the back door. She straightened the furniture around fiercely, as if by erasing every sign she could force from memory the thought of the scenes that had just passed. She took her brother's coat that hung against the wall, and an old pipe from the mantle, and hid them in the room that was hers. Then she looked about for something else to be done.

A shadow darkened the sunny doorway. Looking up, she saw the man she believed to be her brother's murderer.

"I came back, Bess, to see if I could do anything for you."

The tone was kind; but the girl involuntarily put her hand to her throat, and caught her breath. She would like to speak out and tell him what she thought, but she dared not. She did not even dare let her thought appear in her eyes. The dull, statue-like look came over her face that she had worn at the grave. The man thought it was the stupefaction of grief.

"I told you I didn't want any help," she said, trying to speak in the same tone she had used when she thanked the men.

"Yes, but you're all alone," said the man insinuatingly; she felt a menace in the thought, "and I am sorry for you!"

He came nearer, but her face was cold. Instinctively she glanced to the cupboard door behind which lay her brother's belt with two pistols.

"You're very kind," she forced herself to say; "but I'd rather be alone now." It was hard to speak so when she would have liked to dash on him, and call down curses for the death of her brother; but she looked into his evil face, and a fear of herself worse than death stole into her heart.

He took encouragement from her gentle dignity. Where did she get that manner so imperial, she, born in a mountain cabin and bred on the wilds? How could she speak with an accent so different from those about her? The brother was not so, not so much so; the mother had been plain and quiet. He had not known her father, for he had lately come to this State in hiding from another. He wondered, with his wide knowledge of the world, over her wild, haughty beauty, and gloated over it. He liked to think just what worth was within his easy grasp. A prize for the asking, and here alone, unprotected.

"But it ain't good for you to be alone, you know, and I've come to protect you. Besides, you need cheering up, little girl." He came closer. "I love you, Bess, you know, and I'm going to take care of you now. You're all alone. Poor little girl."

He was so near that she almost felt his breath against her cheek. She faced him desperately, growing white to the lips. Was there nothing on earth or in heaven to save her? Mother! Father! Brother! All gone! Ah! Could she but have known that the quarrel which ended her wild young brother's life had been about her, perhaps pride in him would have salved her grief, and choked her horror.

While she watched the green lights play in the evil eyes above her, she gathered all the strength of her young life into one effort, and schooled herself to be calm. She controlled her involuntary shrinking from the man, only drew herself back gently, as a woman with wider experience and gentler breeding might have done.

"Remember," she said, "that my brother just lay there dead!" and she pointed to the empty centre of the room. The dramatic attitude was almost a condemnation to the guilty man before her. He drew back as if the sheriff had entered the room, and looked instinctively to where the coffin had been but a short time before, then laughed nervously and drew himself together.

The girl caught her breath, and took courage. She had held him for a minute; could she not hold him longer?

"Think!" she said. "He is but just buried. It is not right to talk of such things as love in this room where he had just gone out. You must leave me alone for a little while. I cannot talk and think now. We must respect the dead, you know." She looked appealing at him, acting her part desperately, but well. It was as if she were trying to charm a lion or an insane man.

He stood admiring her. She argued well. He was half-minded to humor her, for somehow when she spoke of the dead he could see the gleam in her brother's eyes just before he shot him. Then there was promise in this wooing. She was no girl to be lightly won, after all. She could hold her own, and perhaps she would be the better for having her way for a little. At any rate, there was more excitement in such game.

She saw that she was gaining, and her breath came freer.

"Go!" she said with a flickering smile. "Go! For — a little while," and then she tried to smile again.

He made a motion to take her in his arms and kiss her; but she drew back suddenly, and spread her hands before her, motioning him back.

"I tell you you must not now. Go! Go! or I will never speak to you again."

He looked into her eyes, and seemed to feel a power that he must obey. Half sullenly he drew back toward the door.

"But, Bess, this ain't the way to treat a fellow," he whined. "I came way back here to take care of you. I tell you I love you, and I'm going to have you. There ain't any other fellow going to run off with you —"

"Stop!" she cried tragically. "Don't you see you're not doing right? My brother is just dead. I must have some time to mourn. It is only decent." She was standing now with her back to the little cupboard behind whose door lay the two pistols. Her hand was behind her on the wooden latch.

"You don't respect my trouble!" she said, catching her breath, and putting her hand to her eyes. "I don't believe you care for me when you don't do what I say."

The man was held at bay. He was almost conquered by her sign of tears. It was a new phase of her to see her melt into weakness so. He was charmed.

"How long must I stay away?" he faltered.

She could scarcely speak, so desperate she felt. O if she dared but say, "Forever," and shout it at him! She was desperate enough to try her chances at shooting him if she but had the pistols, and was sure they were loaded — a desperate chance indeed against the best shot on the Pacific coast, and a desperado at that.

She pressed her hands to her throbbing temples, and tried to think. At last she faltered out,

"Three days!"

He swore beneath his breath, and his brows drew down in heavy frowns that were not good to see. She shuddered at what it would be to be in his power forever. How he would play with her and toss her aside! Or kill her, perhaps, when he had tired of her! Her life on the mountain had made her familiar with evil characters.

He came a step nearer, and she felt she was losing ground.

Straightening up, she said coolly:

"You must go away at once, and not think of coming back at least until to-morrow night. Go!" With wonderful control she smiled at him, one frantic, brilliant smile; and to her great wonder he drew back. At the door he paused, a softening look upon his face.

"Mayn't I kiss you before I go?"

She shuddered involuntarily, but put out her hands in protest again. "Not to-night!" She shook her head, and tried to smile.

He thought he understood her, but turned away half satisfied. Then she heard his step coming back to the door again, and she went to meet him. He must not come in. She had gained in sending him out, if she could but close the door fast. It was in the doorway that she faced him as he stood with one foot ready to enter again. The crafty look was out upon his face plainly now, and in the sunlight she could see it.

"You will be all alone to-night."

"I am not afraid," calmly. "And no one will trouble me. Don't you know what they say about the spirit of a man —" she stopped; she had almost said "a man who has been murdered" — "coming back to his home the first night after he is buried?" It was her last frantic effort.

The man before her trembled, and looked around nervously.

"You better come away to-night with me," he said, edging away from the door.

"See, the sun is going down! You must go now," she said imperiously; and reluctantly the man mounted his restless horse, and rode away down the mountain.

She watched him silhouetted against the blood-red globe of the sun as it sank lower and lower. She could see every outline of his slouch-hat and muscular shoulders as he turned now and then and saw her standing still alone at her cabin door. Why he was going he could not tell; but he went, and he frowned as he rode away, with the wicked gleam still in his eye; for he meant to return.

At last he disappeared; and the girl, turning, looked up, and there rode the white ghost of the moon overhead. She was alone.

Chapter 2
The Flight

A great fear settled down upon the girl as she realized that she was alone and, for a few hours at least, free. It was a miraculous escape. Even now she could hear the echo of the man's last words, and see his hateful smile as he waved his good-by and promised to come back for her to-morrow.

She felt sure he would not wait until the night. It might be he would return even yet. She cast another reassuring look down the darkening road, and strained her ear; but she could no longer hear hoof-beats. Nevertheless, it behooved her to hasten. He had blanched at her suggestion of walking spirits; but, after all, his courage might arise. She shuddered to think of his returning later, in the night. She must fly somewhere at once.

Instantly her dormant senses seemed to become alert. Fully fledged plans flashed through her brain. She went into the cabin, and barred the door. She made every movement swiftly, as if she had not an instant to spare. Who could tell? He might return even before dark. He had been hard to deter, and she did not feel at all secure. It was her one chance of safety to get away speedily, whither it mattered little, only so she was away and hidden.

Her first act inside the cottage was to get the belt from the cupboard and buckle it around her waist. She examined and loaded the pistols. Her throat seemed seized with sudden constriction when she discovered that the barrels had been empty and the weapons would have done her no good even if she could have reached them.

She put into her belt the sharp little knife her brother used to carry, and then began to gather together everything eatable that she could carry with her. There was not much that could be easily carried — some dried beef, a piece of cheese, some corn-meal, a piece of pork, a handful of cheap coffee-berries, and some pieces of hard corn bread. She hesitated over a pan half full of baked beans, and finally added them to the store. They were bulky, but she ought to take them if she could. There was nothing else in the house that seemed advisable to take in the way of edibles. Their stores had been running low, and the trouble of the last day or two had put housekeeping entirely out of her mind. She had not cared to eat, and now it occurred to her that food had not passed her lips that day. With strong self-control she forced herself to eat a few of the dry pieces of corn bread, and to drink some cold coffee that stood in the little coffee-pot. This she did while she worked, wasting not one minute.

There were some old flour-sacks in the house. She put the food into two of them, with the pan of beans on the top, adding a tin cup, and tied them securely together. Then she went into her little shed room, and put on the few extra garments in her wardrobe. They were not many, and that was the easiest way to carry them. Her mother's wedding-ring, sacredly kept in a box since the mother's death, she slipped upon her finger. It seemed the closing act of her life in the cabin, and she paused and bent her head as if to ask the mother's permission that she might wear the ring. It seemed a kind of protection to her in her lonely situation.

There were a few papers and an old letter or two yellow with years, which the mother had always guarded sacredly. One was the certificate of her mother's marriage. The girl did not know what the others were. She had never looked into them closely, but she knew that her mother had counted them precious. These she pinned into the bosom of her calico gown. Then she was ready.

She gave one swift glance of farewell about the cabin where she had spent nearly all of her life that she could remember, gathered up the two flour-sacks and an old coat of her father's that hung on the wall, remembering at the last minute to put into its pocket the few matches and the single candle left in the house, and went out from the cabin, closing the door behind her.

She paused, looking down the road, and listened again; but no sound came to her save a distant howl of a wolf. The moon rode high and clear by this time; and it seemed not so lonely here, with everything bathed in soft silver, as it had in the darkening cabin with its flickering candle.

The girl stole out from the cabin and stealthily across the patch of moonlight into the shadow of the shackly barn where stamped the poor, ill-fed, faithful horse that her brother had ridden to his death upon. All her movements were stealthy as a cat's.

She laid the old coat over the horse's back, swung her brother's saddle into place — she had none of her own, and could ride his, or without any; it made no difference, for she was perfectly at home on horseback — and strapped the girths with trembling fingers that were icy cold with excitement. Across the saddle-bows she hung the two flour-sacks containing her provisions. Then with added caution she tied some old burlap about each

of the horse's feet. She must make no sound and leave no track as she stole
forth into the great world.

The horse looked curiously down and whinnied at her, as she tied his
feet up clumsily. He did not seem to like his new habiliments, but he suffered anything at her hand.

"Hush!" she murmured softly, laying her cold hands across his nostrils;
and he put his muzzle into her palm, and seemed to understand.

She led him out into the clear moonlight then, and paused a second,
looking once more down the road that led away in front of the cabin; but
no one was coming yet, though her heart beat high as she listened, fancying
every falling bough or rolling stone was a horse's hoof-beat.

There were three trails leading away from the cabin, for they could hardly be dignified by the name of road. One led down the mountain toward
the west, and was the way they took to the nearest clearing five or six miles
beyond and to the supply store some three miles further. One led off to the
east, and was less travelled, being the way to the great world; and the third
led down behind the cabin, and was desolate and barren under the moon.
It led down, back, and away to desolation, where five graves lay stark and
ugly at the end. It was the way they had taken that afternoon.

She paused just an instant as if hesitating which way to take. Not the
way to the west — ah, any but that! To the east? Yes, surely, that must be
the trail she would eventually strike; but she had a duty yet to perform.
That prayer was as yet unsaid, and before she was free to seek safety — if
safety there were for her in the wide world — she must take her way down
the lonely path. She walked, leading the horse, which followed her with
muffled tread and arched neck as if he felt he were doing homage to the
dead. Slowly, silently, she moved along into the river of moonlight and
dreariness; for the moonlight here seemed cold, like the graves it shone
upon, and the girl, as she walked with bowed head, almost fancied she saw
strange misty forms flit past her in the night.

As they came in sight of the graves, something dark and wild with plumy
tail slunk away into the shadows, and seemed a part of the place. The girl
stopped a moment to gain courage in full sight of the graves, and the horse
snorted, and stopped too, with his ears a-quiver, and a half-fright in his
eyes.

She patted his neck and soothed him incoherently, as she buried her face
in his mane for a moment, and let the first tears that had dimmed her eyes
since the blow had fallen come smarting their way out. Then, leaving the
horse to stand curiously watching her, she went down and stood at the
head of the new-heaped mound. She tried to kneel, but a shudder passed

through her. It was as if she were descending into the place of the dead herself; so she stood up and raised her eyes to the wide white night and the moon riding so high and far away.

"Our Father," she said in a voice that sounded miles away to herself. Was there any Father, and could He hear her? And did He care? "Which art in heaven —" but heaven was so far away and looked so cruelly serene to her in her desolateness and danger! "hallowed be thy name. Thy kingdom come —" whatever that might mean. "Thy will be done in earth, as it is in heaven." It was a long prayer to pray, alone with the pale moonrain and the graves, and a distant wolf, but it was her mother's wish. Her will being done here over the dead — was that anything like the will of the Father being done in heaven? Her untrained thoughts hovered on the verge of great questions, and then slipped back into her pathetic self and its fear, while her tongue hurried on through the words of the prayer.

Once the horse stirred and breathed a soft protest. He could not understand why they were stopping so long in this desolate place, for nothing apparently. He had looked and looked at the shapeless mound before which the girl was standing; but he saw no sign of his lost master, and his instincts warned him that there were wild animals about. Anyhow, this was no place for a horse and a maid to stop in the night.

A few loose stones rattled from the horse's motion. The girl started, and looked hastily about, listening for a possible pursuer; but everywhere in the white sea of moonlight there was empty, desolate space. On to the "Amen" she finished then, and with one last look at the lonely graves she turned to the horse. Now they might go, for the duty was done, and there was no time to be lost.

Somewhere over toward the east across the untravelled wilderness of white light was the trail that started to the great world from the little cabin she had left. She dared not go back to the cabin to take it, lest she find herself already followed. She did not know the way across this lonely plain, and neither did the horse. In fact, there was no way, for it was all one arid plain so situated that human travellers seldom came near it, so large and so barren that one might wander for hours and gain no goal, so dry that nothing would grow.

With another glance back on the way she had come, the girl mounted the horse and urged him down into the valley. He stepped cautiously into the sandy plain, as if he were going into a river and must try its depth. He did not like the going here, but he plodded on with his burdens. The girl was light; he did not mind her weight; but he felt this place uncanny, and now and then would start on a little spurt of haste, to get into a better way.

He liked the high mountain trails, where he could step firmly and hear the twigs crackle under his feet, not this muffled, velvet way where one made so little progress and had to work so hard.

The girl's heart sank as they went on, for the sand seemed deep and drifted in places. She felt she was losing time. The way ahead looked endless, as if they were but treading sand behind them which only returned in front to be trodden over again. It was to her like the valley of the dead, and she longed to get out of it. A great fear lest the moon should go down and leave her in this low valley alone in the dark took hold upon her. She felt she must get away, up higher. She turned the horse a little more to the right, and he paused, and seemed to survey the new direction and to like it. He stepped up more briskly, with a courage that could come only from an intelligent hope for better things. And at last they were rewarded by finding the sand shallower, and now and then a bit of rock cropping out for a firmer footing.

The young rider dismounted, and untied the burlap from the horse's feet. He seemed to understand, and to thank her as he nosed about her neck. He thought, perhaps, that this mission was over and they were going to strike out for home now.

The ground rose steadily before them now, and at times grew quite steep; but the horse was fresh as yet, and clambered upward with good heart; and the rider was used to rough places, and felt no discomfort from her position. The fear of being followed had succeeded to the fear of being lost, for the time being; and instead of straining her ears on the track behind she was straining her eyes to the wilderness before. The growth of sage-brush was dense now, and trees were ahead.

After that the way seemed steep, and the rider's heart stood still with fear lest she could never get up and over to the trail which she knew must be somewhere in that direction, though she had never been far out on its course herself. That it led straight east into all the great cities she never doubted, and she must find it before she was pursued. That man would be angry, *angry* if he came and found her gone! He was not beyond shooting her for giving him the slip in this way.

The more she thought over it, the more frightened she became, till every bit of rough way, and every barrier that kept her from going forward quickly, seemed terrible to her. A bob-cat shot across the way just ahead, and the green gleam of its eyes as it turned one swift glance at this strange intruder in its chosen haunts made her catch her breath and put her hand on the pistols.

They were climbing a long time — it seemed hours to the girl — when at last they came to a space where a better view of the land was possible. It was high, and sloped away on three sides. To her looking now in the clear night the outline of a mountain ahead of her became distinct, and the lay of the land was not what she had supposed. It brought her a curious sense of being lost. Over there ought to be the familiar way where the cabin stood, but there was no sign of anything she had ever seen before, though she searched eagerly for landmarks. The course she had chosen, and which had seemed the only one, would take her straight up, up over the mountain, a way well-nigh impossible, and terrible even if it were possible.

It was plain she must change her course, but which way should she go? She was completely turned around. After all, what mattered it? One way might be as good as another, so it led not home to the cabin which could never be home again. Why not give the horse his head, and let him pick out a safe path? Was there danger that he might carry her back to the cabin again, after all? Horses did that sometimes. But at least he could guide through this maze of perplexity till some surer place was reached. She gave him a sign, and he moved on, nimbly picking a way for his feet.

They entered a forest growth where weird branches let the pale moon through in splashes and patches, and grim moving figures seemed to chase them from every shadowy tree-trunk. It was a terrible experience to the girl. Sometimes she shut her eyes and held to the saddle, that she might not see and be filled with this frenzy of things, living or dead, following her. Sometimes a real black shadow crept across the path, and slipped into the engulfing darkness of the undergrowth to gleam with yellow-lighted eyes upon the intruders.

But the forest did not last forever, and the moon was not yet gone when they emerged presently upon the rough mountain-side. The girl studied the moon then, and saw by the way it was setting that after all they were going in the right general direction. That gave a little comfort until she made herself believe that in some way she might have made a mistake and gone the wrong way from the graves, and so be coming up to the cabin after all.

It was a terrible night. Every step of the way some new horror was presented to her imagination. Once she had to cross a wild little stream, rocky and uncertain in its bed, with slippery, precipitous banks; and twice in climbing a steep incline she came sharp upon sheer precipices down into a rocky gorge, where the moonlight seemed repelled by dark, bristling evergreen trees growing half-way up the sides. She could hear the rush and clamor of a tumbling mountain stream in the depths below. Once she fancied she heard a distant shot, and the horse pricked up his ears, and went forward excitedly.

But at last the dawn contended with the night, and in the east a faint pink flush crept up. Down in the valley a mist like a white feather rose gently into a white cloud, and obscured everything. She wished she might carry the wall of white with her to shield her. She had longed for the dawn; and now, as it came with sudden light and clear revealing of the things about her, it was almost worse than night, so dreadful were the dangers when clearly seen, so dangerous the chasms, so angry the mountain torrents.

With the dawn came the new terror of being followed. The man would have no fear to come to her in the morning, for murdered men were not supposed to haunt their homes after the sun was up, and murderers were always courageous in the day. He might the sooner come, and find her gone, and perhaps follow; for she felt that he was not one easily to give up an object he coveted, and she had seen in his evil face that which made her fear unspeakably.

As the day grew clearer, she began to study the surroundings. All seemed utter desolation. There was no sign that anyone had ever passed that way before; and yet, just as she had thought that, the horse stopped and snorted, and there in the rocks before them lay a man's hat riddled with shot. Peering fearfully around, the girl saw a sight which made her turn icy cold and begin to tremble; for there, below them, as if he had fallen from his horse and rolled down the incline, lay a man on his face.

For the instant fear held her riveted, with the horse, one figure like a statue, girl and beast; the next, sudden panic took hold upon her. Whether the man were dead or not, she must make haste. It might be he would come to himself and pursue her, though there was that in the rigid attitude of the figure down below that made her sure he had been dead some time. But how had he died? Scarcely by his own hand. Who had killed him? Were there fiends lurking in the fastnesses of the mountain growth above her?

With guarded motion she urged her horse forward, and for miles beyond the horse scrambled breathlessly, the girl holding on with shut eyes, not daring to look ahead for fear of seeing more terrible sights, not daring to look behind for fear of — what she did not know.

At last the way sloped downward, and they reached more level ground, with wide stretches of open plain, dotted here and there with sage-brush and greasewood.

She had been hungry back there before she came upon the dead man; but now the hunger had gone from her, and in its place was only faintness. Still, she dared not stop long enough to eat. She must make as much time as possible here in this open space, and now she was where she could be seen more easily if any one were in pursuit.

But the horse had decided that it was time for breakfast. He had had one or two drinks of water on the mountain, but there had been no time for him to eat. He was decidedly hungry, and the plain offered nothing in the shape of breakfast. He halted, lingered, and came to a neighing stop, looking around at his mistress. She roused from her lethargy of trouble, and realized that his wants — if not her own — must be attended to.

She must sacrifice some of her own store of eatables, for by and by they would come to a good grazing-place perhaps, but now there was nothing.

The corn-meal seemed the best for the horse. She had more of it than of anything else. She poured a scanty portion out on a paper, and the beast smacked his lips appreciatively over it, carefully licking every grain from the paper, as the girl guarded it lest his breath should blow any away. He snuffed hungrily at the empty paper, and she gave him a little more meal, while she ate some of the cold beans, and scanned the horizon anxiously. There was nothing but sage-brush in sight ahead of her, and more hills further on where dim outlines of trees could be seen. If she could but get up higher where she could see farther, and perhaps reach a bench where there would be grass and some shelter.

It was only a brief rest she allowed; and then, hastily packing up her stores, and retaining some dry corn bread and a few beans in her pocket, she mounted and rode on.

The morning grew hot, and the way was long. As the ground rose again, it was stony and overgrown with cactus. A great desolation took possession of the girl. She felt as if she were in an endless flight from an unseen pursuer, who would never give up until he had her.

It was high noon by the glaring sun when she suddenly saw another human being. At first she was not quite sure whether he were human. It was only a distant view of a moving speck; but it was coming toward her, though separated by a wide valley that had stretched already for miles. He was moving along against the sky-line on a high bench on one side of the valley, and she mounted as fast as her weary beast would go to the top of another, hoping to find a grassy stretch and a chance to rest.

But the sight of the moving speck startled her. She watched it breathlessly as they neared each other. Could it be a wild beast? No, it must be a horse and rider. A moment later there came a puff of smoke as from a rifle discharged, followed by the distant echo of the discharge. It was a man, and he was yet a great way off. Should she turn and flee before she was discovered? But where? Should she go back? No, a thousand times, no! Her enemy was there. This could not be the one from whom she fled. He was coming from the opposite direction, but he might be just as bad. Her experience taught her that men were to be shunned. Even fathers and brothers were terribly uncertain, sorrow-bringing creatures.

She could not go back to the place where the dead man lay. She must not go back. And forward she was taking the only course that seemed at all possible through the natural obstructions of the region. She shrank to her saddle, and urged the patient horse on. Perhaps she could reach the bench and get away out of sight before the newcomer saw her.

But the way was longer to the top, and steeper than it had seemed at first, and the horse was tired. Sometimes he stopped of his own accord, and snorted appealingly to her with his head turned inquiringly as if to know how long and how far this strange ride was to continue. Then the man in the distance seemed to ride faster. The valley between them was not so wide here. He was quite distinctly a man now, and his horse was going rapidly. Once it seemed as if he waved his arms; but she turned her head, and urged her horse with sudden fright. They were almost to the top now. She dismounted and clambered alongside of the animal up the steep incline, her breath coming in quick gasps, with the horse's breath hot upon her cheek as they climbed together.

At last! They were at the top! Ten feet more and they would be on a level, where they might disappear from view. She turned to look across the valley, and the man was directly opposite. He must have ridden hard to get there so soon. Oh, horror! He was waving his hands and calling. She could distinctly hear a cry! It chilled her senses, and brought a frantic, unreasoning fear. Somehow she felt he was connected with the one from whom she fled. Some emissary of his sent out to foil her in her attempt for safety, perhaps.

She clutched the bridle wildly, and urged the horse up with one last effort; and just as they reached high ground she heard the wild cry ring clear and distinct, "Hello! Hello!" and then something else. It sounded like "Help!" but she could not tell. Was he trying to deceive her? Pretending he would help her?

She flung herself into the saddle, giving the horse the signal to run; and, as the animal obeyed and broke into his prairie run, she cast one fearful glance behind her. The man was pursuing her at a gallop! He was crossing the valley. There was a stream to cross, but he would cross it. He had determination in every line of his flying figure. His voice was pursuing her, too. It seemed as if the sound reached out and clutched her heart, and tried to draw her back as she fled. And now her pursuers were three: her enemy, the dead man upon the mountain, and the voice.

Chapter 3
The Pursuit

Straight across the prairie she galloped, not daring to stop for an instant, with the voice pursuing her. For hours it seemed to ring in her ears, and even after she was far beyond any possibility of hearing it she could not be sure but there was now and then a faint echo of it ringing yet, "Hello!" — ringing like some strange bird amid the silence of the world.

There were cattle and sheep grazing on the bench, and the horse would fain have stopped to dine with them; but the girl urged him on, seeming to make him understand the danger that might be pursuing them.

It was hours before she dared stop for the much-needed rest. Her brain had grown confused with the fright and weariness. She felt that she could not much longer stay in the saddle. She might fall asleep. The afternoon sun would soon be slipping down behind the mountains. When and where dared she rest? Not in the night, for that would be almost certain death, with wild beasts about.

A little group of greasewood offered a scanty shelter. As if the beast understood her thoughts he stopped with a neigh, and looked around at her. She scanned the surroundings. There were cattle all about. They had looked up curiously from their grazing as the horse flew by, but were now going quietly about their business. They would serve as a screen if any should be still pursuing her. One horse among the other animals in a landscape would not be so noticeable as one alone against the sky. The greasewood was not far from sloping ground where she might easily flee for hiding if danger approached.

The horse had already begun to crop the tender grass at his feet as if his life depended upon a good meal. The girl took some more beans from the pack she carried, and mechanically ate them, though she felt no appetite, and her dry throat almost refused to swallow. She found her eyes shutting even against her will; and in desperation she folded the old coat into a pillow, and with the horse's bridle fastened in her belt she lay down.

The sun went away; the horse ate his supper; and the girl slept. By and by the horse drowsed off too, and the bleating sheep in the distance, the lowing of the cattle, the sound of night-birds, came now and again from the distance; but still the girl slept on. The moon rose full and round, shining with flickering light through the cottonwoods; and the girl stirred in a dream and thought some one was pursuing her, but slept on again. Then out through the night rang a vivid human voice, "Hello! Hello!" The horse roused from his sleep, and stamped his feet nervously, twitching at his bridle; but the relaxed hand that lay across the leather strap did not quicken, and the girl slept on. The horse listened, and thought he heard a sound good to his ear. He neighed, and neighed again; but the girl slept on.

The first ray of the rising sun at last shot through the gray of dawning, and touched the girl full in the face as it slid under the branches of her sheltering tree. The light brought her acutely to her senses. Before she opened her eyes she seemed to be keenly and painfully aware of much that had gone on during her sleep. With another flash her eyes flew open. Not because she willed it, but rather as if the springs that held the lids shut had unexpectedly been touched and they sprang back because they had to.

She shrank, as her eyes opened, from a new day, and the memory of the old one. Then before her she saw something which kept her motionless, and almost froze the blood in her veins. She could not stir nor breathe, and for a moment even thought was paralyzed. There before her but a few feet away stood a man! Beyond him, a few feet from her own horse, stood his horse. She could not see it without turning her head, and that she dared not do; but she knew it was there, felt it even before she noticed the double stamping and breathing of the animals. Her keen senses seemed to make the whole surrounding landscape visible to her without the moving of a muscle. She knew to a nicety exactly how her weapons lay, and what movement would bring her hand to the trigger of her pistol; yet she stirred not.

Gradually she grew calm enough to study the man before her. He stood almost with his back turned toward her, his face just half turned so that one cheek and a part of his brow were visible. He was broad-shouldered and well built. There was strength in every line of his body. She felt how powerless she would be in his grasp. Her only hope would be in taking him unaware. Yet she moved not one atom.

He wore a brown flannel shirt, open at the throat, brown leather belt and boots; in short, his whole costume was in harmonious shades of brown, and looked new as if it had been worn but a few days. His soft felt sombrero was rolled back from his face, and the young red sun tinged the short brown curls to a ruddy gold. He was looking toward the rising sun. The gleam of it shot across his brace of pistols in his belt, and flashed twin rays into her eyes. Then all at once the man turned and looked at her.

Instantly the girl sprang to her feet, her hands upon her pistol, her eyes meeting with calm, desperate defiance the blue ones that were turned to her.

She was braced against a tree, and her senses were measuring the distance between her horse and herself, and deciding whether escape were possible.

"Good morning," said the man politely. "I hope I haven't disturbed your nap."

The girl eyed him solemnly, and said nothing. This was a new kind of man. He was not like the one from whom she had fled, nor like any she had ever seen; but he might be a great deal worse. She had heard that the world was full of wickedness.

"You see," went on the man with an apologetic smile, which lit up his eyes in a wonderfully winning way, "you led me such a desperate race nearly all day yesterday that I was obliged to keep you in sight when I finally caught you."

He looked for an answering smile, but there was none. Instead, the girl's dark eyes grew wide and purple with fear. He was the same one, then, that she had seen in the afternoon, the voice who had cried to her; and he had been pursuing her. He was an enemy, perhaps, sent by the man from whom she fled. She grasped her pistol with trembling fingers, and tried to think what to say or do.

The young man wondered at the formalities of the plains. Were all these Western maidens so reticent?

"Why did you follow me? Who did you think I was?" she asked breathlessly at last.

"Well, I thought you were a man," he said, "at least, you appeared to be a human being, and not a wild animal. I hadn't seen anything but wild animals for six hours, and very few of those; so I followed you."

The girl was silent. She was not reassured. It did not seem to her that her question was directly answered. The young man was playing with her.

"What right had you to follow me?" she demanded fiercely.

"Well, now that you put it in that light, I'm not sure that I had any right at all, unless it may be the claim that every human being has upon all creation."

His arms were folded now across his broad brown flannel chest, and the pistols gleamed in his belt below like fine ornaments. He wore a philosophical expression, and looked at his companion as if she were a new specimen of the human kind, and he was studying her variety, quite impersonally, it is true, but interestingly. There was something in his look that angered the girl.

"What do you want?" She had never heard of the divine claims of all the human family. Her one instinct at present was fear.

An expression that was almost bitter flitted over the young man's face, as of an unpleasant memory forgotten for the instant.

"It really wasn't of much consequence when you think of it," he said with a shrug of his fine shoulders. "I was merely lost, and was wanting to inquire where I was — and possibly the way to somewhere. But I don't know as 'twas worth the trouble."

The girl was puzzled. She had never seen a man like this before. He was not like her wild, reckless brother, nor any of his associates.

"This is Montana," she said, "or was, when I started," she added with sudden thought.

"Yes? Well, it was Montana when I started, too; but it's as likely to be the Desert of Sahara as anything else. I'm sure I've come far enough, and found it barren enough."

"I never heard of that place," said the girl seriously; "is it in Canada?"

"I believe not," said the man with sudden gravity; "at least, not that I know of. When I went to school, it was generally located somewhere in Africa."

"I never went to school," said the girl wistfully; "but —" with a sudden resolve — "I'll go now."

"Do!" said the man. "I'll go with you. Let's start at once; for, now that I think of it, I haven't had anything to eat for over a day, and there might be something in that line near a schoolhouse. Do you know the way?"

"No," said the girl, slowly studying him — she began to feel he was making fun of her; "but I can give you something to eat."

"Thank you!" said the man. "I assure you I shall appreciate anything from hardtack to bisque ice-cream."

"I haven't any of those," said the girl, "but there are plenty of beans left; and, if you will get some wood for a fire, I'll make some coffee."

"Agreed," said the man. "That sounds better than anything I've heard for forty-eight hours."

The girl watched him as he strode away to find wood, and frowned for an instant; but his face was perfectly sober, and she turned to the business of getting breakfast. For a little her fears were allayed. At least, he would do her no immediate harm. Of course she might fly from him now while his back was turned; but then of course he would pursue her again, and she had little chance of getting away. Besides, he was hungry. She could not leave him without something to eat.

"We can't make coffee without water," she said as he came back with a bundle of sticks.

He whistled.

"Could you inform me where to look for water?" he asked.

She looked into his face, and saw how worn and gray he was about his eyes; and a sudden compassion came upon her.

"You'd better eat something first," she said, "and then we'll go and hunt for water. There's sure to be some in the valley. We'll cook some meat."

She took the sticks from him, and made the fire in a businesslike way. He watched her, and wondered at her grace. Who was she, and how had she wandered out into this waste place? Her face was both beautiful and interesting. She would make a fine study if he were not so weary of all human nature, and especially woman. He sighed as he thought again of himself.

The girl caught the sound, and, turning with the quickness of a wild creature, caught the sadness in his face. It seemed to drive away much of her fear and resentment. A half-flicker of a smile came to her as their eyes met. It seemed to recognize a comradeship in sorrow. But her face hardened again almost at once into disapproval as he answered her look.

The man felt a passing disappointment. After a minute, during which the girl had dropped her eyes to her work again, he said: "Now, why did you look at me in that way? Ought I to be helping you in some way? I'm awkward, I know, but I can obey if you'll just tell me how."

The girl seemed puzzled; then she replied almost sullenly:

"There's nothing more to do. It's ready to eat."

She gave him a piece of the meat and the last of the corn bread in the tin cup, and placed the pan of beans beside him; but she did not attempt to eat anything herself.

He took a hungry bite or two, and looked furtively at her.

"I insist upon knowing why you looked —" he paused and eyed her — "why you look at me in that way. I'm not a wolf if I am hungry, and I'm not going to eat you up."

The look of displeasure deepened on the girl's brow. In spite of his hunger the man was compelled to watch her. She seemed to be looking at a flock of birds in the sky. Her hand rested lightly at her belt. The birds were coming towards them, flying almost over their heads.

Suddenly the girl's hand was raised with a quick motion, and something gleamed in the sun across his sight. There was a loud report, and one of the birds fell almost at his feet, dead. It was a sage-hen. Then the girl turned and walked towards him with as haughty a carriage as ever a society belle could boast.

"You were laughing at me," she said quietly.

It had all happened so suddenly that the man had not time to think.

Several distinct sensations of surprise passed over his countenance. Then, as the meaning of the girl's act dawned upon him, and the full intention of her rebuke, the color mounted in his nice, tanned face. He set down the tin cup, and balanced the bit of corn bread on the rim, and arose.

"I beg your pardon," he said. "I never will do it again. I couldn't have shot that bird to save my life," and he touched it with the tip of his tan leather boot as if to make sure it was a real bird.

The girl was sitting on the ground, indifferently eating some of the cooked pork. She did not answer. Somehow the young man felt uncomfortable. He sat down, and took up his tin cup, and went at his breakfast again; but his appetite seemed in abeyance.

"I've been trying myself to learn to shoot during the last week," he began soberly. "I haven't been able yet to hit anything but the side of a barn. Say, I'm wondering, suppose I had tried to shoot at those birds just now and had missed, whether you wouldn't have laughed at me — quietly, all to yourself, you know. Are you quite sure?"

The girl looked up at him solemnly, without saying a word for a full minute.

"Was what I said as bad as that?" she asked slowly.

"I'm afraid it was," he answered thoughtfully; "but I was a blamed idiot for laughing at you. A girl that shoots like that may locate the Desert of Sahara in Canada if she likes, and Canada ought to be proud of the honor."

She looked into his face for an instant, and noted his earnestness; and all at once she broke into a clear ripple of laughter. The young man was astonished anew that she had understood him enough to laugh. She must be unusually keen-witted, this lady of the desert.

"If 'twas as bad as that," she said in quite another tone, "you c'n laugh."

They looked at each other then in mutual understanding, and each fell to eating his portion in silence. Suddenly the man spoke.

"I am eating your food that you had prepared for your journey, and I have not even said, 'Thank you' yet, nor asked if you have enough to carry you to a place where there is more. Where are you going?"

The girl did not answer at once; but, when she did, she spoke thoughtfully, as if the words were a newly made vow from an impulse just received.

"I am going to school," she said in her slow way, "to learn to 'sight' the Desert of Sahara."

He looked at her, and his eyes gave her the homage he felt was her due; but he said nothing. Here evidently was an indomitable spirit, but how did she get out into the wilderness? Where did she come from, and why was she alone? He had heard of the freedom of Western women, but surely such girls as this did not frequent so vast a waste of uninhabited territory as his experience led him to believe this was. He sat studying her.

The brow was sweet and thoughtful, with a certain keen inquisitiveness about the eyes. The mouth was firm; yet there were gentle lines of grace about it. In spite of her coarse, dark calico garb, made in no particular fashion except with an eye to covering with the least possible fuss and trouble, she was graceful. Every movement was alert and clean-cut. When she turned to look full in his face, he decided that she had almost beautiful eyes.

She had arisen while he was watching her, and seemed to be looking off with sudden apprehension. He followed her gaze, and saw several dark figures moving against the sky.

"It's a herd of antelope," she said with relief; "but it's time we hit the trail." She turned, and put her things together with incredible swiftness, giving him very little opportunity to help, and mounted her pony without more words.

For an hour he followed her at high speed as she rode full tilt over rough and smooth, casting furtive, anxious glances behind her now and then, which only half included him. She seemed to know that he was there and was following; that was all.

The young man felt rather amused and flattered. He reflected that most women he knew would have ridden by his side, and tried to make him talk. But this girl of the wilderness rode straight ahead as if her life depended upon it. She seemed to have nothing to say to him, and to be anxious neither to impart her own history nor to know his.

Well, that suited his mood. He had come out into the wilderness to think and to forget. Here was ample opportunity. There had been a little too much of it yesterday, when he wandered from the rest of his party who had come out to hunt; and for a time he had felt that he would rather be back in his native city with a good breakfast and all his troubles than to be alone in the vast waste forever. But now there was human company, and a possibility of getting somewhere sometime. He was content.

The lithe, slender figure of the girl ahead seemed one with the horse it rode. He tried to think what this ride would be if another woman he knew were riding on that horse ahead, but there was very small satisfaction in that. In the first place, it was highly improbable, and the young man was of an intensely practical turn of mind. It was impossible to imagine the haughty beauty in a brown calico riding a high-spirited horse of the wilds. There was but one parallel. If she had been there, she would, in her present state of mind, likely be riding imperiously and indifferently ahead instead of by his side where he wanted her. Besides, he came out to the plains to forget her. Why think of her?

The sky was exceedingly bright and wide. Why had he never noticed this wilderness in skies at home? There was another flock of birds. What if he should try to shoot one? Idle talk. He would probably hit anything but the birds. Why had that girl shot that bird, anyway? Was it entirely because she might need it for food? She had picked it up significantly with the other things, and fastened it to her saddle-bow without a word. He was too ignorant to know whether it was an edible bird or not, or she was merely carrying it to remind him of her skill.

And what sort of a girl was she? Perhaps she was escaping from justice. She ran from him yesterday, and apparently stopped only when utterly exhausted. She seemed startled and anxious when the antelopes came into sight. There was no knowing whether her company meant safety, after all. Yet his interest was so thoroughly aroused in her that he was willing to risk it.

Of course he might go more slowly and gradually, let her get ahead, and he slip out of sight. It was not likely he had wandered so many miles away from human habitation but that he would reach one sometime; and, now that he was re-enforced by food, perhaps it would be the better part of wisdom to part with this strange maiden. As he thought, he unconsciously slackened his horse's pace. The girl was several yards ahead, and just vanishing behind a clump of sage-brush. She vanished, and he stopped for an instant, and looked about him on the desolation; and a great loneliness settled upon him like a frenzy. He was glad to see the girl riding back toward him with a smile of good fellowship on her face.

"What's the matter?" she called. "Come on! There's water in the valley."

The sound of water was good; and life seemed suddenly good for no reason whatever but that the morning was bright, and the sky was wide, and there was water in the valley. He rode forward, keeping close beside her now, and in a moment there gleamed below in the hot sunshine the shining of a sparkling stream.

"You seem to be running away from someone," he explained. "I thought you wanted to get rid of me, and I would give you a chance."

She looked at him surprised.

"I am running away," she said, "but not from you."

"From whom, then, may I ask? It might be convenient to know, if we are to travel in the same company."

She looked at him keenly.

"Who are you, and where do you belong?"

Chapter 4
The Two Fugitives

"I'm not anybody in particular," he answered, "and I'm not just sure where I belong. I live in Pennsylvania, but I didn't seem to belong there exactly, at least not just now, and so I came out here to see if I belonged anywhere else. I concluded yesterday that I didn't. At least, not until I came in sight of you. But I suspect I am running away myself. In fact, that is just what I am doing, running away from a woman!"

He looked at her with his honest hazel eyes, and she liked him. She felt he was telling her the truth, but it seemed to be a truth he was just finding out for himself as he talked.

"Why do you run away from a woman? How could a woman hurt you? Can she shoot?"

He flashed her a look of amusement and pain mingled.

"She uses other weapons," he said. "Her words are darts, and her looks are swords."

"What a queer woman! Does she ride well?"

"Yes, in an automobile!"

"What is that?" She asked the question shyly as if she feared he might laugh again; and he looked down, and perceived that he was talking far above her. In fact, he was talking to himself more than to the girl.

There was a bitter pleasure in speaking of his lost lady to this wild creature who almost seemed of another kind, more like an intelligent bird or flower.

"An automobile is a carriage that moves about without horses," he answered her gravely. "It moves by machinery."

"I should not like it," said the girl decidedly. "Horses are better than machines. I saw a machine once. It was to cut wheat. It made a noise, and did not go fast. It frightened me."

"But automobiles go very fast, faster than any horses. And they do not all make a noise."

The girl looked around apprehensively.

"My horse can go very fast. You do not know how fast. If you see her coming, I will change horses with you. You must ride to the nearest bench and over, and then turn backward on your tracks. She will never find you that way. And I am not afraid of a woman.''

The man broke into a hearty laugh, loud and long. He laughed until the tears rolled down his cheeks; and the girl, offended, rode haughtily beside him. Then all in a moment he grew quite grave.

"Excuse me," he said. "I am not laughing at you now, though it looks that way. I am laughing out of the bitterness of my soul at the picture you put before me. Although I am running away from her, the lady will not come out in her automobile to look for me. She does not want me!"

"She does not want you! And yet you ran away from her?"

"That's exactly it," he said. "You see, *I* wanted *her!*"

"Oh!" She gave a sharp, quick gasp of intelligence, and was silent. After a full minute she rode quite close to his horse, and laid her small brown hand on the animal's mane.

"I am sorry," she said simply.

"Thank you," he answered. "I'm sure I don't know why I told you. I never told anyone before."

There was a long silence between them. The man seemed to have forgotten her as he rode with his eyes upon his horse's neck, and his thoughts apparently far away.

At last the girl said softly, as if she were rendering return for the confidence given her, "I ran away from a man."

The man lifted his eyes courteously, questioningly, and waited.

"He is big and dark and handsome. He shoots to kill. He killed my brother. I hate him. He wants me, and I ran away from him. But he is a coward. I frightened him away. He is afraid of dead men that he has killed."

The young man gave his attention now to the extraordinary story which the girl told as if it were a common occurrence.

"But where are your people, your family and friends? Why do they not send the man away?"

"They're all back there in the sand," she said with a sad little flicker of a smile and a gesture that told of tragedy. "I said the prayer over them. Mother always wanted it when we died. There wasn't anybody left but me. I said it, and then I came away. It was cold moonlight, and there were noises. The horse was afraid. But I said it. Do you suppose it will do any good?"

She fastened her eyes upon the young man with her last words as if demanding an answer. The color came up to his cheeks. He felt embarrassed at such a question before her trouble.

"Why, I should think it ought to," he stammered. "Of course it will," he added with more confident comfort.

"Did you ever say the prayer?"

"Why — I — yes, I believe I have," he answered somewhat uncertainly.

"Did it do any good?" She hung upon his words.

"Why, I — believe — yes, I suppose it did. That is, praying is always a good thing. The fact is, it's a long time since I've tried it. But of course it's all right."

A curious topic for conversation between a young man and woman on a ride through the wilderness. The man had never thought about prayer for so many minutes consecutively in the whole of his life; at least, not since the days when his nurse tried to teach him "Now I lay me."

"Why don't you try it about the lady?" asked the girl suddenly.

"Well, the fact is, I never thought of it."

"Don't you believe it will do any good?"

"Well, I suppose it might."

"Then let's try it. Let's get off now, quick, and both say it. Maybe it will help us both. Do you know it all through? Can't you say it?" This last anxiously, as he hesitated and looked doubtful.

The color came into the man's face. Somehow this girl put him in a very bad light. He couldn't shoot; and, if he couldn't pray, what would she think of him?

"Why, I think I could manage to say it with help," he answered uneasily. "But what if that man should suddenly appear on the scene?"

"You don't think the prayer is any good, or you wouldn't say that." She said it sadly, hopelessly.

"O, why certainly," he said, "only I thought there might be some better time to try it; but, if you say so, we'll stop right here." He sprang to the ground, and offered to assist her; but she was beside him before he could get around his horse's head.

Down she dropped, and clasped her hands as a little child might have done, and closed her eyes.

"Our Father," she repeated slowly, precisely, as if every word belonged to a charm and must be repeated just right or it would not work. The man's mumbling words halted after hers. He was reflecting upon the curious tableau they would make to the chance passer-by on the desert if there were any passers-by. It was strange, this aloneness. There was a wideness here that made praying seem more natural than it would have been at home in the open country.

The prayer, by reason of the unaccustomed lips, went slowly; but, when it was finished, the girl sprang to her saddle again with a businesslike expression.

"I feel better," she said with a winning smile. "Don't you? Don't you think He heard?"

"Who heard?"

"Why, 'our Father.' "

"O certainly! That is, I've always been taught to suppose He did. I haven't much experimental knowledge in this line, but I dare say it'll do some good somewhere. Now do you suppose we could get some of that very sparkling water? I feel exceedingly thirsty."

They spurred their horses, and were soon beside the stream, refreshing themselves.

"Did you ride all night?" asked the girl.

"Pretty much," answered the man. "I stopped once to rest a few minutes; but a sound in the distance stirred me up again, and I was afraid to lose my chance of catching you, lest I should be hopelessly lost. You see, I went out with a party hunting, and I sulked behind. They went off up a steep climb, and I said I'd wander around below till they got back, or perhaps ride back to camp; but, when I tried to find the camp, it wasn't where I had left it."

"Well, you've got to lie down and sleep awhile," said the girl decidedly. "You can't keep going like that. It'll kill you. You lie down, and I'll watch, and get dinner. I'm going to cook that bird."

He demurred, but in the end she had her way; for he was exceedingly weary, and she saw it. So he let her spread the old coat down for him while he gathered some wood for a fire, and then he lay down and watched her simple preparations for the meal. Before he knew it he was asleep.

When he came to himself, there was a curious blending of dream and reality. He thought his lady was coming to him across the rough plains in an automobile, with gray wings like those of the bird the girl had shot, and his prayer as he knelt in the sand was drawing her, while overhead the air was full of a wild, sweet music from strange birds that mocked and called and trilled. But, when the automobile reached him and stopped, the lady withered into a little, old, dried-up creature of ashes; and the girl of the plains was sitting in her place radiant and beautiful.

He opened his eyes, and saw the rude little dinner set, and smelt the delicious odor of the roasted bird. The girl was standing on the other side of the fire, gravely whistling a most extraordinary song, like unto all the birds of the air at once.

She had made a little cake out of the corn-meal, and they feasted royally.

"I caught two fishes in the brook. We'll take them along for supper," she said as they packed the things again for starting. He tried to get her to take a rest also, and let him watch; but she insisted that they must go on, and promised to rest just before dark. "For we must travel hard at night, you know," she added fearfully.

He questioned her more about the man who might be pursuing, and came to understand her fears.

"The scoundrel!" he muttered, looking at the delicate features and clear, lovely profile of the girl. He felt a strong desire to throttle the evil man.

He asked a good many questions about her life, and was filled with wonder over the flower-like girl who seemed to have blossomed in the wilderness with no hand to cultivate her save a lazy, clever, drunken father, and a kind but ignorant mother. How could she have escaped being coarsened amid such surroundings? How was it, with such brothers as she had, that she had come forth as lovely and unhurt as she seemed? He somehow began to feel a great anxiety for her lonely future and a desire to put her in the way of protection. But at present they were still in the wilderness; and he began to be glad that he was here too, and might have the privilege of protecting her now, if there should be need.

As it grew toward evening, they came upon a little grassy spot in a coulee where the horses might rest and eat. Here they stopped, and the girl threw herself under a shelter of trees, with the old coat for a pillow, and rested, while the man paced up and down at a distance, gathering wood for a fire, and watching the horizon. As night came on, the city-bred man longed for shelter. He was by no means a coward where known quantities were concerned, but to face wild animals and drunken brigands in a strange, wild plain with no help near was anything but an enlivening prospect. He could not understand why they had not come upon some human habitation by this time. He had never realized how vast this country was before. When he came westward on the train he did not remember to have traversed such long stretches of country without a sign of civilization, though of course a train went so much faster than a horse that he had no adequate means of judging. Then, besides, they were on no trail now, and had probably gone in a most round-about way to anywhere. In reality they had twice come within five miles of little homesteads, tucked away beside a stream in a fertile spot; but they had not known it. A mile further to the right at one spot would have put them on the trail and made their way easier and shorter, but that they could not know.

The girl did not rest long. She seemed to feel her pursuit more as the darkness crept on, and kept anxiously looking for the moon.

"We must go toward the moon," she said as she watched the bright spot coming in the east.

They ate their supper of fish and cornbread with the appetite that grows on horseback, and by the time they had started on their way again the moon spread a path of silver before them, and they went forward feeling as if they had known each other a long time. For a while their fears and hopes were blended in one.

Meantime, as the sun sank and the moon rose, a traveller rode up the steep ascent to the little lonely cabin which the girl had left. He was handsome and dark and strong, with a scarlet kerchief knotted at his throat; and he rode slowly, cautiously, looking furtively about and ahead of him. He was doubly armed, and his pistols gleamed in the moonlight, while an ugly knife nestled keenly in a secret sheath.

He was wicked, for the look upon his face was not good to see; and he was a coward, for he started at the flutter of a night-bird hurrying late to its home in a rock by the wayside. The mist rising from the valley in wreaths of silver gauze startled him as he rounded the trail to the cabin, and for an instant he stopped and drew his dagger, thinking the ghost he feared was walking thus early. A draught from the bottle he carried in his pocket steadied his nerves, and he went on, but stopped again in front of the cabin; for there stood another horse, and there in the doorway stood a figure in the darkness! His curses rang through the still air and smote the moonlight. His pistol flashed forth a volley of fire to second him.

In answer to his demand who was there came another torrent of profanity. It was one of the comrades of the day before. He explained that he and two others had come up to pay a visit to the pretty girl. They had had a wager as to who could win her, and they had come to try; but she was not here. The door was fastened. They had forced it. There was no sign of her about. The other two had gone down to the place where her brother was buried to see whether she was there. Women were known to be sentimental. She might be that kind. He had agreed to wait here, but he was getting uneasy. Perhaps, if the other two found her, they might not be fair.

The last comer with a mighty oath explained that the girl belonged to him, and that no one had a right to her. He demanded that the other come with him to the grave, and see what had become of the girl; and then they would all go and drink together — but the girl belonged to him.

They rode to the place of the graves, and met the two others returning; but there was no sign of the girl, and the three taunted the one, saying that the girl had given him the slip. Amid much argument as to whose she was and where she was, they rode on cursing through God's beauty. They passed the bottle continually, that their nerves might be the steadier; and, when they came to the deserted cabin once more, they paused and discussed what to do.

At last it was agreed that they should start on a quest after her, and with oaths, and coarse jests, and drinking, they started down the trail of which the girl had gone in search by her roundabout way.

Chapter 5
A Night Ride

It was a wonderful night that the two spent wading the sea of moonlight together on the plain. The almost unearthly beauty of the scene grew upon them. They had none of the loneliness that had possessed each the night before, and might now discover all the wonders of the way.

Early in the way they came upon a prairie-dogs' village, and the man would have lingered watching with curiosity, had not the girl urged him on. It was the time of night when she had started to run away, and the same apprehension that filled her then came upon her with the evening. She longed to be out of the land which held the man she feared. She would rather bury herself in the earth and smother to death than be caught by him. But, as they rode on, she told her companion much of the habits of the curious little creatures they had seen; and then, as the night settled down upon them, she pointed out the dark, stealing creatures that slipped from their way now and then, or gleamed with a fearsome green eye from some temporary refuge.

At first the cold shivers kept running up and down the young man as he realized that here before him in the sage-brush was a real live animal about which he had read so much, and which he had come out bravely to hunt. He kept his hand upon his revolver, and was constantly on the alert, nervously looking behind lest a troop of coyotes or wolves should be quietly stealing upon him. But, as the girl talked fearlessly of them in much the same way as we talk of a neighbor's fierce dog, he grew gradually calmer, and was able to watch a dark, velvet-footed moving object ahead without starting.

By and by he pointed to the heavens, and talked of the stars. Did she know that constellation? No? Then he explained. Such and such stars were so many miles from the earth. He told their names, and a bit of mythology connected with the name, and then went on to speak of the moon, and the possibility of its once having been inhabited.

The girl listened amazed. She knew certain stars as landmarks, telling east from west and north from south; and she had often watched them one by one coming out, and counted them her friends; but that they were worlds, and that the inhabitants of this earth knew anything whatever about the heavenly bodies, she had never heard. Question after question she plied him with, some of them showing extraordinary intelligence and thought, and others showing deeper ignorance than a little child in our kindergartens would show.

He wondered more and more as their talk went on. He grew deeply interested in unfolding the wonders of the heavens to her; and, as he studied her pure profile in the moonlight with eager, searching, wistful gaze, her beauty impressed him more and more. In the East the man had a friend, an artist. He thought how wonderful a theme for a painting this scene would make. The girl in picturesque hat of soft felt, riding with careless ease and grace; horse, maiden, plain, bathed in a sea of silver.

More and more as she talked the man wondered how this girl reared in the wilds had acquired a speech so free from grammatical errors. She was apparently deeply ignorant, and yet with a very few exceptions she made no serious errors in English. How was it to be accounted for?

He began to ply her with questions about herself, but could not find that she had ever come into contact with people who were educated. She had not even lived in any of the miserable little towns that flourish in the wildest of the West, and not within several hundred miles of a city. Their nearest neighbors in one direction had been forty miles away, she said, and said it as if that were an everyday distance for a neighbor to live.

Mail? They had had a letter once that she could remember, when she was a little girl. It was just a few lines in pencil to say that her mother's father had died. He had been killed in an accident of some sort, working in the city where he lived. Her mother had kept the letter and cried over it till almost all the pencil marks were gone.

No, they had no mail on the mountain where their homestead was.

Yes, her father went there first because he thought he had discovered gold, but it turned out to be a mistake; so, as they had no other place to go to, and no money to go with, they had just stayed there; and her father and brothers had been cow-punchers, but she and her mother had scarcely ever gone away from home. There were the little children to care for; and, when they died, her mother did not care to go, and would not let her go far alone.

O, yes, she had ridden a great deal, sometimes with her brothers, but not often. They went with rough men, and her mother felt afraid to have her go. The men all drank. Her brothers drank. Her father drank too. She stated it as if it were a sad fact common to all mankind, and ended with the statement which was almost, not quite, a question, "I guess you drink too."

"Well," said the young man hesitatingly, "not that way. I take a glass of wine now and then in company, you know —"

"Yes, I know," sighed the girl. "Men are all alike. Mother used to say so. She said men were different from women. They had to drink. She said they all did it. Only she said her father never did; but he was very good, though he had to work hard."

"Indeed," said the young man, his color rising in the moonlight, "indeed, you make a mistake. I don't drink at all, not that way. I'm not like them. I — why, I only — well, the fact is, I don't care a red cent about the stuff anyway; and I don't want you to think I'm like them. If it will do you any good, I'll never touch it again, not a drop."

He said it earnestly. He was trying to vindicate himself. Just why he should care to do so he did not know, only that all at once it was very necessary that he should appear different in the eyes of this girl from the other men she had known.

"Will you really?" she asked, turning to look in his face. "Will you promise that?"

"Why, certainly I will," he said, a trifle embarrassed that she had taken him at his word. "Of course I will. I tell you it's nothing to me. I only took a glass at the club occasionally when the other men were drinking, and sometimes when I went to banquets, class banquets, you know, and dinners —"

Now the girl had never heard of class banquets, but to take a glass occasionally when the other men were drinking was what her brothers did; and so she sighed, and said: "Yes, you may promise, but I know you won't keep it. Father promised too; but, when he got with the other men, it did no good. Men are all alike."

"But I'm not," he insisted stoutly. "I tell you I'm not. I don't drink, and I won't drink. I promise you solemnly here under God's sky that I'll never drink another drop of intoxicating liquor again if I know it as long as I live."

He put out his hand toward her, and she put her own into it with a quick grasp for just an instant.

"Then you're not like other men, after all," she said with a glad ring in her voice. "That must be why I wasn't so very much afraid of you when I woke up and found you standing there."

A distinct sense of pleasure came over him at her words. Why it should make him glad that she had not been afraid of him when she had first seen him in the wilderness he did not know. He forgot all about his own troubles. He forgot the lady in the automobile. Right then and there he dropped her out of his thoughts. He did not know it; but she was forgotten, and he did not think about her any more during that journey. Something had erased her. He had run away from her, and he had succeeded most effectually, more so than he knew.

There in the desert the man took his first temperance pledge, urged thereto by a girl who had never heard of a temperance pledge in her life, had never joined a woman's temperance society, and knew nothing about women's crusades. Her own heart had taught her out of a bitter experience just how to use her God-given influence.

They came to a long stretch of level ground then, smooth and hard; and the horses as with common consent set out to gallop shoulder to shoulder in a wild, exhilarating skim across the plain. Talking was impossible. The man reflected that he was making great strides in experience, first a prayer and then a pledge, all in the wilderness. If anyone had told him he was going into the West for this, he would have laughed him to scorn.

Towards morning they rode more slowly. Their horses were growing jaded. They talked in lower tones as they looked toward the east. It was as if they feared they might waken someone too soon. There is something awesome about the dawning of a new day, and especially when one has been sailing a sea of silver all night. It is like coming back from an unreal world into a sad, real one. Each was almost sorry that the night was over. The new day might hold so much of hardship or relief, so much of trouble or surprise; and this night had been perfect, a jewel cut to set in memory with every facet flashing to the light. They did not like to get back to reality from the converse they had held together. It was an experience for each which would never be forgotten.

Once there came the distant sound of shots and shouts. The two shrank nearer each other, and the man laid his strong hand protectingly on the mane of the girl's horse; but he did not touch her hand. The lady of his thoughts had sometimes let him hold her jewelled hand, and smiled with drooping lashes when he fondled it; and, when she had tired of him, other admirers might claim the same privilege. But this woman of the wilderness — he would not even in his thoughts presume to touch her little brown, firm hand. Somehow she had commanded his honor and respect from the first minute, even before she shot the bird.

Once a bob-cat shot across their path but a few feet in front of them, and later a kit-fox ran growling up with ruffled fur; but the girl's quick shot soon put it to flight, and they passed on through the dawning morning of the first real Sabbath day the girl had ever known.

"It is Sunday morning at home," said the man gravely as he watched the sun lift its rosy head from the mist of mountain and valley outspread before them. "Do you have such an institution out here?"

The girl grew white about the lips. "Awful things happen on Sunday," she said with a shudder.

He felt a great pity rising in his heart for her, and strove to turn her thoughts in other directions. Evidently there was a recent sorrow connected with the Sabbath.

"You are tired," said he, "and the horses are tired. See! We ought to stop and rest. The daylight has come, and nothing can hurt us. Here is a good place, and sheltered. We can fasten the horses behind these bushes, and no one will guess we are here."

She assented, and they dismounted. The man cut an opening into a clump of thick growth with his knife, and there they fastened the weary horses, well hidden from sight if anyone chanced that way. The girl lay down a few feet away in a spot almost entirely surrounded by sage-brush which had reached an unusual height and made a fine hiding-place. Just outside the entrance of this natural chamber the man lay down on a fragrant bed of sage-brush. He had gathered enough for the girl first, and spread out the old coat over it; and she had dropped asleep almost as soon as she lay down. But, although his own bed of sage-brush was tolerably comfortable, even to one accustomed all his life to the finest springs and hair mattress that money could buy, and although the girl had insisted that he must rest too, for he was weary and there was no need to watch, sleep would not come to his eyelids.

He lay there resting and thinking. How strange was the experience through which he was passing! Came ever a wealthy, college-bred, society man into the like before? What did it all mean? His being lost, his wandering for a day, the sight of this girl and his pursuit, the prayer under the open sky, and that night of splendor under the moonlight riding side by side. It was like some marvellous tale.

And this girl! Where was she going? What was to become of her? Out in the world where he came from, were they ever to reach it, she would be nothing. Her station in life was beneath his so far that the only recognition she could have would be one which would degrade her. This solitary journey they were taking, how the world would lift up its hands in horror at it! A girl without a chaperon! She was impossible! And yet it all seemed right and good, and the girl was evidently recognized by the angels; else how had she escaped from degradation thus far?

Ah! How did he know she had? But he smiled at that. No one could look into that pure, sweet face, and doubt that she was as good as she was beautiful. If it was not so, he hoped he would never find it out. She seemed to him a woman yet unspoiled, and he shrank from the thought of what the world might do to her — the world and its cultivation, which would not be for her, because she was friendless and without money or home. The world would have nothing but toil to give her, with a meagre living.

Where was she going, and what was she proposing to do? Must he not try to help her in some way? Did not the fact that she had saved his life demand so much from him? If he had not found her, he must surely have starved before he got out of this wild place. Even yet starvation was not an impossibility; for they had not reached any signs of habitation yet, and there was but one more portion of corn-meal and a little coffee left. They had but two matches now, and there had been no more flights of birds, nor brooks with fishes.

In fact, the man found a great deal to worry about as he lay there, too weary with the unaccustomed exercise and experiences to sleep.

He reflected that the girl had told him very little, after all, about her plans. He must ask her. He wished he knew more of her family. If he were only older and she younger, or if he had the right kind of a woman friend to whom he might take her, or send her! How horrible that that scoundrel was after her! Such men were not men, but beasts, and should be shot down.

Far off in the distance, it might have been in the air or in his imagination, there sometimes floated a sound as of faint voices or shouts; but they came and went, and he listened, and by and by heard no more. The horses breathed heavily behind their sage-brush stable, and the sun rose higher and hotter. At last sleep came, troubled, fitful, but sleep, oblivion. This time there was no lady in an automobile.

It was high noon when he awoke, for the sun had reached around the sage-brush, and was pouring full into his face. He was very uncomfortable, and moreover an uneasy sense of something wrong pervaded his mind. Had he or had he not, heard a strange, low, sibilant, writhing sound just as he came to consciousness? Why did he feel that something, someone, had passed him but a moment before?

He rubbed his eyes open, and fanned himself with his hat. There was not a sound to be heard save a distant hawk in the heavens, and the breathing of the horses. He stepped over, and made sure that they were all right, and then came back. Was the girl still sleeping? Should he call her? But what should he call her? She had no name to him as yet. He could not say, "My dear madam" in the wilderness, nor yet "mademoiselle."

Perhaps it was she who had passed him. Perhaps she was looking about for water, or for fire-wood. He cast his eyes about, but the thick growth of sage-brush everywhere prevented his seeing much. He stepped to the right and then to the left of the little enclosure where she had gone to sleep, but there was no sign of life.

At last the sense of uneasiness grew upon him until he spoke.

"Are you awake yet?" he ventured; but the words somehow stuck in his throat, and would not sound out clearly. He ventured the question again, but it seemed to go no further than the gray-green foliage in front of him. Did he catch an alert movement, the sound of attention, alarm? Had he perhaps frightened her?

His flesh grew creepy, and he was angry with himself that he stood here actually trembling and for no reason. He felt that there was danger in the air. What could it mean? He had never been a believer in premonitions or superstitions of any kind. But the thought came to him that perhaps that evil man had come softly while he slept, and had stolen the girl away. Then all at once a horror seized him, and he made up his mind to end this suspense and venture in to see whether she were safe.

Chapter 6
A Christian Endeavor Meeting
in the Wilderness

He stepped boldly around the green barrier, and his first glance told him she was lying there still asleep; but the consciousness of another presence held him from going away. There, coiled on the ground with venomous fangs extended and eyes glittering like slimy jewels, was a rattlesnake, close beside her.

For a second he gazed with a kind of fascinated horror, and his brain refused to act. Then he knew he must do something, and at once. He had read of serpents and travellers' encounters with them, but no memory of what was to be done under such circumstances came. Shoot? He dared not. He would be more likely to kill the girl than the serpent, and in any event would precipitate the calamity. Neither was there any way to awaken the girl and drag her from peril, for the slightest movement upon her part would bring the poisoned fangs upon her.

He cast his eyes about for some weapon, but there was not a stick or a stone in sight. He was a good golf-player; if he had a loaded stick, he could easily take the serpent's head off, he thought; but there was no stick. There was only one hope, he felt, and that would be to attract the creature to himself; and he hardly dared move lest the fascinated gaze should close upon the victim as she lay there sweetly sleeping, unaware of her new peril.

Suddenly he knew what to do. Silently he stepped back out of sight, tore off his coat, and then cautiously approached the snake again, holding the coat up before him. There was an instant's pause when he calculated whether the coat could drop between the snake and the smooth brown arm in front before the terrible fangs would get there; and then the coat dropped, the man bravely holding one end of it as a wall between the serpent and the girl, crying to her in an agony of frenzy to awaken and run.

There was a terrible moment in which he realized that the girl was saved and he himself was in peril of death, while he held to the coat till the girl was on her feet in safety. Then he saw the writhing coil at his feet turn and fasten its eyes of fury upon him. He was conscious of being uncertain whether his fingers could let go the coat, and whether his trembling knees could carry him away before the serpent struck; then it was all over, and he and the girl were standing outside the sage-brush, with the sound of the pistol dying away among the echoes, and the fine ache of his arm where her fingers had grasped him to drag him from danger.

The serpent was dead. She had shot it. She took that as coolly as she had taken the bird in its flight. But she stood looking at him with great eyes of gratitude, and he looked at her amazed that they were both alive, and scarcely understanding all that had happened.

The girl broke the stillness.

"You are what they call a 'tenderfoot,' " she said significantly.

"Yes," he assented humbly, "I guess I am. I couldn't have shot it to save anybody's life."

"You are a tenderfoot, and you couldn't shoot," she continued eulogistically, as if it were necessary to have it all stated plainly, "but you — you are what my brother used to call 'a white man.' You couldn't shoot; but you could risk your life, and hold that coat, and look death in the face. *You* are no tenderfoot."

There was eloquence in her eyes, and in her voice there were tears. She turned away to hide if any were in her eyes. But the man put out his hand on her sure little brown one, and took it firmly in his own, looking down upon her with his own eyes filled with tears of which he was not ashamed.

"And what am I to say to you for saving my life?" he said.

"I? O, that was easy," said the girl, rousing to the commonplace. "I can always shoot. Only you were hard to drag away. You seemed to want to stay there and die with your coat."

"They laughed at me for wearing that coat when we started away. They said a hunter never bothered himself with extra clothing," he mused as they walked away from the terrible spot.

"Do you think it was the prayer?" asked the girl suddenly.

"It may be!" said the man with wondering accent.

Then quietly, thoughtfully, they mounted and rode onward.

Their way, due east, led them around the shoulder of a hill. It was tolerably smooth, but they were obliged to go single file, so there was very little talking done.

It was nearly the middle of the afternoon when all at once a sound reached them from below, a sound so new that it was startling. They stopped their horses, and looked at each other. It was the faint sound of singing wafted on the light breeze, singing that came in whiffs like a perfume, and then died out. Cautiously they guided their horses on around the hill, keeping close together now. It was plain they were approaching some human being or beings. No bird could sing like that. There were indistinct words to the music.

They rounded the hillside, and stopped again side by side. There below them lay the trail for which they had been searching, and just beneath them, nestled against the hill, was a little schoolhouse of logs, weatherboarded, its windows open; and behind it and around it were horses tied, some of them tied, some of them hitched to wagons, but most of them with saddles.

The singing was clear and distinct now. They could hear the words. "O, that will be glory for me, glory for me, glory for me —"

"What is it?" she whispered.

"Why, I suspect it is a Sunday school or something of the kind."

"O! A school! Could we go in?"

"If you like," said the man, enjoying her simplicity. "We can tie our horses here behind the building, and they can rest. There is fresh grass in this sheltered place; see?"

He led her down behind the schoolhouse to a spot where the horses could not be seen from the trail. The girl peered curiously around the corner into the window. There sat two young girls about her own age, and one of them smiled at her. It seemed an invitation. She smiled back, and went on to the doorway reassured. When she entered the room, she found them pointing to a seat near a window, behind a small desk.

There were desks all over the room at regular intervals, and a larger desk up in front. Almost all the people sat at desks.

There was a curious wooden box in front at one side of the big desk, and a girl sat before it pushing down some black and white strips that looked like sticks, and making her feet go, and singing with all her might. The curious box made music, the same music the people were singing. Was it a piano? she wondered. She had heard of pianos. Her father used to talk about them. O, and what was that her mother used to want? A "cab'net-organ." Perhaps this was a cab'net-organ. At any rate, she was entranced with the music.

Up behind the man who sat at the big desk was a large board painted black with some white marks on it. The sunlight glinted across it, and she could not tell what they were; but, when she moved a little, she saw quite clearly it was a large cross with words beneath it — "He will hide me."

It was a strange place. The girl looked around shyly, and felt submerged in the volume of song that rolled around her, from voices untrained, perhaps, but hearts that knew whereof they sang. To her it was heavenly music, if she had the least conception of what such music was like. "Glory," "glory," "glory!" The words seemed to fit the day, and the sunshine, and the deliverance that had come to her so recently. She looked around for her companion and deliverer to enjoy it with him, but he had not come in yet.

The two girls were handing her a book now and pointing to the place. She could read. Her mother had taught her just a little before the other children were born, but not much in the way of literature had ever come in her way. She grasped the book eagerly, hungrily, and looked where the finger pointed. Yes, there were the words. "Glory for me!" "Glory for me!" Did that mean her? Was there glory for her anywhere in the world? She sighed with the joy of the possibility, as the "Glory Song" rolled along, led by the enthusiasm of one who had recently come from a big city where it had been sung in a great revival service. Some kind friend had given some copies of a leaflet containing it and a few other new songs to this little handful of Christians, and they were singing them as if they had been a thousand strong.

The singing ceased and the man at the big desk said, "Let us have the verses."

" 'The eternal God is thy refuge, and underneath are the everlasting arms,' " said a careworn woman in the front seat.

" 'He shall cover thee with his feathers, and under his wings shalt thou trust,' " said a young man next.

" 'In the time of trouble he shall hide me in his pavilion; in the secret of his tabernacle shall he hide me,' " read the girl who had handed the book. The slip of paper she had written it on fluttered to the floor at the feet of the stranger, and the stranger stooped and picked it up, offering it back; but the other girl shook her head, and the stranger kept it, looking wonderingly at the words, trying to puzzle out a meaning.

There were other verses repeated, but just then a sound smote upon the girl's ear which deadened all others. In spite of herself she began to tremble. Even her lips seemed to her to move with the weakness of her fear. She looked up, and the man was just coming toward the door; but her eyes grew dizzy, and a faintness seemed to come over her.

Up the trail on horseback, with shouts and ribald songs, rode four rough men, too drunk to know where they were going. The little schoolhouse seemed to attract their attention as they passed, and just for deviltry they shouted out a volley of oaths and vile talk to the worshippers within. One in particular, the leader, looked straight into the face of the young man as he returned from fastening the horses and was about to enter the schoolhouse, and pretended to point his pistol at him, discharging it immediately into the air. This was the signal for some wild firing as the men rode on past the schoolhouse, leaving a train of curses behind them to haunt the air and struggle with the "Glory Song" in the memories of those who heard.

The girl looked out from her seat beside the window, and saw the evil face of the man from whom she had fled. She thought for a terrible minute, which seemed ages long to her, that she was cornered now. She began to look about on the people there helplessly, and wonder whether they would save her, would help her, in her time of need. Would they be able to fight and prevail against those four terrible men mad with liquor?

Suppose he said she was his — his wife, perhaps, or sister, who had run away. What could they do? Would they believe her? Would the man who had saved her life a few minutes ago believe her? Would anybody help her?

The party passed, and the man came in and sat down beside her quietly enough; but without a word or a look he knew at once who the man was he had just seen. His soul trembled for the girl, and his anger rose hot. He felt that a man like that ought to be wiped off the face of the earth in some way, or placed in solitary confinement the rest of his life.

He looked down at the girl, trembling, brave, white, beside him; and he felt like gathering her in his arms and hiding her himself, such a frail, brave, courageous little soul she seemed. But the calm nerve with which she had shot the serpent was gone now. He saw she was trembling and ready to cry. Then he smiled upon her, a smile the like of which he had never given to a human being before; at least, not since he was a tiny baby and smiled confidingly into his mother's face. Something in that smile was like sunshine to a nervous chill.

The girl felt the comfort of it, though she still trembled. Down her eyes drooped to the paper in her shaking hands. Then gradually, letter by letter, word by word, the verse spoke to her. Not all the meaning she gathered, for "pavilion" and "tabernacle" were unknown words to her, but the hiding she could understand. She had been hidden in her time of trouble. Someone had done it. "He" — the word would fit the man by her side, for he had helped to hide her, and to save her more than once; but just now there came a dim perception that it was some other He, some One greater who had worked this miracle and saved her once more to go on perhaps to better things.

There were many things said in that meeting, good and wise and true. They might have been helpful to the girl if she had understood, but her thoughts had much to do. One grain of truth she had gathered for her future use. There was a "hiding" somewhere in this world, and she had had it in a time of trouble. One moment more out upon the open, and the terrible man might have seen her.

There came a time of prayer in which all heads were bowed, and a voice here and there murmured a few soft little words which she did not comprehend; but at the close they all joined in "the prayer"; and, when she heard the words, "Our Father," she closed her eyes, which had been curiously open and watching, and joined her voice softly with the rest. Somehow it seemed to connect her safety with "our Father," and she felt a stronger faith than ever in her prayer.

The young man listened intently to all he heard. There was something strangely impressive to him in this simple worship out in what to him was a vast wilderness. He felt more of the true spirit of worship than he had ever felt at home sitting in the handsomely upholstered pew beside his mother and sister while the choir-boys chanted the processional and the light filtered though costly windows of many colors over the large and cultivated congregation. There was something about the words of these people that went straight to the heart more than all the intonings of the cultured voices he had ever heard. Truly they meant what they said, and God had been a reality to them in many a time of trouble. That seemed to be the theme of the afternoon, the saving power of the eternal God, made perfect through the need and the trust of His people. He was reminded more than once of the incident of the morning and the miraculous saving of his own and his companion's life.

When the meeting was over, the people gathered in groups and talked with one another. The girl who had handed the book came over and spoke to the strangers, putting out her hand pleasantly. She was the missionary's daughter.

"What is this? School?" asked the stranger eagerly.

"Yes, this is the schoolhouse," said the missionary's daughter; "but this meeting is Christian Endeavor. Do you live near here? Can't you come every time?"

"No, I live a long way off," said the girl sadly. "That is, I did. I don't live anywhere now. I'm going away."

"I wish you lived here. Then you could come to our meeting. Did you have a Christian Endeavor where you lived?"

"No. I never saw one before. It's nice. I like it."

Another girl came up now, and put out her hand in greeting. "You must come again," she said politely.

"I don't know," said the visitor. "I sha'n't be coming back soon."

"Are you going far?"

"As far as I can. I'm going East."

"O," said the inquisitor; and then, seeing the missionary's daughter was talking to someone else, she whispered, nodding toward the man, "Is he your husband?"

The girl looked startled, while a slow color mounted into her cheeks.

"No," said she gravely, thoughtfully. "But — he saved my life a little while ago."

"Oh!" said the other, awestruck. "My! And ain't he handsome? How did he do it?"

But the girl could not talk about it. She shuddered.

"It was a dreadful snake," she said, "and I was — I didn't see it. It was awful! I can't tell you about it."

"My!" said the girl. "How terrible!"

The people were passing out now. The man was talking with the missionary, asking the road to somewhere. The girl suddenly realized that this hour of preciousness was over, and life was to be faced again. Those men, those terrible men! She had recognized the others as having been among her brother's funeral train. Where were they, and why had they gone that way? Were they on her track? Had they any clue to her whereabouts? Would they turn back pretty soon, and catch her when the people were gone home?

It appeared that the nearest town was Malta, sixteen miles away, down in the direction where the party of men had passed. There were only four houses near the schoolhouse, and they were scattered in different directions along the stream in the valley. The two stood still near the door after the congregation had scattered. The girl suddenly shivered. As she looked down the road, she seemed again to see the coarse face of the man she feared, and to hear his loud laughter and oaths. What if he should come back again? "I cannot go that way!" she said, pointing down the trail toward Malta. "I would rather die with wild beasts."

"No!" said the man with decision. "On no account can we go that way. Was that the man you ran away from?"

"Yes." She looked up at him, her eyes filled with wonder over the way in which he had coupled his lot with hers.

"Poor little girl!" he said with deep feeling. "You would be better off with the beasts. Come, let us hurry away from here!"

They turned sharply away from the trail, and followed down behind a family who were almost out of sight around the hill. There would be a chance of getting some provisions, the man thought. The girl thought of nothing except to get away. They rode hard, and soon came within hailing-distance of the people ahead of them, and asked a few questions.

No, there were no houses to the north until you were over the Canadian line, and the trail was hard to follow. Few people went that way. Most went down to Malta. Why didn't they go to Malta? There was a road there, and stores. It was by all means the best way. Yes, there was another house about twenty miles away on this trail. It was a large ranch, and was near to another town that had a railroad. The people seldom came this way, as there were other places more accessible to them. The trail was little used, and might be hard to find in some places; but, if they kept the Cottonwood Creek in sight, and followed on to the end of the valley, and then crossed the bench to the right, they would be in sight of it, and couldn't miss it. It was a good twenty miles beyond their house; but, if the travellers didn't miss the way, they might reach it before dark. Yes, the people could supply a few provisions at their house if the strangers didn't mind taking what was at hand.

The man in the wagon tried his best to find out where the two were going and what they were going for; but the man from the East baffled his curiosity in a most dexterous manner, so that, when the two rode away from the two-roomed log house where the kind-hearted people lived, they left no clue to their identity or mission beyond the fact that they were going quite a journey, and had got a little off their trail and run out of provisions.

They felt comparatively safe from pursuit for a few hours at least, for the men could scarcely return and trace them very soon. They had not stopped to eat anything; but all the milk they could drink had been given to them, and its refreshing strength was racing through their veins. They started upon their long ride with the pleasure of their companionship strong upon them.

"What was it all about?" asked the girl as they settled into a steady gait after a long gallop across a smooth level place.

He looked at her questioningly.

"The school. What did it mean? She said it was a Christian Endeavor. What is that?"

"Why, some sort of a religious meeting, or something of that kind, I suppose," he answered lamely. "Did you enjoy it?"

"Yes," she answered solemnly, "I liked it. I never went to such a thing before. The girl said they had one everywhere all over the world. What do you think she meant?"

"Why, I don't know, I'm sure, unless it's some kind of a society. But it looked to me like a prayer meeting. I've heard about prayer meetings, but I never went to one, though I never supposed they were so interesting. That was a remarkable story that old man told of how he was taken care of that night among the Indians. He evidently believes that prayer helps people."

"Don't you?" she asked quickly.

"O, certainly!" he said, "but there was something so genuine about the way the old man told it that it made you feel it in a new way."

"It is all new to me," said the girl. "But mother used to go to Sunday school and church and prayer meeting. She's often told me about it. She used to sing sometimes. One song was 'Rock of Ages.' Did you ever hear that?

'Rock of Ages, cleft for me,
Let me hide myself in Thee.' "

She said it slowly and in a singsong voice, as if she were measuring the words off to imaginary notes. "I thought about that the night I started. I wished I knew where that rock was. Is there a rock anywhere that they call the Rock of Ages?"

The young man was visibly embarrassed. He wanted to laugh, but he would not hurt her in that way again. He was not accustomed to talking religion: yet here by this strange girl's side it seemed perfectly natural that he, who knew so very little experimentally himself about it, should be trying to explain the Rock of Ages to a soul in need. All at once it flashed upon him that it was for just such souls in need as this one that the Rock of Ages came into the world.

"I've heard the song. Yes, I think they sing it in all churches. It's quite common. No, there isn't any place called Rock of Ages. It refers — that is, I believe — why, you see the thing is figurative — that is, a kind of picture of things. It refers to the Deity."

"O! Who is that?" asked the girl.

"Why — God." He tried to say it as if he had been telling her it was Mr. Smith or Mr. Jones, but somehow the sound of the word on his lips thus shocked him. He did not know how to go on. "It just means God will take care of people."

"Oh!" she said, and this time a light of understanding broke over her face. "But," she added, "I wish I knew what it meant, the meeting, and why they did it. There must be some reason. They wouldn't do it for nothing. And how do you know it's all so? Where did they find it out?"

The man felt he was beyond his depth; so he sought to change the subject. "I wish you would tell me about yourself," he said gently. "I should like to understand you better. We have travelled together for a good many hours now, and we ought to know more about each other."

"What do you want to know?" She asked it gravely. "There isn't much to tell but what I've told you. I've lived on a mountain all my life, and helped mother. The rest all died. The baby first, and my two brothers, and father, and mother, and then John. I said the prayer for John, and ran away."

"Yes, but I want to know about your life. You know I live in the East where everything is different. It's all new to me out here. I want to know, for instance, how you come to talk so well. You don't talk like a girl that never went to school. You speak as if you had read and studied. You make so few mistakes in your English. You speak quite correctly. That is not usual, I believe, when people have lived all their lives away from school, you know. You don't talk like the girls I have met since I came out here."

"Father always made me speak right. He kept at every one of us children when we said a word wrong, and made us say it over again. It made him angry to hear words said wrong. He made mother cry once when she said 'done' when she ought to have said 'did.' Father went to school once, but mother only went a little while. Father knew a great deal, and when he was sober he used to teach us things once in a while. He taught me to read. I can read anything I ever saw."

"Did you have many books and magazines?" he asked innocently.

"We had three books!" she answered proudly, as if that were a great many. "One was a grammar. Father bought it for mother before they were married, and she always kept it wrapped up in paper carefully. She used to get it out for me to read in sometimes; but she was very careful with it, and when she died I put it in her hands. I thought she would like to have it close to her, because it always seemed so much to her. You see father bought it. Then there was an almanac, and a book about stones and earth. A man who was hunting for gold left that. He stopped over night at our house, and asked for something to eat. He hadn't any money to pay for it; so he left that book with us, and said when he found the gold he would come and buy it back again. But he never came back."

"Is that all that you have ever read?" he asked compassionately.

"O, no! We got papers sometimes. Father would come home with a whole paper wrapped around some bundle. Once there was a beautiful story about a girl; but the paper was torn in the middle, and I never knew how it came out."

There was great wistfulness in her voice. It seemed to be one of the regrets of her girlhood that she did not know how that other girl in the story fared. All at once she turned to him.

"Now tell me about your life," she said. "I'm sure you have a great deal to tell."

His face darkened in a way that made her sorry.

"O, well," said he as if it mattered very little about his life, "I had a nice home — have yet, for the matter of that. Father died when I was little, and mother let me do just about as I pleased. I went to school because the other fellows did, and because that was the thing to do. After I grew up I liked it. That is, I liked some studies; so I went to a university.''

"What is that?"

"O, just a higher school where you learn grown-up things. Then I travelled. When I came home, I went into society a good deal. But'' — and his face darkened again — ''I got tired of it all, and thought I would come out here for a while and hunt, and I got lost, and I found you!'' He smiled into her face. ''Now you know the rest.''

Something passed between them in that smile and glance, a flash of the recognition of souls, and a gladness in each other's company, that made the heart warm. They said no more for some time, but rode quietly side by side.

They had come to the end of the valley, and were crossing the bench. The distant ranch could quite distinctly be seen. The silver moon had come up, for they had not been hurrying, and a great beauty pervaded everything. They almost shrank from approaching the buildings and people. They had enjoyed the ride and the companionship. Every step brought them nearer to what they had known all the time was an indistinct future from which they had been joyously shut away for a little time till they might know each other.

Chapter 7
Bad News

They found rest for the night at the ranch house. The place was wide and hospitable. The girl looked about her with wonder on the comfortable arrangements for work. If only her mother had had such a kitchen to work in, and such a pleasant, happy home, she might have been living yet. There was a pleasant-faced, sweet-voiced woman with gray hair whom the men called "mother." She gave the girl a kindly welcome, and made her sit down to a nice warm supper, and, when it was over, led her to a little room where her own bed was, and told her she might sleep with her. The girl lay down in a maze of wonder, but was too weary with the long ride to keep awake and think about it.

They slept, the two travellers, a sound and dreamless sleep, wherein seemed peace and moonlight, and a forgetting of sorrows.

Early the next morning the girl awoke. The woman by her side was already stirring. There was breakfast to get for the men. The woman asked her a few questions about her journey.

"He's your brother, ain't he, dearie?" asked the woman as she was about to leave the room.

"No," said the girl.

"O," said the woman, puzzled, "then you and he's goin' to be married in the town."

"O, no!" said the girl with scarlet cheeks, thinking of the lady in the automobile.

"Not goin' to be married, dearie? Now that's too bad. Ain't he any kind of relation to you? Not an uncle nor cousin nor nothin?"

"No."

"Then how be's you travellin' 'lone with him? It don't seem just right. You's a sweet, good girl; an' he's a fine man. But harm's come to more'n one. Where'd you take up with each other? Be he a neighbor? He looks like a man from way off, not hereabouts. You sure he ain't deceivin' you, dearie?"

The girl flashed her eyes in answer.

"Yes, I'm sure. He's a good man. He prays to our Father. No, he's not a neighbor, nor an uncle, nor a cousin. He's just a man that got lost. We were both lost on the prairie in the night; and he's from the East, and got lost from his party of hunters. He had nothing to eat, but I had; so I gave him some. Then he saved my life when a snake almost stung me. He's been good to me.''

The woman looked relieved.

"And where you goin', dearie, all 'lone? What your folks thinkin' 'bout to let you go 'lone this way?''

"They're dead," said the girl with great tears in her eyes.

"Dearie me! And you so young! Say, dearie, s'pose you stay here with me. I'm lonesome, an' there's no women near by here. You could help me and be comp'ny. The men would like to have a girl round. There's plenty likely men on this ranch could make a good home for a girl sometime. Stay here with me, dearie.''

Had this refuge been offered the girl during her first night in the wilderness, with what joy and thankfulness she would have accepted! Now it suddenly seemed a great impossibility for her to stay. She must go on. She had a pleasant ride before her, and delightful companionship; and she was going to school. The world was wide, and she had entered it. She had no mind to pause thus on the threshold, and never see further than Montana. Moreover, the closing words of the woman did not please her.

"I cannot stay," she said decidedly. "I'm going to school. And I do not want a man. I have just run away from a man, a dreadful one. I am going to school in the East. I have some relations there, and perhaps I can find them.''

"You don't say so!" said the woman, looking disappointed. She had taken a great fancy to the sweet young face. "Well, dearie, why not stay here a little while, and write to your folks, and then go on with someone who is going your way? I don't like to see you go off with that man. It ain't the proper thing. He knows it himself. I'm afraid he's deceivin' you. I can see by his clo'es he's one of the fine young fellows that does as they please. He won't think any good of you if you keep travellin' 'lone with him. It's all well 'nough when you get lost, an' he was nice to help you out and save you from snakes; but he knows he ain't no business travellin' 'lone with you, you pretty little creature.''

"You must not talk so!" said the girl, rising and flashing her eyes again. "He's a good man. He's what my brother called 'a white man all through.' Besides, he's got a lady, a beautiful lady, in the East. She rides in some kind of a grand carriage that goes of itself, and he thinks a great deal of her.''

The woman looked as if she were but half convinced.

"It may seem all right to you, dearie," she said sadly; "but I'm old, and I've seen things happen. You'd find his fine lady wouldn't go jantin' round the world 'lone with him unless she's married. I've lived East, and I know; and what's more, he knows it too. He may mean all right, but you never can trust folks."

The woman went away to prepare breakfast then, and left the girl feeling as if the whole world was against her, trying to hold her. She was glad when the man suggested that they hurry their breakfast and get away as quickly as possible. She did not smile when the old woman came out to bid her good-by, and put a detaining hand on the horse's bridle, saying "You better stay with me, after all, hadn't you, dearie?"

The man looked inquiringly at the two women, and saw like a flash the suspicion of the older woman, read the trust and haughty anger in the beautiful younger face, and then smiled down on the old woman whose kindly hospitality had saved them for a while from the terrors of the open night, and said:

"Don't you worry about her, auntie. I'm going to take good care of her, and perhaps she'll write you a letter some day, and tell you where she is and what she's doing."

Half reassured, the old woman gave him her name and address; and he wrote them down in a little red notebook.

When they were well started on their way, the man explained that he had hurried because from conversation with the men he had learned that this ranch where they had spent the night was on the direct trail from Malta to another small town. It might be that the pursuers would go further than Malta. Did she think they would go so far? They must have come almost a hundred miles already. Would they not be discouraged?

But the girl looked surprised. A hundred miles on horseback was not far. Her brother often used to ride a hundred miles just to see a fight or have a good time. She felt sure the men would not hesitate to follow a long distance if something else did not turn them aside.

The man's face looked sternly out from under his wide hat. He felt a great responsibility for the girl since he had seen the face of the man who was pursuing her.

Their horses were fresh, and the day was fine. They rode hard as long as the road was smooth, and did little talking. The girl was turning over in her mind the words the woman had spoken to her. But the thing that stuck there and troubled her was, "And he knows it is so."

Was she doing something for which this man by her side would not respect her? Was she overstepping some unwritten law of which she had never heard, and did he know it, and yet encourage her in it?

That she need fear him in the least she would not believe. Had she not watched the look of utmost respect on his face as he stood quietly waiting for her to awake the first morning they had met? Had he not had opportunity again and again to show her dishonor by word or look? Yet he had never been anything but gentle and courteous to her. She did not call things by these names, but she felt the gentleman in him.

Besides, there was the lady. He had told about her at the beginning. He evidently honored the lady. The woman had said that the lady would not ride with him alone. Was it true? Would he not like to have the lady ride alone with him when she was not his relative in any way? Then was there a difference between his thought of the lady and of herself? Of course, there was some; he loved the lady, but he should not think less honorably of her than of any lady in the land.

She sat straight and proudly in her man's saddle, and tried to make him feel that she was worthy of respect. She had tried to show him this when she had shot the bird. Now she recognized that there was a fine something, higher than shooting or prowess of any kind, which would command respect. It was something she felt belonged to her, yet she was not sure she commanded it. What did she lack, and how could she secure it?

He watched her quiet, thoughtful face, and the lady of his former troubled thoughts was as utterly forgotten by him as if she had never existed. He was unconsciously absorbed in the study of eye and lip and brow. His eyes were growing accustomed to the form and feature of this girl beside him, and he took pleasure in watching her.

They stopped for lunch in a coulee under a pretty cluster of cedar-trees a little back from the trail, where they might look over the way they had come and be warned against pursuers. About three o'clock they reached a town. Here the railroad came directly from Malta, but there was but one train a day each way.

The man went to the public stopping-place and asked for a room, and boldly demanded a private place for his "sister" to rest for a while. "She is my little sister," he told himself in excuse for the word. "She is my sister to care for. That is, if she were my sister, this is what I should want some good man to do for her."

He smiled as he went on his way after leaving the girl to rest. The thought of a sister pleased him. The old woman at the ranch had made him careful for the girl who was thus thrown in his company.

He rode down through the rough town to the railway station, but a short distance from the rude stopping-place; and there he made inquiries concerning roads, towns, etc., in the neighboring locality, and sent a telegram to the friends with whom he had been hunting when he got lost. He said he would be at the next town about twenty miles away. He knew that by this time they would be back home and anxious about him, if they were not already sending out searching parties for him. His message read:

"Hit the trail all right. Am taking a trip for my health. Send mail to me at —"

Then after careful inquiry as to directions, and learning that there was more than one route to the town he had mentioned in his telegram, he went back to his companion. She was ready to go, for the presence of other people about her made her uneasy. She feared again there would be objection to their further progress together. Somehow the old woman's words had grown into a shadow which hovered over her. She mounted her horse gladly, and they went forward. He told her what he had just done, and how he expected to get his mail the next morning when they reached the next town. He explained that there was a ranch half-way there where they might stop all night.

She was troubled at the thought of another ranch. She knew there would be more questions, and perhaps other disagreeable words said; but she held her peace, listening to his plans. Her wonder was great over the telegram. She knew little or nothing about modern discoveries. It was a mystery to her how he could receive word by morning from a place that it had taken them nearly two days to leave behind, and how had he sent a message over a wire? Yes, she had heard of telegrams, but had never been quite sure they were true. When he saw that she was interested, he went on to tell her of other wonderful triumphs of science, the telephone, the electric light, gas, and the modern system of waterworks. She listened as if it were all a fairy tale. Sometimes she looked at him, and wondered whether it could be true, or whether he were not making fun of her; but his earnest, honest eyes forbade doubt.

At the ranch they found two women, a mother and her daughter. The man asked frankly whether they could take care of this young friend of his overnight, saying that she was going on to the town in the morning, and was in his care for the journey. This seemed to relieve all suspicion. The two girls eyed each other, and then smiled.

"I'm Myrtle Baker," said the ranch-owner's daughter. "Come; I'll take you where you can wash your hands and face, and then we'll have some supper."

Myrtle Baker was a chatterer by nature. She talked incessantly; and, though she asked many questions, she did not wait for half of them to be answered. Besides, the traveller had grown wary. She did not intend to talk about the relationship between herself and her travelling companion. There was a charm in Myrtle's company which made the girl half regret leaving the next morning, as they did quite early, amid protests from Myrtle and her mother, who enjoyed a visitor in their isolated home.

But the ride that morning was constrained. Each felt in some subtle way that their pleasant companionship was coming to a crisis. Ahead in that town would be letters, communications from the outside world of friends, people who did not know or care what these two had been through together, and who would not hesitate to separate them with a firm hand. Neither put this thought into words, but it was there in their hearts, in the form of a vague fear. They talked very little, but each was feeling how pleasant the journey had been, and dreading what might be before.

They wanted to stay in this Utopia of the plains, forever journeying together, and never reaching any troublesome futures where were laws and opinions by which they must abide.

But the morning grew bright, and the road was not half long enough. Though at the last they walked their horses, they reached the town before the daily train had passed through. They went straight to the station, and found that the train was an hour late; but a telegram had arrived for the man. He took it nervously, his fingers trembling. He felt a premonition that it contained something unpleasant.

The girl sat on her horse by the platform, watching him through the open station door where he was standing as he tore open the envelope. She saw a deathly pallor overspread his face, and a look of anguish as if an arrow had pierced his heart. She felt as if the arrow had gone on into her own heart, and then she sat and waited. It seemed hours before he glanced up, with an old, weary look in his eyes. The message read:

"Your mother seriously ill. Wants you immediately. Will send your baggage on morning train. Have wired you are coming."

It was signed by his cousin with whom he had been taking his hunting-trip, and who was bound by business to go further West within a few days more.

The strong young man was almost bowed under this sudden shock. His mother was very dear to him. He had left her well and happy. He must go to her at once, of course; but what should he do with the girl who had within the last two days taken so strong a hold upon his — he hesitated, and called it "protection." That word would do in the present emergency.

Then he looked, and saw her own face pale under the tan, and stepped out to the platform to tell her.

Chapter 8
The Parting

She took the news like a Spartan. Her gentle pity was simply expressed, and then she had held her peace. He must go. He must leave her. She knew that the train would carry him to his mother's bedside quicker than a horse could go. She felt by the look in his eyes and the set of his mouth that he had already decided that. Of course he must go. And the lady was there too! His mother and the lady! The lady would be sorry by this time, and would love him. Well, it was all right. He had been good to her. He had been a strong, bright angel God had sent to help her out of the wilderness; and now that she was safe the angel must return to his heaven. This was what she thought.

He had gone into the station to inquire about the train. It was an hour late. He had one short hour in which to do a great deal. He had very little money with him. Naturally men do not carry a fortune when they go into the wilderness for a day's shooting. Fortunately he had his railroad return ticket to Philadelphia. That would carry him safely. But the girl. She of course had no money. And where was she going? He realized that he had failed to ask her many important questions. He hurried out, and explained to her.

"The train is an hour late. We must sell our horses, and try to get money enough to take us East. It is the only way. Where do you intend going?"

But the girl stiffened in her seat. She knew it was her opportunity to show that she was worthy of his honor and respect.

"I cannot go with you," she said very quietly.

"But you must," said he impatiently. "Don't you see there is no other way? I must take this train and get to my mother as soon as possible. She may not be living when I reach her if I don't." Something caught in his throat as he uttered the horrible thought that kept coming to his mind.

"I know," said the girl quietly. "You must go, but I must ride on."

"And why? I should like to know. Don't you see that I cannot leave you here alone? Those villains may be upon us at any minute. In fact, it is a good thing for us to board the train and get out of their miserable country as fast as steam can carry us. I am sorry you must part with your horse, for I know

56

you are attached to it; but perhaps we can arrange to sell it to someone who will let us redeem it when we send the money out. You see I have not money enough with me to buy you a ticket. I couldn't get home myself if I hadn't my return ticket with me in my pocket. But surely the sale of both horses will bring enough to pay your way."

"You are very kind, but I must not go." The red lips were firm, and the girl was sitting very erect. She looked as she had done after she had shot the bird.

"But why?"

"I cannot travel alone with you. It is not your custom where you come from. The woman on the ranch told me. She said you knew girls did not do that, and that you did not respect me for going alone with you. She said it was not right, and that you knew it."

He looked at her impatient, angry, half ashamed that she should face him with these words.

"Nonsense!" said he. "This is a case of necessity. You are to be taken care of, and I am the one to do it."

"But it is not the custom among people where you live, is it?"

The clear eyes faced him down, and he had to admit that it was not.

"Then I can't go," she said decidedly.

"But you must. If you don't, I won't go."

"But you must," said the girl, "and I mustn't. If you talk that way, I'll run away from you. I've run away from one man, and I guess I can from another. Besides, you're forgetting the lady."

"What lady?"

"Your lady. The lady who rides in a carriage without horses."

"Hang the lady!" he said inelegantly. "Do you know that the train will be along here in less than an hour, and we have a great deal to do before we can get on board? There's no use stopping to talk about this matter. We haven't time. If you will just trust things to me, I'll attend to them all, and I'll answer your questions when we get safely on the train. Every instant is precious. Those men might come around that corner over there any minute. That's all bosh about respect. I respect you more than any woman I ever met. And it's my business to take care of you."

"No, it's not your business," said the girl bravely, "and I can't let you. I'm nothing to you, you know."

"You're every — that is — why, you surely know you're a great deal to me. Why, you saved my life, you know!"

"Yes, and you saved mine. That was beautiful, but that's all."

"Isn't that enough? What are you made of, anyway, to sit there when there's so much to be done, and those villains on our track, and insist that you won't be saved? Respect you! Why a lion in the wilderness would have to respect you. You're made of iron and steel and precious stones. You've the courage of a — a — I was going to say a man, but I mean an angel. You're pure as snow, and true as the heavenly blue, and firm as a rock; and, if I had never respected you before, I would have to now. I respect, I honor, I — I — I pray for you!'' he finished fiercely.

He turned his back to hide his emotions.

She lifted her eyes to his when he turned again, and her own were full of tears.

"Thank you!" She said it very simply. "That makes me — very — glad! But I cannot go with you."

"Do you mean that?" he asked her desperately.

"Yes," steadily.

"Then I shall have to stay too."

"But you can't! You must go to your mother. I won't be stayed with. And what would she think? Mothers are — everything!" she finished. "You must go quick and get ready. What can I do to help?"

He gave her a look which she remembered long years afterward. It seemed to burn and sear its way into her soul. How was it that a stranger had the power to scorch her with anguish this way? And she him?

He turned, still with that desperate, half-frantic look in his face, and accosted two men who stood at the other end of the platform. They were not in particular need of a horse at present; but they were always ready to look at a bargain, and they walked speculatively down the uneven boards of the platform with him to where his horse stood, and inspected it.

The girl watched the whole proceeding with eyes that saw not but into the future. She put in a word about the worth of the saddle once when she saw it was going lower than it should. Three other men gathered about before the bargain was concluded, and the horse and its equipment sold for about half its value.

That done, the man turned toward the girl and motioned to her to lead her horse away to a more quiet place, and set him down to plead steadily against her decision. But the talk and the horse-selling had taken more time than he realized. The girl was more decided than ever in her determination not to go with him. She spoke of the lady again. She spoke of his mother, and mothers in general, and finished by reminding him that God would take care of her, and of him, too.

Then they heard the whistle of the train, and saw it growing from a speck to a large black object across the plain. To the girl the sight of this strange machine, that seemed more like a creature rushing toward her to snatch all beauty and hope and safety from her, sent a thrill of horror. To the man it seemed like a dreaded fate that was tearing him asunder. He had barely time to divest himself of his powder-horn, and a few little things that might be helpful to the girl in her journey, before the train was halted at the station. Then he took from his pocket the money that had been paid him for his horse; and, selecting a five-dollar bill for himself, he wrapped the rest in an envelope bearing his own name and address. The envelope was one addressed by the lady at home. It had contained some gracefully worded refusal of a request. But he did not notice now what envelope he gave her.

"Take this," he said. "It will help a little. Yes, you must! I cannot leave you — I *will* not — unless you do," when he saw that she hesitated and looked doubtful. "I owe you all and more for saving my life. I can never repay you. Take it. You may return it sometime when you get plenty more of your own, if it hurts your pride to keep it. Take it, please. Yes, I have plenty for myself. You will need it, and you must stop at nice places overnight. You will be very careful, won't you? My name is on that envelope. You must write to me and let me know that you are safe."

"Someone is calling you, and that thing is beginning to move again," said the girl, an awesome wonder in her face. "You will be left behind! O, hurry! Quick! Your mother!"

He half turned toward the train, and then came back.

"You haven't told me your name!" he gasped. "Tell me quick!"

She caught her breath.

"Elizabeth!" she answered, and waved him from her.

The conductor of the train was shouting to him, and two men shoved him toward the platform. He swung himself aboard with the accustomed ease of a man who has travelled; but he stood on the platform, and shouted, "Where are you going!" as the train swung noisily off.

She did not hear him, but waved her hand, and gave him a bright smile that was brimming with unshed tears. It seemed like instant, daring suicide in him to stand on that swaying, clattering house as it moved off irresponsibly down the plane of vision. She watched him till he was out of sight, a mere speck on the horizon of the prairie; and then she turned her horse slowly into the road, and went her way into the world alone.

The man stood on the platform, and watched her as he whirled away — a little brown girl on a little brown horse, so stanch and firm and stubborn and good. Her eyes were dear, and her lips as she smiled; and her hand was beautiful as it waved him good-by. She was dear, dear, dear! Why had he not known it? Why had he left her? Yet how could he stay? His mother was dying perhaps. He must not fail her in what might be her last summons. Life and death were pulling at his heart, tearing him asunder.

The vision of the little brown girl and the little brown horse blurred and faded. He tried to look, but could not see. He brought his eyes to nearer vision to fix their focus for another look, and straight before him whirled a shackly old saloon, rough and tumble, its character apparent from the men who were grouped about its doorway and from the barrels and kegs in profusion outside. From the doorway issued four men, wiping their mouths and shouting hilariously. Four horses stood tied to a fence nearby. They were so instantly passed, and so vaguely seen, that he could not be sure in the least, but those four men reminded him strongly of the four who had passed the schoolhouse on Sunday.

He shuddered, and looked back. The little brown horse and the little brown girl were one with the little brown station so far away, and presently the saloon and men were blotted out in one blur of green and brown and yellow.

He looked to the ground in his despair. He *must* go back. He could not leave her in such peril. She was his to care for by all the rights of manhood and womanhood. She had been put in his way. It was his duty.

But the ground whirled by under his madness, and showed him plainly that to jump off would be instant death. Then the thought of his mother came again, and the girl's words, "I am nothing to you, you know."

The train whirled its way between two mountains and the valley, and the green and brown and yellow blur was gone from sight. He felt as if he had just seen the coffin close over the girl's sweet face, and he had done it.

By and by he crawled into the car, pulled his slouch-hat down over his eyes, and settled down in a seat; but all the time he was trying to see over again that old saloon and those four men, and to make out their passing identity. Sometimes the agony of thinking it all over, and trying to make out whether those men had been the pursuers, made him feel frantic; and it seemed as if he must pull the bell-cord, and make the train stop, and get off to walk back. Then the utter hopelessness of ever finding her would come over him, and he would settle back in his seat again and try to sleep. But the least drowsiness would bring a vision of the girl galloping alone over the prairie with the four men in full pursuit behind. "Elizabeth, Elizabeth!" the car-wheels seemed to say.

Elizabeth — that was all he had of her. He did not know the rest of her name, nor where she was going. He did not even know where she had come from, just "Elizabeth" and "Montana." If anything happened to her, he would never know. Oh! why had he left her? Why had he not *made* her go with him? In a case like that a man should assert his authority. But, then, it was true he had none, and she had said she would run away. She would have done it too. O, if it had been anything but sickness and possible death at the other end — and his mother, his own little mother! Nothing else would have kept him from staying to protect Elizabeth.

What a fool he had been! There were questions he might have asked, and plans they might have made, all those beautiful days and those moon-silvered nights. If any other man had done the same, he would have thought him lacking mentally. But here he had maundered on, and never found out the all-important things about her. Yet how did he know then how important they were to be? It had seemed as if they had all the world before them in the brilliant sunlight. How could he know that modern improvements were to seize him in the midst of a prairie waste, and whirl him off from her when he had just begun to know what she was, and to prize her company as a most precious gift dropped down from heaven at his feet?

By degrees he came out of his hysterical frenzy, and returned to a somewhat normal state of mind. He reasoned himself several times into the belief that those men were not in the least like the men he had seen Sunday. He knew that one could not recognize one's own brother at that distance and that rate of passing speed. He tried to think that Elizabeth would be cared for. She had come through many a danger, and was it likely that the God in whom she trusted, who had guarded her so many times in her great peril, would desert her now in her dire need? Would He not raise up help for her somewhere? Perhaps another man as good as he, and as trust-worthy as he had tried to be, would find her and help her.

But that thought was not pleasant. He put it away impatiently. It cut him. Why had she talked so much about the lady? The lady! Ah! How was it the lady came no more into his thoughts? The memory of her haughty face no more quickened his heart-beats. Was he fickle that he could lose what he had supposed was a lifelong passion in a few days?

The darkness was creeping on. Where was Elizabeth? Had she found a refuge for the night? Or was she wandering on an unknown trail, hearing voices and oaths through the darkness, and seeing the gleaming of wild eyes low in the bushes ahead? How could he have left her? How could he? He must go back even yet. He must, he must, *he must!*

And so it went on through the long night.

The train stopped at several places to take on water; but there seemed to be no human habitation near, or else his eyes were dim with his trouble.

Once, when they stopped longer than the other times, he got up and walked the length of the car and down the steps to the ground. He even stood there, and let the train start jerkily on till his car had passed him, and the steps were just sliding by, and tried to think whether he would not stay, and go back in some way to find her. Then the impossibility of the search, and of his getting back in time to do any good, helped him to spring on board just before it was too late. He walked back to his seat saying to himself, "Fool! Fool!"

It was not till morning that he remembered his baggage and went in search for it. There he found a letter from his cousin, with other letters and telegrams explaining the state of affairs at home. He came back to his seat laden with a large leather grip and a suitcase. He sat down to read his letters, and these took his mind away from his troubled thoughts for a little while. There was a letter from his mother, sweet, graceful, half wistfully offering her sympathy. He saw she guessed the reason why he had left her and gone to this far place. Dear little mother! What would she say if she knew his trouble now? And then would return his heart-frenzy over Elizabeth's peril. O to know that she was protected, hidden!

Fumbling in his pocket, he came upon a slip of paper, the slip the girl had given Elizabeth in the schoolhouse on Sunday afternoon. "For in the time of trouble he shall hide me in his pavilion; in the secret of his tabernacle shall he hide me."

Ah! God had hidden her then. Why not again? And what was that he had said to her himself, when searching for a word to cover his emotion? "I pray for you!" Why could he not pray? She had made him pray in the wilderness. Should he not pray for her who was in peril now? He leaned back in the hot, uncomfortable car-seat, pulling his hat down closer over his eyes, and prayed as he had never prayed before. "Our Father" he stumbled through as far as he could remember, and tried to think how her sweet voice had filled in the places where he had not known it the other time. Then, when he was done, he waited and prayed, "Our Father, care for Elizabeth," and added, "For Jesus' sake. Amen." Thereafter through the rest of his journey, and for days and weeks stretching ahead, he prayed that prayer, and sometimes found in it his only solace from the terrible fear that possessed him lest some harm had come to the girl, whom it seemed to him now he had deserted in cold blood.

Chapter 9
In a Trap

Elizabeth rode straight out to the east, crossing the town as rapidly as possible, going full gallop where the streets were empty. On the edge of the town she crossed another trail running back the way that they had come; but without swerving she turned out toward the world, and soon passed into a thick growth of trees, around a hill.

Not three minutes elapsed after she had passed the crossing of the trails before the four men rode across from the other direction, and, pausing, called to one another, looking this way and that:

"What d'ye think, Bill? Shall we risk the right hand 'r the left?"

"Take the left hand fer luck," answered Bill. "Let's go over to the ranch and ask. Ef she's been hereabouts, she's likely there. The old woman 'll know. Come on, boys!"

And who shall say that the angel of the Lord did not stand within the crossing of the ways and turn aside the evil men?

Elizabeth did not stop her fierce ride until about noon. The frenzy of her fear of pursuit had come upon her with renewed force. Now that she was alone and desolate she dared not look behind her. She had been strong enough as she smiled her farewell; but, when the train had dwindled into a mere speck in the distance, her eyes were dropping tears thick and fast upon the horse's mane. So in the first heaviness of her loneliness she rode as if pursued by enemies close at hand.

But the horse must rest if she did not, for he was her only dependence now. So she sat her down in the shade of a tree, and tried to eat some dinner. The tears came again as she opened the pack which the man's strong hands had bound together for her. How little she had thought at breakfast-time that she would eat the next meal alone!

It was all well enough to tell him he must go, and say she was nothing to him; but it was different now to face the world without a single friend when one had learned to know how good a friend could be. Almost it would have been better if he had never found her, never saved her from the serpent, never ridden beside her and talked of wonderful new things to her; for now that he was gone the emptiness and loneliness were so much harder to bear; and now she was filled with a longing for things that could not be hers.

It was well he had gone so soon, well she had no longer to grow into the charm of his society; for he belonged to the lady, and was not hers. Thus she ate her dinner with the indifference of sorrow.

Then she took out the envelope, and counted over the money. Forty dollars he had given her. She knew he had kept but five for himself. How wonderful that he should have done all that for her! It seemed a very great wealth in her possession. Well, she would use it as sparingly as possible, and thus be able the sooner to return it all to him. Some she must use, she supposed, to buy food; but she would do with as little as she could. She might sometimes shoot a bird, or catch a fish; or there might be berries fit for food by the way. Nights she must stop by the way at a respectable house. That she had promised. He had told her of awful things that might happen to her if she lay down in the wilderness alone. Her lodging would sometimes cost her something. Yet often they would take her in for nothing. She would be careful of the money.

She studied the name on the envelope. George Trescott Benedict, 2 — Walnut Street, Philadelphia, Penn. The letters were large and angular, not easy to read; but she puzzled them out. It did not look like his writing. She had watched him as he wrote the old woman's address in his little red book. He wrote small, round letters, slanting backwards, plain as print, pleasant writing to read. Now the old woman's address would never be of any use, and her wish that Elizabeth should travel alone was fulfilled.

There was a faint perfume from the envelope like wildwood flowers. She breathed it in, and wondered at it. Was it perfume from something he carried in his pocket, some flower his lady had once given him? But this was not a pleasant thought. She put the envelope into her bosom after studying it again carefully until she knew the words by heart.

Then she drew forth the papers of her mother's that she had brought from home, and for the first time read them over.

The first was the marriage certificate. That she had seen before, and had studied with awe; but the others had been kept in a box that was never opened by the children. The mother kept them sacredly, always with the certificate on the top.

The largest paper she could not understand. It was something about a mine. There were a great many "herebys" and "whereases" and "agreements" in it. She put it back into the wrapper as of little account, probably something belonging to her father, which her mother had treasured for old time's sake.

Then came a paper which related to the claim where their little log home had stood, and upon the extreme edge of which the graves were. That, too, she laid reverently within its wrapper.

Next came a bit of pasteboard whereon was inscribed, "Mrs. Merrill Wilton Bailey, Rittenhouse Square, Tuesdays." That she knew was her grandmother's name, though she had never seen the card before — her father's mother. She looked at the card in wonder. It was almost like a distant view of the lady in question. What kind of a place might Rittenhouse Square be, and where was it? There was no telling. It might be near that wonderful Desert of Sahara that the man had talked about. She laid it down with a sigh.

There was only one paper left, and that was a letter written in pale pencil lines. It said:

"My dear Bessie: Your pa died last week. He was killed falling from a scaffold. He was buried on Monday with five carriages and everything nice. We all got new black dresses, and have enough for a stone. If it don't cost too much, we'll have an angel on the top. I always thought an angel pointing to heaven was nice. We wish you was here. We miss you very much. I hope your husband is good to you. Why don't you write to us? You haven't wrote since your little girl was born. I s'pose you call her Bessie like you. If anything ever happens to you, you can send her to me. I'd kind of like her to fill your place. Your sister has got a baby girl too. She calls her Lizzie. We couldn't somehow have it natural to call her 'Lizabeth, and Nan wanted her called for me. I was always Lizzie, you know. Now you must write soon.

"Your loving mother,

"ELIZABETH BRADY."

There was no date nor address to the letter, but an address had been pencilled on the outside in her mother's cramped school-girl hand. It was dim but still readable, "Mrs. Elizabeth Brady, 18 — Flora Street, Philadelphia."

Elizabeth studied the last word, then drew out the envelope again, and looked at that. Yes, the two names were the same. How wonderful! Perhaps she would sometime, sometime, see him again, though of course he belonged to the lady. But perhaps, if she went to school and learned very fast, she might sometime meet him at church — he went to church, she was sure — and then he might smile, and not be ashamed of his friend who had saved his life. Saved his life! Nonsense! She had not done much. He would not feel any such ridiculous indebtedness to her when he got back to home and friends and safety. He had saved her much more than she had saved him.

She put the papers all back in safety, and after having prepared her few belongings for taking up the journey, she knelt down. She would say the prayer before she went on. It might be that would keep the terrible pursuers away.

She said it once, and then with eyes still closed she waited a moment. Might she say it for him, who was gone away from her? Perhaps it would help him, and keep him from falling from that terrible machine he was riding on. Hitherto in her mind prayers had been only for the dead, but now they seemed also to belong to all who were in danger or trouble. She said the prayer over once more, slowly, then paused a moment, and added: "Our Father, hide him from trouble. Hide George Trescott Benedict. And hide me, please, too."

Then she mounted her horse, and went on her way.

It was a long and weary way. It reached over mountains and through valleys, across winding, turbulent streams and broad rivers that had few bridges. The rivers twice led her further south than she meant to go, in her ignorance. She had always felt that Philadelphia was straight ahead east, as straight as one could go to the heart of the sun.

Night after night she lay down in strange homes, some poorer and more forlorn than others; and day after day she took up her lonely travel again.

Gradually, as the days lengthened, and mountains piled themselves behind her, and rivers stretched like barriers between, she grew less and less to dread her pursuers, and more and more to look forward to the future. It seemed so long a way! Would it never end?

Once she asked a man whether he knew where Philadelphia was. She had been travelling then for weeks, and thought she must be almost there. But he said "Philadelphia? O, Philadelphia is in the East. That's a long way off. I saw a man once who came from there."

She set her firm little chin then, and travelled on. Her clothes were much worn, and her skin was brown as a berry. The horse plodded on with a dejected air. He would have liked to stop at a number of places they passed, and remain for life, what there was left of it; but he obediently walked on over any kind of an old road that came in his way, and solaced himself with whatever kind of a bite the roadside afforded. He was becoming a much-travelled horse. He knew a threshing-machine by sight now, and considered it no more than a prairie bobcat.

At one stopping-place a good woman advised Elizabeth to rest on Sundays. She told her God didn't like people to do the same on His day as on other days, and it would bring her bad luck if she kept up her incessant riding. It was bad for the horse too. So, the night being Saturday, Elizabeth remained with the woman over the Sabbath, and heard read aloud the fourteenth chaper of John. It was a wonderful revelation to her. She did not altogether understand it. In fact, the Bible was an unknown book. She had never known that it was different from other books. She had heard it spoken of by her mother, but only as a book. She did not know it was a book of books.

She carried the beautiful thoughts with her on the way, and pondered them. She wished she might have the book. She remembered the name of it, Bible, the Book of God. Then God had written a book! Some day she would try to find it and read it.

"Let not your heart be troubled"; so much of the message drifted into her lonesome, ignorant soul, and settled down to stay. She said it over nights when she found a shelter in some unpleasant place, or days when the road was rough or a storm came up and she was compelled to seek shelter by the roadside under a haystack or in a friendly but deserted shack. She thought of it the day there was no shelter and she was drenched to the skin. She wondered afterward when the sun came out and dried her nicely whether God had really been speaking the words to her troubled heart, "Let not your heart be troubled."

Every night and every morning she said "Our Father" twice, once for herself and once for the friend who had gone out into the world, it seemed about a hundred years ago.

But one day she came across a railroad track. It made her heart beat wildly. It seemed now that she must be almost there. Railroads were things belonging to the East and civilization. But the way was lonely still for days, and then she crossed more railroads, becoming more and more frequent, and came into the line of towns that stretched along beside the snake-like tracks.

She fell into the habit of staying overnight in a town, and then riding on to the next in the morning; but now her clothes were becoming so dirty and ragged that she felt ashamed to go to nice-looking places lest they should turn her out; so she sought shelter in barns and small, mean houses. But the people in these houses were distressingly dirty, and she found no place to wash.

She had lost track of the weeks or the months when she reached her first great city, the only one she had come near in her uncharted wanderings.

Into the outskirts of Chicago she rode undaunted, her head erect, with the carriage of a queen. She had passed Indians and cowboys in her journeying; why should she mind Chicago? Miles and miles of houses and people. There seemed to be no end to it. Nothing but houses everywhere and hurried-looking people, many of them working hard. Surely this must be Philadelphia.

A large, beautiful building attracted her attention. There were handsome grounds about it, and girls playing some game with a ball and curious webbed implements across a net of cords. Elizabeth drew her horse to the side of the road, and watched a few minutes. One girl was skillful, and hit the ball back every time. Elizabeth almost exclaimed out loud once when a particularly fine ball was played. She rode reluctantly on when the game was finished, and saw over the arched gateway the words, "Janeway School for Girls."

Ah! This was Philadelphia at last, and here was her school. She would go in at once before she went to her grandmother's. It might be better.

She dismounted, and tied the horse to an iron ring in a post by the sidewalk. Then she went slowly, shyly up the steps into the charmed circles of learning. She knew she was shabby, but her long journey would explain that. Would they be kind to her, and let her study?

She stood some time before the door, with a group of laughing girls not far away whispering about her. She smiled at them; but they did not return the salutation, and their actions made her more shy. At last she stepped into the open door, and a maid in cap and apron came forward. "You must not come in here, miss," she said imperiously. "This is a school."

"Yes," said Elizabeth gravely, smiling. "I want to see the teacher."

"She's busy. You can't see her," snapped the maid.

"Then I will wait till she is ready. I've come a great many miles, and I must see her."

The maid retreated at this, and an elegant woman in trailing black silk and gold-rimmed glasses approached threateningly. This was a new kind of beggar, of course, and must be dealt with at once.

"What do you want?" she asked frigidly.

"I've come to school," said Elizabeth confidingly. "I know I don't look very nice, but I've had to come all the way from Montana on horseback. If you could let me go where I can have some water and a thread and needle, I can make myself look better."

The woman eyed the girl incredulously.

"You have come to school!" she said; and her voice was large, and frightened Elizabeth. "You have come all the way from Montana! Impossible! You must be crazy."

"No, ma'am, I'm not crazy," said Elizabeth. "I just want to go to school."

The woman perceived that this might be an interesting case for benevolently inclined people. It was nothing but an annoyance to herself. "My dear girl," — her tone was bland and disagreeable now — "are you aware that it takes money to come to school?"

"Does it?" said Elizabeth. "No, I didn't know it, but I have some money. I could give you ten dollars right now; and, if that is not enough, I might work some way, and earn more."

The woman laughed disagreeably.

"It is impossible," she said. "The yearly tuition here is five hundred dollars. Besides, we do not take girls of your class. This is a finishing school for young ladies. You will have to inquire further," and the woman swept away to laugh with her colleagues over the queer character, the new kind of tramp, she had just been called to interview. The maid came pertly forward, and said that Elizabeth could no longer stand where she was.

Bewilderment and bitter disappointment in her face, Elizabeth went slowly down to her horse, the great tears welling up into her eyes. As she rode away, she kept turning back to the school grounds wistfully. She did not notice the passers-by, nor know that they were commenting upon her appearance. She made a striking picture in her rough garments, with her wealth of hair, her tanned skin, and tear-filled eyes. An artist noticed it, and watched her down the street, half thinking he would follow and secure her as a model for his next picture.

A woman, gaudily bedecked in soiled finery, her face giving evidence of the frequent use of rouge and powder, watched her, and followed, pondering. At last she called, "My dear, my dear, wait a minute." She had to speak several times before Elizabeth saw that she was talking to her. Then the horse was halted by the sidewalk.

"My dear," said the woman, "you look tired and disappointed. Don't you want to come home with me for a while, and rest?"

"Thank you," said Elizabeth, "but I am afraid I must go on. I only stop on Sundays."

"But just come home with me for a little while," coaxed the wheedling tones. "You look so tired, and I've some girls of my own. I know you would enjoy resting and talking with them."

The kindness in her tones touched the weary girl. Her pride had been stung to the quick by the haughty woman in the school. This woman would soothe her with kindness.

"Do you live far from here?" asked Elizabeth.

"Only two or three blocks," said the woman. "You ride along by the sidewalk, and we can talk. Where are you going? You look as if you had come a long distance."

"Yes," said the girl wearily, "from Montana. I am going to school. Is this Philadelphia?"

"This is Chicago," said the woman. "There are finer schools here than

in Philadelphia. If you'd like to come and stay at my house awhile, I will
see about getting you into a school.''

"Is it hard work to get people into schools?" asked the girl wonderingly.
"I thought they would want people to teach."

"No, it's very hard," said the lying woman; "but I think I know a school
where I can get you in. Where are your folks? Are they in Montana?"

"They are all dead," said Elizabeth, "and I have come away to school."

"Poor child!" said the woman glibly. "Come right home with me, and
I'll take care of you. I know a nice way you can earn your living, and then
you can study if you like. But you're quite big to go to school. It seems to
me you could have a good time without that. You are a pretty girl; do you
know it? You only need pretty clothes to make you a beauty. If you come
with me, I will let you earn some beautiful new clothes."

"You are very kind," said the girl gravely. "I do need new clothes; and,
if I could earn them, that would be all the better." She did not quite like
the woman; yet of course that was foolish.

After a few more turns they stopped in front of a tall brick building with
a number of windows. It seemed to be a good deal like other buildings; in
fact, as she looked up the street, Elizabeth thought there were miles of
them just alike. She tied her horse in front of the door and went in with the
woman. The woman told her to sit down a minute until she called the lady
of the house, who would tell her more about the school. There were a
number of pretty girls in the room, and they made very free to speak to
her. They twitted her about her clothes, and in a way reminded Elizabeth
of the girls in the school she had just interviewed.

Suddenly she spoke up to the group. An idea had occurred to her. This
was the school, and the woman had not liked to say so until she spoke to
the leader about her.

"Is this a school?" she asked shyly.

Her question was met with a shout of derisive laughter.

"School!" cried the boldest, prettiest one. "School for scandal! School
for morals!"

There was one, a thin, pale girl with dark circles under her eyes, a sad
droop to her mouth, and bright scarlet spots in her cheeks. She came over
to Elizabeth, and whispered something to her. Elizabeth started forward,
unspeakable horror in her face.

She fled to the door where she had come in, but found it fastened. Then
she turned as if she had been brought to bay by a pack of lions.

Chapter 10
Philadelphia at Last

"Open this door!" she commanded. "Let me out of here at once."

The pale girl started to do so, but the pretty one held her back. "No, Nellie; Madam will be angry with us all if you open that door." Then she turned to Elizabeth, and said:

"Whoever enters that door never goes out again. You are nicely caught, my dear."

There was a sting of bitterness and self-pity in the taunt at the end of the words. Elizabeth felt it, as she seized her pistol from her belt, and pointed it at the astonished group. They were not accustomed to girls with pistols. "Open that door, or I will shoot you all!" she cried.

Then, as she heard someone descending the stairs, she rushed again into the room where she remembered the windows were open. They were guarded by wire screens; but she caught up a chair, and dashed it through one, plunging out into the street in spite of detaining hands that reached for her, hands much hindered by the gleam of the pistol and the fear that it might go off in their midst.

It took but an instant to wrench the bridle from its fastening and mount her horse; then she rode forward through the city at a pace that only millionaires and automobiles were allowed to take. She met and passed her first automobile without a quiver. Her eyes were dilated, her lips set; angry, frightened tears were streaming down her cheeks, and she urged her poor horse forward until a policeman here and there thought it his duty to make a feeble effort to detain her. But nothing impeded her way. She fled through a maze of wagons, carriages, automobiles, and trolley-cars, until she passed the whirl of the great city, and at last was free again and out in the open country.

She came toward evening to a little cottage on the edge of a pretty suburb. The cottage was covered with roses, and the front yard was full of great old-fashioned flowers. On the porch sat a plain little old lady in a rocking-chair, knitting. There was a little gate with a path leading up to the door, and at the side another open gate with a road leading around to the back of the cottage.

Elizabeth saw, and murmering, "O 'our Father,' please hide me!" she dashed into the driveway, and tore up to the side of the piazza at a full gallop. She jumped from the horse; and, leaving him standing panting with his nose to the fence, and a tempting strip of clover in front of him where he could graze when he should get his breath, she ran up the steps, and flung herself in a miserable little heap at the feet of the astonished old lady.

"O, please, please, won't you let me stay here a few minutes, and tell me what to do? I am so tired, and I have had such a dreadful, awful time!"

"Why, dearie me!" said the old lady. "Of course I will. Poor child; sit right down in this rocking-chair, and have a good cry. I'll get you a glass of water and something to eat, and then you shall tell me all about it."

She brought the water, and a tray with nice broad slices of brown bread and butter, a generous piece of apple pie, some cheese, and a glass pitcher of creamy milk.

Elizabeth drank the water, but before she could eat she told the terrible tale of her last adventure. It seemed awful for her to believe, and she felt she must have help somewhere. She had heard there were bad people in the world. In fact, she had seen men who were bad, and once a woman had passed their ranch whose character was said to be questionable. She wore a hard face, and could drink and swear like the men. But that sin should be in this form, with pretty girls and pleasant, wheedling women for agents, she had never dreamed; and this in the great, civilized East! Almost better would it have been to remain in the desert alone, and risk the pursuit of that awful man, than to come all this way to find the world gone wrong.

The old lady was horrified, too. She had heard more than the girl of licensed evil; but she had read it in the paper as she had read about the evils of the slave-traffic in Africa, and it had never really seemed true to her. Now she lifted up her hands in horror, and looked at the beautiful girl before her with something akin to awe that she had been in one of those dens of iniquity and escaped. Over and over she made the girl tell what was said, and how it looked, and how she pointed her pistol, and how she got out; and then she exclaimed in wonder, and called her escape a miracle.

They were both weary from excitement when the tale was told. Elizabeth ate her lunch; then the old lady showed her where to put the horse, and made her go to bed. It was only a wee little room with a cot-bed white as snow where she put her; but the roses peeped in at the window, and the box covered with an old white curtain contained a large pitcher of fresh water and a bowl and soap and towels. The old lady brought her a clean white nightgown, coarse and mended in many places, but smelling of rose leaves; and in the morning she tapped at the door quite early before the girl was up, and came in with an armful of clothes.

"I had some boarders last summer," she explained, "and, when they went away, they left these things and said I might put them into the home-mission box. But I was sick when they sent it off this winter; and, if you ain't a home mission, then I never saw one. You put 'em on. I guess they'll fit. They may be a mite large, but she was about your size. I guess your clothes are about worn out; so you just leave 'em here fer the next one, and use these. There's a couple of extra shirt-waists you can put in a bundle for a change. I guess folks won't dare fool with you if you have some clean, nice clothes on."

Elizabeth looked at her gratefully, and wrote her down in the list of saints with the woman who read the fourteenth chapter of John. The old lady had neglected to mention that from her own meagre wardrobe she had supplied some under-garments, which were not included in those the boarders had left.

Bathed and clothed in clean, sweet garments, with a white shirt-waist and a dark-blue serge skirt and coat, Elizabeth looked a different girl. She surveyed herself in the little glass over the box-washstand and wondered. All at once vanity was born within her, and an ambition to be always thus clothed, with a horrible remembrance of the woman of the day before, who had promised to show her how to earn some pretty clothes. It flashed across her mind that pretty clothes might be a snare. Perhaps they had been to those girls she had seen in that house.

With much good advice and kindly blessings from the old lady, Elizabeth fared forth upon her journey once more, sadly wise in the wisdom of the world, and less sweetly credulous than she had been, but better fitted to fight her way.

The story of her journey from Chicago to Philadelphia would fill a volume if it were written, but it might pall upon the reader from the very variety of its experiences. It was made slowly and painfully, with many haltings and much lessening of the scanty store of money that had seemed so much when she received it in the wilderness. The horse went lame, and had to be watched over and petted, and finally, by the advice of a kindly farmer, taken to a veterinary surgeon, who doctored him for a week before he finally said it was safe to let him hobble on again. After that the girl was more careful of the horse. If he should die, what would she do?

One dismal morning, late in November, Elizabeth, wearing the old overcoat to keep her from freezing, rode into Philadelphia.

Armed with instructions from the old lady in Chicago, she rode boldly up to a policeman, and showed him the address of the grandmother to whom she had decided to go first, her mother's mother. He sent her on in the right direction, and in due time with the help of other policemen she reached the right number on Flora Street.

It was a narrow street, banked on either side by small, narrow brick houses of the older type. Here and there gleamed out a scrap of a white marble door-step, but most of the houses were approached by steps of dull stone or of painted wood. There was a dejected and dreary air about the place. The street was swarming with children in various stages of the soiled condition.

Elizabeth timidly knocked at the door after being assured by the interested urchins who surrounded her that Mrs. Brady really lived there, and had not moved away or anything. It did not seem wonderful to the girl, who had lived her life thus far in a mountain shack, to find her grandmother still in the place from which she had written fifteen years before. She did not yet know what a floating population most cities contain.

Mrs. Brady was washing when the knock sounded through the house. She was a broad woman, with a face on which the cares and sorrows of the years had left a not too heavy impress. She still enjoyed life, even though a good part of it was spent at the wash-tub, washing other people's fine clothes. She had some fine ones of her own up-stairs in her clothes-press; and, when she went out, it was in shiny satin, with a bonnet bobbing with jet and a red rose, though of late years, strictly speaking, the bonnet had become a hat again, and Mrs. Brady was in style with the other old ladies.

The perspiration was in little beads on her forehead and trickling down the creases in her well-cushioned neck toward her ample bosom. Her gray hair was neatly combed, and her calico wrapper was open at the throat even on this cold day. She wiped on her apron the soapsuds from her plump arms steaming pink from the hot suds, and went to the door.

She looked with disfavor upon the peculiar person on the door-step attired in a man's overcoat. She was prepared to refuse the demands of the Salvation Army for a nickel for Christmas dinners; or to silence the bananaman, or the fish-man, or the man with shoe-strings and pins and pencils for sale; or to send the photograph-agent on his way; yes, even the man who sold albums for postcards. She had no time to bother with anybody this morning.

But the young person in the rusty overcoat, with the dark-blue serge Eton jacket under it, which might have come from Wanamaker's two years ago, who yet wore a leather belt with gleaming pistols under the Eton jacket, was a new species. Mrs. Brady was taken off her guard; else Elizabeth might have found entrance to her grandmother's home as difficult as she had found entrance to the finishing school of Madame Janeway.

"Are you Mrs. Brady?" asked the girl. She was searching the forbidding face before her for some sign of likeness to her mother, but found none. The cares of Elizabeth Brady's daughter had outweighed those of the mother, or else they sat upon a nature more sensitive.

"I am," said Mrs. Brady, imposingly.

"Grandmother, I am the baby you talked about in that letter," she announced, handing Mrs. Brady the letter she had written nearly eighteen years before.

The woman took the envelope gingerly in the wet thumb and finger that still grasped a bit of the gingham apron. She held it at arm's length, and squinted up her eyes, trying to read it without her glasses. It was some new kind of beggar, of course. She hated to touch these dirty envelopes, and this one looked old and worn. She stepped back to the parlor table where her glasses were lying, and, adjusting them, began to read the letter.

"For the land sakes! Where'd you find this?" she said, looking up suspiciously. "It's against the law to open letters that ain't your own. Didn't me daughter ever get it? I wrote it to her meself. How come you by it?"

"Mother read it to me long ago when I was little," answered the girl, the slow hope fading from her lips as she spoke. Was every one, was even her grandmother, going to be cold and harsh with her? "Our Father, hide me!" her heart murmured, because it had become a habit; and her listening thought caught the answer, "Let not your heart be troubled."

"Well, who are you?" said the uncordial grandmother, still puzzled. "You ain't Bessie, me Bessie. Fer one thing, you're 'bout as young as she was when she went off 'n' got married, against me 'dvice, to that drunken, lazy dude." Her brow was lowering, and she proceeded to finish her letter.

"I am Elizabeth," said the girl with a trembling voice, "the baby you talked about in that letter. But please don't call father that. He wasn't ever bad to us. He was always good to mother, even when he was drunk. If you talk like that about him, I shall have to go away."

"Fer the land sakes! You don't say," said Mrs. Brady, sitting down hard in astonishment on the biscuit upholstery of her best parlor chair. "Now you ain't Bessie's child! Well, I *am clear* beat. And growed up so big! You look strong, but you're kind of thin. What makes your skin so black? Your ma never was dark, ner your pa, neither."

"I've been riding a long way in the wind and sun and rain."

"Fer the land sakes!" as she looked through the window to the street. "Not on a horse?"

"Yes."

"H'm! What was your ma thinkin' about to let you do that?"

"My mother is dead. There was no one left to care what I did. I had to come. There were dreadful people out there, and I was afraid."

"Fer the land sakes!" That seemed the only remark that the capable Mrs. Brady could make. She looked at her new granddaughter in bewilderment, as if a strange sort of creature had suddenly laid claim to relationship.

"Well, I'm right glad to see you," she said stiffly, wiping her hand again on her apron and putting it out formally for a greeting.

Elizabeth accepted her reception gravely, and sat down. She sat down suddenly, as if her strength had given way and a great strain was at an end. As she sat down, she drooped her head back against the wall; and a gray look spread about her lips.

"You're tired," said the grandmother, energetically. "Come far this morning?"

"No," said Elizabeth, weakly, "not many miles; but I hadn't any more bread. I used it all up yesterday, and there wasn't much money left. I thought I could wait till I got here, but I guess I'm hungry."

"Fer the land sakes!" ejaculated Mrs. Brady as she hustled out to the kitchen, and clattered the frying-pan onto the stove, shoving the boiler hastily aside. She came in presently with a steaming cup of tea, and made the girl drink it hot and strong. Then she established her in the big rocking-chair in the kitchen with a plate of appetizing things to eat, and went on with her washing, punctuating every rub with a question.

Elizabeth felt better after her meal, and offered to help, but the grandmother would not hear to her lifting a finger.

"You must rest first," she said. "It beats me how you ever got here. I'd sooner crawl on me hands and knees than ride a great, scary horse."

Elizabeth sprang to her feet.

"The horse!" she said. "Poor fellow! He needs something to eat worse than I did. He hasn't had a bite of grass all this morning. There was nothing but hard roads and pavements. The grass is all brown, anyway, now. I found some cornstalks by the road, and once a man dropped a big bundle of hay out of his load. If it hadn't been for Robin, I'd never have got here; and here I've sat enjoying my breakfast, and Robin out there hungry!"

"Fer the land sakes!" said the grandmother, taking her arms out of the suds and looked troubled. "Poor fellow! What would he like? I haven't got any hay, but there's some mashed potatoes left, and what is there? Why, there's some excelsior the lamp-shade came packed in. You don't suppose he'd think it was hay, do you? No, I guess it wouldn't taste very good."

"Where can I put him, Grandmother?"

"Fer the land sakes! I don't know," said the grandmother, looking around the room in alarm. "We haven't any place fer horses. Perhaps you might get him into the back yard fer a while till we think what to do. There's a stable, but they charge high to board horses. Lizzie knows one of the fellers that works there. Mabbe he'll tell us what to do. Anyway, you lead him round to the alleyway, and we'll see if we can't get him in the little ash-gate. You don't suppose he'd try to get in the house, do you? I shouldn't like him to come in the kitchen when I was getting supper."

"O no!" said Elizabeth. "He's very good. Where is the back yard?"

This arrangement was finally made, and the two women stood in the kitchen door, watching Robin drink a bucketful of water and eat heartily of the various viands that Mrs. Brady set forth for him, with the exception of the excelsior, which he sniffed at in disgust.

"Now, ain't he smart?" said Mrs. Brady, watching fearfully from the door-step, where she might retreat if the animal showed any tendency to step nearer to the kitchen. "But don't you think he's cold? Wouldn't he like a — a — shawl or something?"

The girl drew the old coat from her shoulders, and threw it over him, her grandmother watching her fearless handling of the horse with pride and awe.

"We're used to sharing this together," said the girl simply.

"Nan sews in an up-town dressmaker's place," explained Mrs. Brady by and by, when the wash was hung out in fearsome proximity to the weary horse's heels, and the two had returned to the warm kitchen to clean up and get supper. "Nan's your ma's sister, you know, older'n her by two years; and Lizzie, that's her girl, she's about 's old 's you. She's got a good place in the ten-cent store. Nan's husband died four years ago, and her and me've been livin' together ever since. It'll be nice fer you and Lizzie to be together. She'll make it lively fer you right away. Prob'ly she can get you a place at the same store. She'll be here at half past six to-night. This is her week to get out early."

The aunt came in first. She was a tall, thin woman with faded brown hair and a faint resemblance to Elizabeth's mother. Her shoulders stooped slightly, and her voice was nasal. Her mouth looked as if it was used to holding pins in one corner and gossiping out of the other. She was one of the kind who always gets into a rocking-chair to sew if they can, and rock as they sew. Nevertheless, she was skillful in her way, and commanded good wages. She welcomed the new niece reluctantly, more excited over her remarkable appearance among her relatives after so long a silence than pleased, Elizabeth felt. But after she had satisfied her curiosity she

she was kind, beginning to talk about Lizzie, and mentally compared this thin, brown girl with rough hair and dowdy clothes to her own stylish daughter. Then Lizzie burst in. They could hear her calling to a young man who had walked home with her, even before she entered the house.

"It's just fierce out, Ma!" she exclaimed. "Grandma, ain't supper ready yet? I never was so hungry in all my life. I could eat a house afire."

She stopped short at sight of Elizabeth. She had been chewing gum — Lizzie was always chewing gum — but her jaws ceased action in sheer astonishment.

"This is your cousin Bessie, come all the way from Montana on horseback, Lizzie. She's your aunt Bessie's child. Her folks is dead now, and she's come to live with us. You must see if you can't get her a place in the ten-cent store 'long with you," said the grandmother.

Lizzie came airily forward, and grasped her cousin's hand in mid-air, giving it a lateral shake that bewildered Elizabeth.

"Pleased to meet you," she chattered glibly, and set her jaws to work again. One could not embarrass Lizzie long. But she kept her eyes on the stranger, and let them wander disapprovingly over her apparel in a pointed way as she took out the long hat-pins from the cumbersome hat she wore and adjusted her ponderous pompadour.

"Lizzie 'll have to help fix you up," said the aunt, noting Lizzie's glance. "You're all out of style. I suppose they get behind times out in Montana. Lizzie, can't you show her how to fix her hair pompadour?"

Lizzie brightened. If there was a prospect of changing things, she was not averse to a cousin of her own age; but she never could take such a dowdy-looking girl into society, not the society of the ten-cent store.

"O, cert!" answered Lizzie affably. "I'll fix you fine. Don't you worry. How'd you get so awful tanned? I s'pose riding. You look like you'd been to the seashore, and lay out on the beach in the sun. But 'tain't the right time o' year quite. It must be great to ride horseback!"

"I'll teach you how if you want to learn," said Elizabeth, endeavoring to show a return of the kindly offer.

"Me? What would I ride? Have to ride a counter, I guess. I guess you won't find much to ride here in the city, 'cept trolley-cars."

"Bessie's got a horse. He's out in the yard now," said the grandmother with pride.

"A horse! All your own? Gee whiz! Won't the girls stare when I tell them? Say, we can borrow a rig at the livery some night, and take a ride. Dan'll go with us, and get the rig for us. Won't that be great?"

Elizabeth smiled. She felt the glow of at last contributing something to the family pleasure. She did not wish her coming to be so entirely a wet blanket as it had seemed at first; for, to tell the truth, she had seen blank dismay on the face of each separate relative as her identity had been made known. Her heart was lonely, and she hungered for someone who "belonged" and loved her.

Supper was put on the table, and the two girls began to get a little acquainted, chattering over clothes and the arrangement of hair.

"Do you know whether there is anything in Philadelphia called 'Christian Endeavor'?" asked Elizabeth after the supper-table was cleared off.

"O, Chrishun 'deavor! Yes, I used t'b'long," answered Lizzie. She had removed the gum from her mouth while she ate her supper, but now it was busy again between sentences. "Yes, we have one down to our church. It was real interesting, too; but I got mad at one of the members, and quit. She was a stuck-up old maid, anyway. She was always turning round and scowling at us girls if we just whispered the least little bit, or smiled; and one night she was leading the meeting, and Jim Forbes got in a corner behind a post, and made mouths at her behind his book. He looked awful funny. It was something fierce the way she always screwed her face up when she sang, and he looked just like her. We girls, Hetty and Em'line and I, got to laughing, and we just couldn't stop; and didn't that old thing stop the singing after one verse, and look right at us, and say she thought Christian Endeavor members should remember whose house they were in, and that the owner was there, and all that rot. I nearly died, I was so mad. Everybody look around, and we girls choked, and got up and went out. I haven't been down since. The lookout committee came to see us 'bout it; but I said I wouldn't go back where I'd been insulted, and I've never been inside the doors since. But she's moved away now. I wouldn't mind going back if you want to go."

"Whose house did she mean it was? Was it her house?"

"O, no, it wasn't her house," laughed Lizzie. "It was the church. She meant it was God's house, I s'pose, but she needn't have been so pernickety. We weren't doing any harm."

"Does God have a house?"

"Why, yes; didn't you know that? Why, you talk like a heathen, Bessie. Didn't you have churches in Montana?"

"Yes, there was a church fifty miles away. I heard about it once, but I never saw it," answered Elizabeth. "But what did the woman mean? Who did she say was there? God? Was God in the church? Did you see Him, and know He was there when you laughed?"

"O, you silly!" giggled Lizzie. "Wouldn't the girls laugh at you, though, if they could hear you talk? Why, of course God was there. He's everywhere, you know," with superior knowledge; "but I didn't see Him. You can't see God."

"Why not?"

"Why, because you can't!" answered her cousin with final logic. "Say, haven't you got any other clothes with you at all? I'd take you down with me in the morning if you was fixed up."

Chapter 11
In Flight Again

When Elizabeth lay down to rest that night, with Lizzie still chattering by her side, she found that there was one source of intense pleasure in anticipation, and that was the prospect of going to God's house to Christian Endeavor. Now perhaps she would be able to find out what it all had meant, and whether it were true that God took care of people and hid them in time of trouble. She felt almost certain in her own little experience that He had cared for her, and she wanted to be quite sure, so that she might grasp this precious truth to her heart and keep it forever. No one could be quite alone in the world if there was a God who cared and loved and hid.

The aunt and the grandmother were up betimes the next morning, looking over some meagre stores of old clothing, and there was found an old dress which it was thought could be furbished over for Elizabeth. They were hard-working people with little money to spare, and everything had to be utilized; but they made a great deal of appearance, and Lizzie was proud as a young peacock. She would not take Elizabeth to the store to face the head man without having her fixed up according to the most approved style.

So the aunt cut and fitted before she went off for the day, and Elizabeth was ordered to sew while she was gone. The grandmother presided at the rattling old sewing-machine, and in two or three days Elizabeth was pronounced to be fixed up enough to do for the present till she could earn some new clothes. With her fine hair snarled into a cushion and puffed out into an enormous pompadour that did not suit her face in the least, and with an old hat and jacket of Lizzie's which did not become her nor fit her exactly, she started out to make her way in the world as a saleswoman. Lizzie had already secured her a place if she suited.

The store was a maze of wonder to the girl from the mountains — so many bright, bewildering things, ribbons and tin pans, glassware and toys, cheap jewelry and candies. She looked about with the dazed eyes of a creature from another world.

But the manager looked upon her with eyes of favor. He saw that her eyes were bright and keen. He was used to judging faces. He saw that she

81

was as yet unspoiled, with a face of refinement far beyond the general run of the girls who applied to him for positions. And he was not beyond a friendly flirtation with a pretty new girl himself; so she was engaged at once, and put on duty at the notion-counter.

The girls flocked around her during the intervals of custom. Lizzie had told of her cousin's long ride, embellished, wherever her knowledge failed, by her extremely wild notions of Western life. She had told how Elizabeth arrived wearing a belt with two pistols, and this gave Elizabeth standing at once among all the people in the store. A girl who could shoot, and who wore pistols in a belt like a real cowboy, had a social distinction all her own.

The novel-reading, theatre-going girls rallied around her to a girl; and the young men in the store were not far behind. Elizabeth was popular from the first. Moreover, as she settled down into the routine of life, and had three meals every day, her cheeks began to round out just a little; and it became apparent that she was unusually beautiful in spite of her dark skin, which whitened gradually under the electric light and high-pressure life of the store.

They went to Christian Endeavor, Elizabeth and her cousin; and Elizabeth felt as if heaven had suddenly dropped down about her. She lived from week to week for that Christian Endeavor.

The store, which had been a surprise and a novelty at first, began to be a trial to her. It wore upon her nerves. The air was bad, and the crowds were great. It was coming on toward Christmas time, and the store was crammed to bursting day after day and night after night, for they kept open evenings now until Christmas. Elizabeth longed for a breath from the mountains, and grew whiter and thinner. Sometimes she felt as if she must break away from it all, and take Robin, and ride into the wilderness again. If it were not for the Christian Endeavor, she would have done so, perhaps.

Robin, poor beast, was well housed and well fed; but he worked for his living as did his mistress. He was a grocer's delivery horse, worked from Monday morning early till Saturday night at ten o'clock, subject to curses and kicks from the grocery boy, expected to stand meekly at the curbstones, snuffing the dusty brick pavements while the boy delivered a box of goods, and while trolleys and beer-wagons and automobiles slammed and rumbled and tooted by him, and then to start on the double-quick to the next stopping-place.

He to be thus under the rod who had trod the plains with a free foot and snuffed the mountain air! It was a great come-down, and his life became a weariness to him. But he earned his mistress a dollar a week besides his board. There would have been some consolation in that to his faithful heart if he only could have known it. Albeit she would have gladly gone without the dollar if Robin could have been free and happy.

One day, one dreadful day, the manager of the ten-cent store came to Elizabeth with a look in his eyes that reminded her of the man in Montana from whom she had fled. He was smiling, and his words were unduly pleasant. He wanted her to go with him to the theatre that evening, and he complimented her on her appearance. He stated that he admired her exceedingly, and wanted to give her pleasure. But somehow Elizabeth had fallen into the habit ever since she left the prairies of comparing all men with George Trescott Benedict; and this man, although he dressed well, and was every bit as handsome, did not compare well. There was a sinister, selfish glitter in his eyes that made Elizabeth think of the serpent on the plain just before she shot it. Therefore Elizabeth declined the invitation.

It happened that there was a missionary meeting at the church that evening. All the Christian endeavorers had been urged to attend. Elizabeth gave this as an excuse; but the manager quickly swept that away, saying she could go to church any night, but she could not go to this particular play with him always. The girl eyed him calmly with much the same attitude with which she might have pointed her pistol at his head, and said gravely,

"But I do not want to go with you."

After that the manager hated her. He always hated girls who resisted him. He hated her, and wanted to do her harm. But he fairly persecuted her to receive his attentions. He was a young fellow, extremely young to be occupying so responsible a position. He undoubtedly had business ability. He showed it in his management of Elizabeth. The girl's life became a torment to her. In proportion as she appeared to be the manager's favorite the other girls became jealous of her. They taunted her with the manager's attentions on every possible occasion. When they found anything wrong, they charged it upon her; and so she was kept constantly going to the manager, which was perhaps just what he wanted.

She grew paler and paler, and more and more desperate. She had run away from one man; she had run away from a woman; but here was a man from whom she could not run away unless she gave up her position. If it had not been for her grandmother, she would have done so at once; but, if she gave up her position, she would be thrown upon her grandmother for support, and that must not be. She understood from the family talk that they were having just as much as they could do already to make both ends meet and keep the all-important god of Fashion satisfied. This god of Fashion had come to seem to Elizabeth an enemy of the living God. It seemed to occupy all people's thoughts, and everything else had to be sacrificed to meet its demands.

She had broached the subject of school one evening soon after she arrived, but was completely squelched by her aunt and cousin.

"You're too old!" sneered Lizzie. "School is for children."

"Lizzie went through grammar school, and we talked about high for her," said the grandmother proudly.

"But I just hated school," grinned Lizzie. "It ain't so nice as it's cracked up to be. Just sit and study all day long. Why, they were always keeping me after school for talking or laughing. I was glad enough when I got through. You may thank your stars you didn't have to go, Bess."

"People who have to earn their bread can't lie around and go to school," remarked Aunt Nan dryly, and Elizabeth said no more.

But later she heard of a night-school, and then she took up the subject once more. Lizzie scoffed at this. She said night-school was only for very poor people, and it was a sort of disgrace to go. But Elizabeth stuck to her point, until one day Lizzie came home with a tale about Temple College. She had heard it was very cheap. You could go for ten cents a night, or something like that. Things that were ten cents appealed to her. She was used to bargain-counters.

She heard it was quite respectable to go there, and they had classes in the evening. You could study gymnastics, and it would make you graceful. She wanted to be graceful. And she heard they had a course in millinery. If it was so, she believed she would go herself, and learn to make the new kinds of bows they were having on hats this winter. She could not seem to get the right twist to the ribbon.

Elizabeth wanted to study geography. At least, that was the study Lizzie said would tell her where the Desert of Sahara was. She wanted to know things, all kinds of things; but Lizzie said such things were only for children, and she didn't believe they taught such baby studies in a college. But she would inquire. It was silly of Bessie to want to know, she thought, and she was half ashamed to ask. But she would find out.

It was about this time that Elizabeth's life at the store grew intolerable.

One morning — it was little more than a week before Christmas — Elizabeth had been sent to the cellar to get seven little red tin pails and shovels for a woman who wanted them for Christmas gifts for some Sunday-school class. She had just counted out the requisite number and turned to go up-stairs when she heard someone step near her, and, as she looked up in the dim light, there stood the manager.

"At last I've got you alone, Bessie, my dear!" He said it with suave triumph in his tones. He caught Elizabeth by the wrists, and before she could wrench herself away he had kissed her.

With a scream Elizabeth dropped the seven tin pails and the seven tin shovels, and with one mighty wrench took her hands from his grasp. Instinctively her hand went to her belt, where were now no pistols. If one had been there she certainly would have shot him in her horror and fury. But, as she had no other weapon, she seized a little shovel, and struck him in the face. Then with the frenzy of the desert back upon her she rushed up the stairs, out through the crowded store, and into the street, hatless and coatless in the cold December air. The passers-by made way for her, thinking she had been sent out on some hurried errand.

She had left her pocketbook, with its pitifully few nickels for car-fare and lunch, in the cloak-room with her coat and hat. But she did not stop to think of that. She was fleeing again, this time on foot, from a man. She half expected he might pursue her, and make her come back to the hated work in the stifling store with his wicked face moving everywhere above the crowds. But she turned not to look back. On over the slushy pavements, under the leaden sky, with a few busy flakes floating above her.

The day seemed pitiless as the world. Where could she go and what should she do? There seemed no refuge for her in the wide world. Instinctively she felt her grandmother would feel that a calamity had befallen them in losing the patronage of the manager of the ten-cent store. Perhaps Lizzie would get into trouble. What should she do?

She had reached the corner where she and Lizzie usually took the car for home. The car was coming now; but she had no hat nor coat, and no money to pay for a ride. She must walk. She paused not, but fled on in a steady run, for which her years on the mountain had given her breath. Three miles it was to Flora Street, and she scarcely slackened her pace after she had settled into the steady half-run, half-walk. Only at the corner of Flora Street she paused, and allowed herself to glance back once. No, the manager had not pursued her. She was safe. She might go in and tell her grandmother without fearing he would come behind her as soon as her back was turned.

Chapter 12
Elizabeth's Declaration of Independence

Mrs. Brady was at the wash-tub again when her most uncommon and unexpected grandchild burst into the room.

She wiped her hands on her apron, and sat down with her usual exclamation. "Fer the land sakes! What's happened? Bessie, tell me quick. Is anything the matter with Lizzie? Where is she?"

But Elizabeth was on the floor at her feet in tears. She was shaking with sobs, and could scarcely manage to stammer out that Lizzie was all right. Mrs. Brady settled back with a relieved sigh. Lizzie was the first grandchild, and therefore the idol of her heart. If Lizzie was all right, she could afford to be patient and find out by degrees.

"It's that awful man, grandmother!" Elizabeth sobbed out.

"What man? That feller in Montana you run away from?" The grandmother sat up with snapping eyes. She was not afraid of a man, even if he did shoot people. She would call in the police and protect her own flesh and blood. Let him come. Mrs. Brady was ready for him.

"No, no, grandmother, the man-man-manager at the ten-cent store," sobbed the girl; "he kissed me! Oh!" and she shuddered as if the memory was the most terrible thing that ever came to her.

"Fer the land sakes! Is that all?" said the woman with much relief and a degree of satisfaction. "Why, that's nothing. You ought to be proud. Many a girl would go boasting round about that. What are you crying for? He didn't hurt you, did he? Why, Lizzie seems to think he's fine. I tell you Lizzie wouldn't cry if he was to kiss her, I'm sure. She'd just laugh, and ask him fer a holiday. Here, sit up, child, and wash your face, and go back to your work. You've evidently struck the manager on the right side, and you're bound to get a rise in your wages. Every girl he takes a notion to gets up and does well. Perhaps you'll get money enough to go to school. Goodness knows what you want to go for. I s'pose it's in the blood, though Bess used to say our pa wa'n't any good at study. But, if you've struck the manager the right way, no telling what he might do. He might even want to marry you."

"Grandmother!"

Mrs. Brady was favored with the flashing of the Bailey eyes. She viewed it in astonishment not unmixed with admiration.

"Well, you certainly have got spirit," she ejaculated. "I don't wonder he liked you. I didn't know you was so pretty, Bessie; you look like your mother when she was eighteen; you really do. I never saw the resemblance before. I believe you'll get on all right. Don't you be afraid. I wish you had your chance if you're so anxious to go to school. I shouldn't wonder ef you'd turn out to be something and marry rich. Well, I must be getting back to me tub. Land sakes, but you did give me a turn. I thought Lizzie had been run over. I couldn't think what else'd make you run off way here without your coat. Come, get up, child, and go back to your work. It's too bad you don't like to be kissed, but don't let that worry you. You'll have lots worse than that to come up against. When you've lived as long as I have and worked as hard, you'll be pleased to have someone admire you. You better wash your face, and eat a bite of lunch, and hustle back. You needn't be afraid. If he's fond of you, he won't bother about your running away a little. He'll excuse you ef 'tis busy times, and not dock your pay neither."

"Grandmother!" said Elizabeth. "Don't! I can never go back to that awful place and that man. I would rather go back to Montana. I would rather be dead."

"Hoity-toity!" said the easy-going grandmother, sitting down to her task, for she perceived some wholesome discipline was necessary. "You can't talk that way, Bess. You got to go to your work. We ain't got money to keep you in idleness, and land knows where you'd get another place as good's this one. Ef you stay home all day, you might make him awful mad; and then it would be no use goin' back, and you might lose Lizzie her place too."

But, though the grandmother talked and argued and soothed by turns, Elizabeth was firm. She would not go back. She would never go back. She would go to Montana if her grandmother said any more about it.

With a sigh at last Mrs. Brady gave up. She had given up once before nearly twenty years ago. Bessie, her oldest daughter, had a will like that, and tastes far above her station. Mrs. Brady wondered where she got them.

"You're fer all the world like yer ma," she said as she thumped the clothes in the wash-tub. "She was jest that way, when she would marry your pa. She could 'a' had Jim Stokes, the groceryman, er Lodge, the milkman, er her choice of three railroad men, all of 'em doing well, and ready to let her walk over 'em; but she *would have* your pa, the drunken, good-for-nothing, slippery dude. The only thing I'm surprised at was that he ever married her. I never expected it. I s'posed they'd run off, and he'd leave her when he got tired of her; but it seems he stuck to her. It's the only good thing he ever done, and I'm not sure but she'd 'a' been better off ef he hadn't 'a' done that."

"Grandmother!" Elizabeth's face blazed.

"Yes, *gran*'mother!" snapped Mrs. Brady. "It's all true, and you might's well face it. He met her in church. She used to go reg'lar. Some boys used to come and set in the back seat behind the girls, and then go home with them. They was all nice enough boys 'cept him. I never had a bit a use for him. He belonged to the swells and the stuck-ups; and he knowed it, and presumed upon it. He jest thought he could wind Bessie round his finger, and he did. If he said, 'Go,' she went, no matter what I'd do. So, when his ma found it out, she was hoppin' mad. She jest came driving round here to me house, and presumed to talk to me. She said Bessie was a designing snip, and a bad girl, and a whole lot of things. Said she was leading her son astray, and would come to no good end, and a whole lot of stuff; and told me to look after her. It wasn't so. Bess got John Bailey to quit smoking for a whole week at a time, and he said if she'd marry him he'd quit drinking too. His ma couldn't 'a' got him to promise that. She wouldn't even believe he got drunk. I told her a few things about her precious son, but she curled her fine, aristocratic lip up, and said, 'Gentlemen never get drunk.' Humph! Gentlemen! That's all she knowed about it. He got drunk all right, and stayed drunk, too. So after that, when I tried to keep Bess at home, she slipped away one night; said she was going to church; and she did too; went to the minister's study in a strange church, and got married, her and John; and then they up and off West. John, he'd sold his watch and his fine diamond stud his ma had give him; and he borrowed some money from some friends of his father's, and he off with three hundred dollars and Bess; and that's all I ever saw more of me Bessie."

The poor woman sat down in her chair, and wept into her apron regardless for once of the soap-suds that rolled down her red, wet arms.

"Is my grandmother living yet?" asked Elizabeth. She was sorry for this grandmother, but did not know what to say. She was afraid to comfort her lest she take it for yielding.

"Yes, they say she is," said Mrs. Brady, sitting up with a show of interest. She was always ready for a bit of gossip. "Her husband's dead, and her other son's dead, and she's all alone. She lives in a big house on Rittenhouse Square. If she was any 'count, she'd ought to provide for you. I never thought about it. But I don't suppose it would be any use to try. You might ask her. Perhaps she'd help you to go to school. You've got a claim on her. She ought to give you her son's share of his father's property, though I've heard she disowned him when he married our Bess. You might fix up in some of Lizzie's best things, and go up there and try. She might give you some money."

"I don't want her money," said Elizabeth stiffly. "I guess there's work somewhere in the world I can do without begging even of grandmothers. But I think I ought to go and see her. She might want to know about father."

Mrs. Brady looked at her granddaughter wonderingly. This was a view of things she had never taken.

"Well," said she resignedly, "go your own gait. I don't know where you'll come up at. All I say is, ef you're going through the world with such high and mighty fine notions, you'll have a hard time. You can't pick out roses and cream and a bed of down every day. You have to put up with life as you find it."

Elizabeth went to her room, the room she shared with Lizzie. She wanted to get away from her grandmother's disapproval. It lay on her heart like lead. Was there no refuge in the world? If grandmothers were not refuges, where should one flee? The old lady in Chicago had understood; why had not Grandmother Brady?

Then came the sweet old words, "Let not your heart be troubled." "In the time of trouble he shall hide me in his pavilion; in the secret of his tabernacle shall he hide me." She knelt down by the bed and said "Our Father." She was beginning to add some words of her own now. She had heard them pray so in Christian Endeavor in the sentence prayers. She wished she knew more about God, and His Book. She had had so little time to ask or think about it. Life seemed all one rush for clothes and position.

At supper-time Lizzie came home much excited. She had been in hot water all the afternoon. The girls had said at lunch-time that the manager was angry with Bessie, and had discharged her. She found her coat and hat, and had brought them home. The pocketbook was missing. There was only fifteen cents in it; but Lizzie was much disturbed, and so was the grandmother. They had a quiet consultation in the kitchen; and, when the aunt came, there was another whispered conversation among the three.

Elizabeth felt disapproval in the air. Aunt Nan came, and sat down beside her, and talked very coldly about expenses and being dependent upon one's relatives, and let her understand thoroughly that she could not sit around and do nothing; but Elizabeth answered by telling her how the manager had been treating her. The aunt then gave her a dose of worldly wisdom, which made the girl shrink into herself. It needed only Lizzie's loud-voiced exhortations to add to her misery and make her feel ready to do anything. Supper was a most unpleasant meal. At last the grandmother spoke up.

"Well, Bessie," she said firmly, "we've decided, all of us, that, if you are going to be stubborn about this, something will have to be done; and I think the best thing is for you to go to Mrs. Bailey and see what she'll do for you. It's her business, anyway."

Elizabeth's cheeks were very red. She said nothing. She let them go on with the arrangements. Lizzie went and got her best hat, and tried it on Elizabeth to see how she would look, and produced a silk waist from her store of garments, and a spring jacket. It wasn't very warm, it is true; but Lizzie explained that the occasion demanded strenuous measures, and the jacket was undoubtedly stylish, which was the main thing to be considered. One could afford to be cold if one was stylish.

Lizzie was up early the next morning. She had agreed to put Elizabeth in battle-array for her visit to Rittenhouse Square. Elizabeth submitted meekly to her borrowed adornings. Her hair was brushed over her face, and curled on a hot iron, and brushed backward in a perfect mat, and then puffed out in a bigger pompadour than usual. The silk waist was put on with Lizzie's best skirt, and she was adjured not to let that drag. Then the best hat with the cheap pink plumes was set atop the elaborate coiffure; the jacket was put on; and a pair of Lizzie's long silk gloves were struggled into. They were a trifle large when on, but to the hands unaccustomed to gloves they were like being run into a mould.

Elizabeth stood it all until she was pronounced complete. Then she came and stood in front of the cheap little glass, and surveyed herself. There were blisters in the glass that twisted her head into a grotesque shape. The hairpins stuck into her head. Lizzie had tied a spotted veil tight over her nose and eyes. The collar of the silk waist was frayed, and cut her neck. The shirt-band was too tight, and the gloves were torture. Elizabeth turned slowly, and went down-stairs, past the admiring aunt and grandmother, who exclaimed at the girl's beauty, now that she was attired to their mind, and encouraging her by saying they were sure her grandmother would want to do something for so pretty a girl.

Lizzie called out to her not to worry, as she flew for her car. She said she had heard there was a variety show in town where they wanted a girl who could shoot. If she didn't succeed with her grandmother, they would try and get her in at the show. The girls at the store knew a man who had charge of it. They said he liked pretty girls, and they thought would be glad to get her. Indeed, Mary James had promised to speak to him last night, and would let her know to-day about it. It would likely be a job more suited to her cousin's liking.

Elizabeth shuddered. Another man! Would he be like all the rest? — all the rest save one!

She walked a few steps in the direction she had been told to go, and then turned resolutely around, and came back. The watching grandmother felt her heart sink. What was this headstrong girl going to do next? Rebel again?

"What's the matter, Bessie?" she asked, meeting her anxiously at the door. "It's bad luck to turn back when you've started."

"I can't go this way," said the girl excitedly. "It's all a cheat. I'm not like this. It isn't mine, and I'm not going in it. I must have my own clothes and be myself when I go to see her. If she doesn't like me and want me, then I can take Robin and go back." And like another David burdened with Saul's armor she came back to get her little sling and stones.

She tore off the veil, and the sticky gloves from her cold hands, and all the finery of silk waist and belt, and donned her old plain blue coat and skirt in which she had arrived in Philadelphia. They had been frugally brushed and sponged, and made neat for a working dress. Elizabeth felt that they belonged to her. Under the jacket, which fortunately was long enough to hide her waist, she buckled her belt with the two pistols. Then she took the battered old felt hat from the closet, and tried to fasten it on; but the pompadour interfered. Relentlessly she pulled down the work of art that Lizzie had created, and brushed and combed her long, thick hair into subjection again, and put it in its long braid down her back. Her grandmother should see her just as she was. She should know what kind of a girl belonged to her. Then, if she chose to be a real grandmother, well and good.

Mrs. Brady was much disturbed in mind when Elizabeth came downstairs. She exclaimed in horror, and tried to force the girl to go back, telling her it was a shame and a disgrace to go in such garments into the sacred precincts of Rittenhouse Square; but the girl was not to be turned back. She would not even wait till her aunt and Lizzie came home. She would go now, at once.

Mrs. Brady sat down in her rocking-chair in despair for full five minutes after she had watched the reprehensible girl go down the street. She had not been so completely beaten since the day when her own Bessie left the house and went away to a wild West to die in her own time and way. The grandmother shed a few tears. The girl was like her own Bessie, and she could not help loving her, though there was a streak of something else about her that made her seem above them all; and that was hard to bear. It must be the Bailey streak, of course. Mrs. Brady did not admire the Baileys, but she was obliged to reverence them.

If she had watched or followed Elizabeth, she would have been still more horrified. The girl went straight to the corner grocery, and demanded her own horse, handing back to the man the dollar he had paid her last Saturday night, and saying she had need of the horse at once. After some parley, in which she showed her ability to stand her own ground, the boy unhitched the horse from the wagon, and got her own old saddle from the stable. Then Elizabeth mounted her horse and rode away to Rittenhouse Square.

Chapter 13
Another Grandmother

Elizabeth's idea in taking the horse along with her was to have all her armor on, as a warrior goes out to meet the foe. If this grandmother proved impossible, why, then so long as she had life and breath and a horse she could flee. The world was wide, and the West was still open to her. She could flee back to the wilderness that gave her breath.

The old horse stopped gravely and disappointedly before the tall, aristocratic house in Rittenhouse Square. He had hoped that city life was now to end, and that he and his dear mistress were to travel back to their beloved prairies. No amount of oats could ever make up to him for his freedom, and the quiet, and the hills. He had a feeling that he should like to go back home and die. He had seen enough of the world.

She fastened the halter to a ring in the sidewalk, which surprised him. The grocer's boy never fastened him. He looked up questioningly at the house, but saw no reason why his mistress should go in there. It was not familiar ground. Coffee and Sons never came up this way.

Elizabeth, as she crossed the sidewalk and mounted the steps before the formidable carved doors, felt that here was the last hope of finding an earthly habitation. If this failed her, then there was the desert, and starvation, and a long, long sleep. But while the echo of the bell still sounded through the high-ceiled hall there came to her the words: "Let not your heart be troubled. . . . In my Father's house are many mansions; if it were not so, I would have told you. I go to prepare a place for you. . . . I will come again and receive you." How sweet that was! Then, even if she died on the desert, there was a home prepared for her. So much she had learned in Christian Endeavor meeting.

The stately butler let her in. He eyed her questioningly at first, and said madam was not up yet; but Elizabeth told him she would wait.

"Is she sick?" asked Elizabeth with a strange constriction about her heart.

"O no, she is not up yet, miss," said the kind old butler, "she never gets up before this. You're from Mrs. Sands, I suppose." Poor soul, for once his butler eyes had been mistaken. He thought she was the little errand-girl from Madam Bailey's modiste.

"No, I'm just Elizabeth," said the girl, smiling. She felt that this man, whoever he was, was not against her. He was old, and he had a kind look.

He still thought she meant she was not the modiste, just her errand-girl. Her quaint dress and the long braid down her back made her look like a child.

"I'll tell her you've come. Be seated," said the butler, and gave her a chair in the dim hall just opposite the parlor door, where she had a glimpse of elegance such as she had never dreamed existed. She tried to think how it must be to live in such a room and walk on velvet. The carpet was deep and rich. She did not know it was a rug, nor that it was woven in some poor peasant's home and then was brought here years afterward at a fabulous price. She only knew it was beautiful in its silvery sheen, with gleaming colors through it like jewels in the dew.

On through another open doorway she caught a glimpse of a painting on the wall. It was a man as large as life, sitting in a chair; and the face and attitude were her father's — her father at his best. She was fairly startled. Who was it? Could it be her father? And how had they made this picture of him? He must be changed in those twenty years he had been gone from home.

Then the butler came back, and before he could speak she pointed toward the picture. "Who is it?" she asked.

"That, miss? That's Mr. John, Madam's husband that's dead a good many years now. But I remember him well."

"Could I look at it? He is so much like my father." She walked rapidly over the ancient rug, unheeding its beauties, while the wondering butler followed a trifle anxiously. This was unprecedented. Mrs. Sands's errand-girls usually knew their place.

"Madam said you was to come right up to her room," said the butler pointedly. But Elizabeth stood rooted to the ground, studying the picture. The butler had to repeat his message. She smiled and turned to follow him, and as she did so saw on a side wall the portraits of two boys.

"Who are they?" she pointed swiftly. They were much like her own two brothers.

"Them are Mr. John and Mr. James, Madam's two sons. They's both of them dead now," said the butler. "At least, Mr. James is, I'm sure. He died two years ago. But you better come right up. Madam will be wondering."

She followed the old man up the velvet-shod stairs that gave back no sound from footfall, and pondered as she went. Then that was her father, that boy with the beautiful face and the heavy wavy hair tossed back from his forehead, and the haughty, imperious, don't-care look. And here was where he had lived. Here amid all this luxury.

Like a flash came the quick contrast of the home in which he had died, and a great wave of reverence for her father rolled over her. From such a home and such surroundings it would not have been strange if he had grown weary of the rough life out West, and deserted his wife, who was beneath him in station. True, he had not been of much use to her, and much of the time had been but a burden and anxiety; but he had stayed and loved her — when he was sober. She forgave him his many trying ways, his faultfindings with her mother's many little blunders — no wonder, when he came from this place.

The butler tapped on a door at the head of the stairs, and a maid swung it open.

"Why, you're not the girl Mrs. Sands sent the other day," said a querulous voice from a mass of lace-ruffled pillows on the great bed.

"I am Elizabeth," said the girl, as if that were full explanation.

"Elizabeth? Elizabeth who? I don't see why she sent another girl. Are you sure you will understand the directions? They're very particular, for I want my frock ready for to-night without fail." The woman sat up, leaning on one elbow. Her lace nightgown and pale-blue silk dressing-sack fell away from a round white arm that did not look as if it belonged to a very old lady. Her gray hair was becomingly arranged, and she was extremely pretty, with small features. Elizabeth looked and marvelled. Like a flash came the vision of the other grandmother at the wash-tub. The contrast was startling.

"I am Elizabeth Bailey," said the girl quietly, as if she would break a piece of hard news gently. "My father was your son John."

"The idea!" said the new grandmother, and promptly fell back upon her pillows with her hand upon her heart. "John, John, my little John. No one has mentioned his name to me for years and years. He never writes to me." She put up a lace-trimmed handkerchief, and sobbed.

"Father died five years ago," said Elizabeth.

"You wicked girl!" said the maid. "Can't you see that Madam can't bear such talk? Go right out of the room!" The maid rushed up with smelling-salts and a glass of water, and Elizabeth in distress came and stood by the bed.

"I'm sorry I made you feel bad, Grandmother," she said when she saw that the fragile, childish creature on the bed was recovering somewhat.

"What right have you to call me that? Grandmother, indeed! I'm not so old as that. Besides, how do I know you belong to me? If John is dead, your mother better look after you. I'm sure I'm not responsible for you. It's her business. She wheedled John away from his home, and carried him off to that awful West, and never let him write to me. She has done it all, and now she may bear the consequences. I suppose she has sent you here to beg, but she has made a mistake. I shall not have a thing to do with her or her children.''

"Grandmother!'' Elizabeth's eyes flashed as they had done to the other grandmother a few hours before. "You must not talk so. I won't hear it. I wouldn't let Grandmother Brady talk about my father, and you can't talk so about mother. She was my mother, and I loved her, and so did father love her; and she worked hard to keep him and take care of him when he drank years and years, and didn't have any money to help her. Mother was only eighteen when she married father, and you ought not to blame her. She didn't have a nice home like this. But she was good and dear, and now she is dead. Father and mother are both dead, and all the other children. A man killed my brother, and then as soon as he was buried he came and wanted me to go with him. He was an awful man, and I was afraid, and took my brother's horse and ran away. I rode all this long way because I was afraid of that man, and I wanted to get to some of my own folks, who would love me, and let me work for them, and let me go to school and learn something. But I wish now I had stayed out there and died. I could have lain down in the sage-brush, and a wild beast would have killed me perhaps, and that would be a great deal better than this; for Grandmother Brady does not understand, and you do not want me; but in my Father's house in heaven there are many mansions, and He went to prepare a place for me; so I guess I will go back to the desert, and perhaps He will send for me. Good-by, Grandmother.''

Then before the astonished woman in the bed could recover her senses from this remarkable speech Elizabeth turned and walked majestically from the room. She was slight and not very tall, but in the strength of her pride and purity she looked almost majestic to the awe-struck maid and the bewildered woman.

Down the stairs walked the girl, feeling that all the wide world was against her. She would never again try to get a friend. She had not met a friend except in the desert. One man had been good to her, and she had let him go away; but he belonged to another woman, and she might not let him stay. There was just one thing to be thankful for. She had knowledge of her Father in heaven, and she knew what Christian Endeavor meant. She could take that with her out into the desert, and no one could take it from her. One wish she had, but maybe that was too much to hope for. If she could have had a Bible of her own! She had no money left. Nothing but her mother's wedding-ring, the papers, and the envelope that had contained the money the man had given her when he left. She could not part with them, unless perhaps someone would take the ring and keep it until she could buy it back. But she would wait and hope.

She walked by the old butler with her hand on her pistol. She did not intend to let anyone detain her now. He bowed pleasantly, and opened the door for her, however; and she marched down the steps to her horse. But just as she was about to mount and ride away into the unknown where no grandmother, be she Brady or Bailey, would ever be able to search her out, no matter how hard she tried, the door suddenly opened again, and there was a great commotion. The maid and the old butler both flew out, and laid hands upon her. She dropped the bridle, and seized her pistol, covering them both with its black, forbidding nozzle.

They stopped, trembling, but the butler bravely stood his ground. He did not know why he was to detain this extraordinary young person, but he felt sure something was wrong. Probably she was a thief, and had taken some of Madam's jewels. He could call the police. He opened his mouth to do so when the maid explained.

"Madam wants you to come back. She didn't understand. She wants to see you and ask about her son. You must come, or you will kill her. She has heart-trouble, and you must not excite her."

Elizabeth put the pistol back into its holster, and, picking up the bridle again, fastened it in the ring, saying simply, "I will come back."

"What do you want?" she asked abruptly when she returned to the bedroom.

"Don't you know that's a disrespectful way to speak?" asked the woman querulously. "What did you have to get into a temper for, and go off like that without telling me anything about my son? Sit down, and tell me all about it."

"I'm sorry, Grandmother," said Elizabeth, sitting down. "I thought you didn't want me and I better go."

"Well, the next time wait until I send you. What kind of a thing have you got on, anyway? That's a queer sort of a hat for a girl to wear. Take it off. You look like a rough boy with that on. You make me think of John when he had been out disobeying me."

Elizabeth took off the offending headgear, and revealed her smoothly parted, thick brown hair in its long braid down her back.

"Why, you're rather a pretty girl if you were fixed up," said the old lady, sitting up with interest now. "I can't remember your mother, but I don't think she had fine features like that."

"They said I looked like Father," said Elizabeth.

"Did they? Well, I believe it's true," with satisfaction. "I couldn't bear if you looked like those low-down —"

"Grandmother!" Elizabeth stood up, and flashed her Bailey eyes.

"You needn't 'grandmother' me all the time," said the lady petulantly. "But you look quite handsome when you say it. Take off that ill-fitted coat. It isn't thick enough for winter, anyway. What in the world have you got round your waist? A belt? Why, that's a man's belt! And what have you got on it? Pistols? Horrors! Marie, take them away quick! I shall faint! I never could bear to be in a room with one. My husband used to have one on his closet shelf, and I never went near it, and always locked the room when he was out. You must put them out in the hall. I cannot breathe where pistols are. Now sit down and tell me all about it, how old you are, and how you got here."

Elizabeth surrendered her pistols with hesitation. She felt that she must obey her grandmother, but was not altogether certain whether it was safe for her to be weaponless until she was sure this was friendly ground.

At the demand she began back as far as she could remember, and told the story of her life, pathetically, simply, without a single claim to pity, yet so earnestly and vividly that the grandmother, lying with her eyes closed, forgot herself completely, and let the tears trickle unbidden and unheeded down her well-preserved cheeks.

When Elizabeth came to the graves in the moonlight, she gasped, and sobbed: "O Johnny, Johnny, my little Johnny! Why did you always be such a bad, bad boy?" and when the ride in the desert was described, and the man from whom she fled, the grandmother held her breath, and said, "O, how fearful!" Her interest in the girl was growing, and kept at white heat during the whole of the story.

There was one part of her experience, however, that Elizabeth passed over lightly, and that was the meeting with George Trescott Benedict. Instinctively she felt that this experience would not find a sympathetic listener. She passed it over by merely saying that she had met a kind gentleman from the East who was lost, and that they had ridden together for a few miles until they reached a town; and he had telegraphed to his friends, and gone on his way. She said nothing about the money he had lent to her, for she shrank from speaking about him more than was necessary. She felt that her grandmother might feel as the old woman of the ranch had felt about their travelling together. She left it to be inferred that she might have had a little money with her from home. At least, the older woman asked no questions about how she secured provisions for the way.

When Elizabeth came to her Chicago experience, her grandmother clasped her hands as if a serpent had been mentioned, and said: "How degrading! You certainly would have been justified in shooting the whole company. I wonder such places are allowed to exist!" But Marie sat with large eyes of wonder, and retailed the story over again in the kitchen afterwards for the benefit of the cook and the butler, so that Elizabeth became henceforth a heroine among them.

Elizabeth passed on to her Philadelphia experience, and found that here her grandmother was roused to blazing indignation, but the thing that roused her was the fact that a Bailey should serve behind a counter in a ten-cent store. She lifted her hands, and uttered a moan of real pain, and went on at such a rate that the smelling-salts had to be brought into requisition again.

When Elizabeth told of her encounter with the manager in the cellar, the grandmother said: "How disgusting! The impertinent creature! He ought to be sued. I will consult the lawyer about the matter. What did you say his name was? Marie, write that down. And so, dear, you did quite right to come to me. I've been looking at you while you talked, and I believe you'll be a pretty girl if you are fixed up. Marie, go to the telephone, and call up Blandeaux, and tell him to send up a hair-dresser at once. I want to see how Miss Elizabeth with look with her hair done low in one of those new coils. I believe it will be becoming. I shall have tried it long ago myself; only it seems a trifle too youthful for hair that is beginning to turn gray."

Elizabeth watched her grandmother in wonder. Here truly was a new phase of woman. She did not care about great facts, but only about little things. Her life was made up of the great pursuit of fashion, just like Lizzie's. Were people in cities all alike? No, for he, the one man she had met in the wilderness, had not seemed to care. Maybe, though, when he got back to the city he did care. She sighed and turned toward the new grandmother.

"Now I have told you everything, Grandmother. Shall I go away? I wanted to go to school; but I see that it costs a great deal of money, and I don't want to be a burden on any one. I came here, not to ask you to take me in, because I did not want to trouble you; but I thought before I went away I ought to see you once because — because you are my grandmother."

"I've never been a grandmother," said the little woman of the world reflectively, "but I don't know but it would be rather nice. I'd like to make you into a pretty girl, and take you out into society. That would be something new to live for. I'm not very pretty myself any more, but I can see that you will be. Do you wear blue or pink? I used to wear pink myself, but I believe you could wear either when you get your complexion in shape. You've tanned it horribly, but it may come out all right. I think you'll take. You say you want to go to school. Why, certainly, I suppose that will be necessary; living out in that barbarous, uncivilized region, of course you don't know much. You seem to speak correctly, but John always was particular about his speech. He had a tutor when he was little who tripped him up every mistake he made. That was the only thing that tutor was good for; he was a linguist. We found out afterwards he was terribly wild, and drank. He did John more harm than good. Marie, I shall want Elizabeth to have the rooms next mine. Ring for Martha to see that everything is in order. Elizabeth, did you ever have your hands manicured? You have a pretty-shaped hand. I'll have the woman attend to it when she comes to shampoo your hair and put it up. Did you bring any clothes along? Of course not. You couldn't on horseback. I suppose you had your trunk sent by express. No trunk? No express? No railroad? How barbarous! How John must have suffered, poor fellow! He, so used to every luxury! Well, I don't see that it was my fault. I gave him everything he wanted except his wife, and he took her without my leave. Poor fellow, poor fellow!''

Mrs. Bailey in due time sent Elizabeth off to the suite of rooms that she said were to be hers exclusively, and arose to bedeck herself for another day. Elizabeth was a new toy, and she anticipated playing with her. It put new zest into a life that had grown monotonous.

Elizabeth, meanwhile, was surveying her quarters, and wondering what Lizzie would think if she could see her. According to orders, the coachman had taken Robin to the stable, and he was already rolling in all the luxuries of a horse of the aristocracy, and congratulating himself on the good taste of his mistress to select such a stopping-place. For his part he was now satisfied not to move further. This was better than the wilderness any day. Oats like these, and hay such as this, were not to be found on the plains.

Toward evening the grave butler, with many a deprecatory glance at the neighborhood, arrived at the door of Mrs. Brady, and delivered himself of the following message to that astonished lady, backed by her daughter and her granddaughter, with their ears stretched to the utmost to hear every syllable:

"Mrs. Merrill Wilton Bailey sends word that her granddaughter, Miss Elizabeth, has reached her home safely, and will remain with her. Miss Elizabeth will come sometime to see Mrs. Brady, and thank her for her kindness during her stay with her."

The butler bowed, and turned away with relief. His dignity and social standing had not been so taxed by the family demands in years. He was glad he might shake off the dust of Flora Street forever. He felt for the coachman. He would probably have to drive the young lady down here sometime, according to that message.

Mrs. Brady, her daughter, and Lizzie stuck their heads out into the lamplighted street, and watched the dignified butler out of sight. Then they went in and sat down in three separate stages of relief and astonishment.

"Fer the land sakes!" ejaculated the grandmother. "Well, now, if that don't beat all!" then after a minute: "The impertinent fellow! And the impidence of the woman! Thank me fer my kindness to me own grandchild! I'd thank her to mind her business, but then that's just like her."

"Her nest is certainly well feathered," said Aunt Nan enviously. "I only wish Lizzie had such a chance."

Said Lizzie: "It's awful queer, her looking like that, too, in that crazy rig! Well, I'm glad she's gone, fer she was so awful queer it was jest fierce. She talked religion a lot to the girls, and then they laughed at her behind her back; and they kep' a telling me I'd be a missionary 'fore long if she stayed with us. I went to Mr. Wray, the manager, and told him my cousin was awfully shy, and she sent word she wanted to be excused fer running away like that. He kind of colored up, and said 'twas all right, and she might come back and have her old place if she wanted, and he'd say no more about it. I told him I'd tell her. But I guess her acting up won't do me a bit of harm. The girls say he'll make up to *me* now. Wish he would. I'd have a fine time. It's me turn to have me wages raised, anyway. He said if Bess and I would come to-morrow ready to stay in the evening, he'd take us to a show that beat everything he ever saw in Philadelphia. I mean to make him take me, anyway. I'm just glad she's out of the way. She wasn't like the rest of us."

Said Mrs. Brady: "It's the Bailey in her. But she said she'd come back and see me, didn't she?" and the grandmother in her meditated over that fact for several minutes.

Chapter 14
In a New World

Meantime the panorama of Elizabeth's life passed on into more peaceful scenes. By means of the telephone and the maid a lot of new and beautiful garments were provided for her, which fitted perfectly, and which bewildered her not a little until they were explained by Marie. Elizabeth had her meals up-stairs until these things had arrived and she had put them on. The texture of the garments was fine and soft, and they were rich with embroidery and lace. The flannels were as soft as the down in a milkweed pod, and everything was of the best. Elizabeth found herself wishing she might share them with Lizzie, — Lizzie who adored rich and beautiful things, and who had shared her meagre outfit with her. She mentioned this wistfully to her grandmother, and in a fit of childish generosity that lady said: "Certainly, get her what you wish. I'll take you downtown some day, and you can pick out some nice things for them all. I hate to be under obligations."

A dozen ready-made dresses had been sent out before the first afternoon was over, and Elizabeth spent the rest of the day in trying on and walking back and forth in front of her grandmother. At last two or three were selected which it was thought would "do" until the dressmaker could be called in to help, and Elizabeth was clothed and allowed to come down into the life of the household.

It was not a large household. It consisted of the grandmother, her dog, and the servants. Elizabeth fitted into it better than she had feared. It seemed pleasanter to her than the house on Flora Street. There was more room, and more air, and more quiet. With her mountain breeding she could not get her breath in a crowd.

She was presently taken in a luxurious carriage, drawn by two beautiful horses, to a large department store, where she sat by the hour and watched her grandmother choose things for her. Another girl might have gone half wild over the delightful experience of being able to have anything in the shops. No so Elizabeth. She watched it all apathetically, as if the goods displayed about had been the leaves upon the trees set forth for her admiration. She could wear but one dress at once, and one hat. Why were so many necessary? Her main hope lay in the words her grandmother had spoken about sending her to school.

The third day of her stay in Rittenhouse Square, Elizabeth had reminded her of it, and the grandmother had said half impatiently: "Yes, yes, child; you shall go of course to a finishing school. That will be necessary. But first I must get you fixed up. You have scarcely anything to put on." So Elizabeth subsided.

At last there dawned a beautiful Sabbath when, the wardrobe seemingly complete, Elizabeth was told to array herself for church, as they were going that morning. With great delight and thanksgiving she put on what she was told; and, when she looked into the great French plate mirror after Marie had put on the finishing touches, she was astonished at herself. It was all true, after all. She was a pretty girl.

She looked down at the beautiful gown of finest broadcloth, with the exquisite finish that only the best tailors can put on a garment, and wondered at herself. The very folds of dark-green cloth seemed to bring a grace into her movements. The green velvet hat with its long curling plumes of green and cream-color seemed to be resting lovingly above the beautiful hair that was arranged so naturally and becomingly.

Elizabeth wore her lovely ermine collar and muff without ever knowing they were costly. They all seemed so fitting and quiet and simple, so much less obtrusive than Lizzie's pink silk waist and cheap pink plumes. Elizabeth liked it, and walked to church beside her grandmother with a happy feeling in her heart.

The church was just across the Square. Its tall brown stone spire and arched doorways attracted Elizabeth when she first came to the place. Now she entered with a kind of delight.

It was the first time she had ever been to a Sabbath morning regular service in church. The Christian Endeavor had been as much as Lizzie had been able to stand. She said she had to work too hard during the week to waste so much time on Sunday in church. "The Sabbath was made for man" and "for rest," she had quoted glibly. For the first time in her life since she left Montana Elizabeth felt as if she had a real home and was like other people. She looked around shyly to see whether perchance her friend of the desert might be sitting near, but no familiar face met her gaze. Then she settled back, and gave herself up to delight in the service.

The organ was playing softly, low, tender music. She learned afterward that the music was Handel's "Largo." She did not know that the organ was one of the finest in the city, nor that the organist was one of the most skillful to be had; she knew only that the music seemed to take her soul and lift it up above the earth so that heaven was all around her, and the very clouds seemed singing to her. Then came the processional, with the wonderful voices of the choir-boys sounding far off, and then nearer. It would be impossible for anyone who had been accustomed all his life to these things to know how it affected Elizabeth.

It seemed as though the Lord Himself was leading the girl in a very special way. At scarcely any other church in a fashionable quarter of the great city would Elizabeth have heard preaching so exactly suited to her needs. The minister was one of those rare men who lived with God, and talked with Him daily. He had one peculiarity which marked him from all other preachers, Elizabeth heard afterward. He would turn and talk with God in a gentle, sweet, conversational tone right in the midst of his sermon. It made the Lord seem very real and very near.

If he had not been the great and brilliant preacher of an old established church, and revered by all denominations as well as his own, the minister would have been called eccentric and have been asked to resign, because his religion was so very personal that it became embarrassing to some. However, his rare gifts, and his remarkable consecration and independence in doing what he thought right, had produced a most unusual church for a fashionable neighborhood.

Most of his church-members were in sympathy with him, and a wonderful work was going forward right in the heart of Sodom, unhampered by fashion or form or class distinctions. It is true there were some who, like Madam Bailey sat calmly in their seats, and let the minister attend to the preaching end of the service without ever bothering their thoughts as to what he was saying. It was all one to them whether he prayed three times or once, so the service got done at the usual hour. But the majority were being led to see that there is such a thing as a close and intimate walk with God upon this earth.

Into this church came Elizabeth, the sweet heathen, eager to learn all that could be learned about the things of the soul. She sat beside her grandmother, and drank in the sermon, and bowed her lovely, reverent head when she became aware that God was in the room and was being spoken to by His servant. After the last echo of the recessional had died away, and the bowed hush of the congregation had grown into a quiet, well-bred commotion of the putting on of wraps and the low Sabbath greetings, Elizabeth turned to her grandmother.

"Grandmother, may I please go and ask that man some questions? He said just what I have been longing and longing to know, and I must ask him more. Nobody else ever told me these things. Who is he? How does he know it is all true?"

The elder woman watched the eager, flushed face of the girl; and her heart throbbed with pride that this beautiful young thing belonged to her. She smiled indulgently.

"The rector, you mean? Why, I'll invite him to dinner if you wish to talk with him. It's perfectly proper that a young girl should understand about religion. It has a most refining influence, and the Doctor is a charming man. I'll invite his wife and daughter too. They move in the best circles, and I have been meaning to ask them for a long time. You might like to be confirmed. Some do. It's a very pretty service. I was confirmed myself when I was about your age. My mother thought it a good thing for a girl before she went into society. Now, just as you are a schoolgirl, is the proper time. I'll send for him this week. He'll be pleased to know you are interested in these things. He has some kind of a young people's club that meets on Sunday. 'Christian Something' he calls it; I don't know just what, but he talks a great deal about it, and wants every young person to join. You might pay the dues, whatever they are, anyway. I suppose it's for charity. It wouldn't be necessary for you to attend the meetings, but it would please the Doctor."

"Is it Christian Endeavor?" asked Elizabeth, with her eyes sparkling.

"Something like that, I believe. Good morning, Mrs. Schuyler. Lovely day, isn't it? for December. No, I haven't been very well. No, I haven't been out for several weeks. Charming service, wasn't it? The Doctor grows more and more brilliant, I think. Mrs. Schuyler, this is my granddaughter, Elizabeth. She has just come from the West to live with me and complete her education. I want her to know your daughter."

Elizabeth passed through the introduction as a necessary interruption to her train of thought. As soon as they were out upon the street again she began.

"Grandmother, was God in that church?"

"Dear me, child! What strange questions you do ask! Why, yes, I suppose He was, in a way. God is everywhere, they say. Elizabeth, you had better wait until you can talk these things over with a person whose business it is. I never understood much about such questions. You look very nice in that shade of green, and your hat is most becoming."

So was the question closed for the time, but not put out of the girl's thoughts.

The Christmas time had come and passed without much notice on the part of Elizabeth, to whom it was an unfamiliar festival. Mrs. Bailey had suggested that she select some gifts for her "relatives on her mother's side," as she always spoke of the Bradys; and Elizabeth had done so with alacrity, showing good sense and good taste in her choice of gifts, as well as deference to the wishes of the one to whom they were to be given. Lizzie, it is true, was a trifle disappointed that her present was not a gold watch or a diamond ring; but on the whole she was pleased.

A new world opened before the feet of Elizabeth. School was filled with wonder and delight. She absorbed knowledge like a sponge in the water, and rushed eagerly from one study to another, showing marvellous aptitude, and bringing to every task the enthusiasm of a pleasure-seeker.

Her growing intimacy with Jesus Christ through the influence of the pastor who knew Him so well caused her joy in life to blossom into loveliness.

The Bible she studied with the zest of a novel-reader, for it was a novel to her; and daily, as she took her rides in the park on Robin, now groomed into self-respecting sleekness, and wearing a saddle of the latest approved style, she marvelled over God's wonderful goodness to her, just a maid of the wilderness.

So passed three beautiful years in peace and quietness. Every month Elizabeth went to see her Grandmother Brady, and to take some charming little gifts; and every summer she and her Grandmother Bailey spent at some of the fashionable watering-places or in the Catskills, the girl always dressed in most exquisite taste, and as sweetly indifferent in her clothes as a bird of the air or a flower of the field.

The first pocket-money she had been given she saved up, and before long had enough to send the forty dollars to the address the man in the wilderness had given her. But with it she sent no word. It was like her to think she had no right.

She went out more and more with her grandmother among the fashionable old families in Philadelphia society, though as yet she was not supposed to be "out," being still in school; but in all her goings she neither saw nor heard of George Trescott Benedict.

Often she looked about upon the beautiful women that came to her grandmother's house, who smiled and talked to her, and wondered which of them might be the lady to whom his heart was bound. She fancied she must be most sweet and lovely in every way, else such as he could not care for her; so she would pick out this one and that one; and then, as some disagreeableness or glaring fault would appear, she would drop that one for another. There were only a few, after all, that she felt were good enough for the man who had become her ideal.

But sometimes in her dreams he would come and talk with her, and smile as he used to do when they rode together; and he would lay his hand on the mane of her horse — there were always the horses in her dreams. She liked to think of it when she rode in the park, and to think how pleasant it would be if he could be riding there beside her, and they might talk of a great many things that had happened since he left her alone. She felt she would like to tell him of how she had found a friend in Jesus Christ. He would be glad to know about it, she was sure. He seemed to be one who was interested in such things, not like other people who were all engaged in the world.

Sometimes she felt afraid something had happened to him. He might have been thrown from that terrible train and killed, perhaps; and no one know anything about it. But as her experience grew wider, and she travelled on the trains herself, of course this fear grew less. She came to understand that the world was wide, and many things might have taken him away from his home.

Perhaps the money she had sent reached him safely, but she had put in no address. It had not seemed right that she should. It would seem to draw his attention to her, and she felt "the lady" would not like that. Perhaps they were married by this time, and had gone far away to some charmed land to live. Perhaps — a great many things. Only this fact remained; he never came any more into the horizon of her life; and therefore she must try to forget him, and be glad that God had given her a friend in him for her time of need. Some day in the eternal home perhaps she would meet him and thank him for his kindness to her, and then they might tell each other all about the journey through the great wilderness of earth after they had parted. The links in Elizabeth's theology had been well supplied by this time, and her belief in the hereafter was strong and simple like a child's.

She had one great longing, however, that he, her friend, who had in a way been the first to help her toward higher things, and to save her from the wilderness, might know Jesus Christ as he had not known Him when they were together. And so in her daily prayer she often talked to her heavenly Father about him, until she came to have an abiding faith that some day, somehow, he would learn the truth about his Christ.

During the third season of Elizabeth's life in Philadelphia her grandmother decided that it was high time to bring out this bud of promise, who was by this time developing into a more beautiful girl than even her fondest hopes had pictured.

So Elizabeth "came out," and Grandmother Brady read her doings and sayings in the society columns with her morning coffee and an air of deep satisfaction. Aunt Nan listened with her nose in the air. She could never understand why Elizabeth should have privileges beyond her Lizzie. It was the Bailey in her, of course, and mother ought not to think well of it. But Grandmother Brady felt that, while Elizabeth's success was doubtless due in large part to the Bailey in her, still, she was a Brady, and the Brady had not hindered her. It was a step upward for the Bradys.

Lizzie listened, and with pride retailed at the ten-cent store the doings of "my cousin, Elizabeth Bailey," and the other girls listened with awe.

And so it came on to be the springtime of the third year that Elizabeth had spent in Philadelphia.

Chapter 15
An Eventful Picnic

It was summer and it was June. There was to be a picnic, and Elizabeth was going.

Grandmother Brady had managed it. It seemed to her that, if Elizabeth could go, her cup of pride would be full to overflowing; so after much argument, pro and con, with her daughter and Lizzie, she set herself down to pen the invitation. Aunt Nan was decidedly against it. She did not wish to have Lizzie outshone. She had been working nights for two weeks on an elaborate organdie, with pink roses all over it, for Lizzie to wear. It had yards and yards of cheap lace and insertion, and a whole bolt of pink ribbons of various widths. The hat was a marvel of impossible roses, just calculated for the worst kind of a wreck if a thunder-shower should come up at a Sunday-school picnic. Lizzie's mother was even thinking of getting her a pink chiffon parasol to carry; but the family treasury was well-nigh depleted, and it was doubtful whether that would be possible. After all that, it did not seem pleasant to have Lizzie put in the shade by a fine-lady cousin in silks and jewels.

But Grandmother Brady had waited long for her triumph. She desired above all things to walk among her friends and introduce her granddaughter, Elizabeth Bailey, and inadvertently remark: "You must have seen me granddaughter's name in the paper often, Mrs. Babcock. She was giving a party in Rittenhouse Square the other day."

Elizabeth would likely be married soon, and perhaps go off somewhere away from Philadelphia — New York or Europe, there was no telling what great fortune might come to her. Now the time was ripe for triumph if ever, and when things are ripe they must be picked. Mrs. Brady proceeded to pick.

She gathered together at great pains pen, paper, and ink. A pencil would be inadequate when the note was going to Rittenhouse Square. She sat down when Nan and Lizzie had left for their day's work, and constructed her sentences with great care.

"Dear Bessie —" Elizabeth had never asked her not to call her that, although she fairly detested the name. But still it had been her mother's name, and was likely dear to her grandmother. It seemed disloyalty to her

mother to suggest that she be called "Elizabeth." So Grandmother Brady serenely continued to call her "Bessie" to the end of her days. Elizabeth decided that to care much about such little things, in a world where there were so many great things, would be as bad as to give one's mind entirely over to the pursuit of fashion.

The letter proceeded laboriously:

"Our Sunday school is going to have a picnic out to Willow Grove. It's on Tuesday. We're going in the trolley. I'd be pleased if you would go 'long with us. We will spend the day, and take our dinner and supper along, and wouldn't get home till late; so you could stay overnight here with us, and not go back home till after breakfast. You needn't bring no lunch; fer we've got a lot of things planned, and it ain't worth while. But if you wanted to bring some candy, you might. I ain't got time to make any, and what you buy at our grocery might not be fine enough for you. I want you to go real bad. I've never took my two granddaughters off to anything yet, and your Grandmother Bailey has you to things all the time. I hope you can manage to come. I am going to pay all the expenses. Your old Christian Deaver you used to 'tend is going to be there; so you'll have a good time. Lizzie has a new pink organdie, with roses on her hat; and we're thinking of getting her a pink umbreller if it don't cost too much. The kind with chiffon flounces on it. You'll have a good time, fer there's lots of side-shows out to Willow Grove, and we're going to see everything there is to see. There's going to be some music too. A man with a name that sounds like swearing is going to make it. I don't remember it just now, but you can see it advertised round on the trolley-cars. He comes to Willow Grove every year. Now please let me hear if you will go at once, as I want to know how much cake to make.

"Your loving grandmother,
"ELIZABETH BRADY."

Elizabeth laughed and cried over this note. It pleased her to have her grandmother show kindness to her. She felt that whatever she did for Grandmother Brady was in a sense showing her love to her own mother; so she brushed aside several engagements, much to the annoyance of her Grandmother Bailey, who could not understand why she wanted to go down to Flora Street for two days and a night just in the beginning of warm weather. True, there was not much going on just now between seasons, and Elizabeth could do as she pleased; but she might get a fever in such a crowded neighborhood. It wasn't in the least wise. However, if she must, she must. Grandmother Bailey was on the whole lenient. Elizabeth was too much of a success, and too willing to please her in all things, for her to care to cross her wishes.

So Elizabeth wrote on her fine note-paper bearing the Bailey crest in silver:

"Dear Grandmother: I shall be delighted to go to the picnic with you, and I'll bring a nice box of candy, Huyler's best. I'm sure you'll think it's the best you ever tasted. Don't get Lizzie a parasol; I'm going to bring her one to surprise her. I'll be at the house by eight o'clock.

"Your loving granddaughter,

"ELIZABETH."

Mrs. Brady read this note with satisfaction and handed it over to her daughter to read with a gleam of triumph in her eyes at the suppertable. She knew the gift of the pink parasol would go far toward reconciling Aunt Nan to the addition to their party. Elizabeth never did things by halves, and the parasol would be all that could possibly be desired without straining the family pocketbook any further.

So Elizabeth went to the picnic in a cool white dimity, plainly made, with tiny frills of itself, edged with narrow lace that did not shout to the unknowing multitude, "I am real!" but was content with being so; and with a white Panama hat adorned with only a white silken scarf, but whose texture was possible only at a fabulous price. The shape reminded Elizabeth of the old felt hat belonging to her brother, which she had worn on her long trip across the continent. She had put it on in the hat-store one day; and her grandmother, when she found how exquisite a piece of weaving the hat was, at once purchased it for her. It was stylish to wear those soft hats in all sorts of odd shapes. Madam Bailey thought it would be just the thing for the seashore.

Her hair was worn in a low coil on her neck, making the general appearance and contour of her head much as it had been three years before. She wore no jewelry, save the unobtrusive gold buckle at her belt and the plain gold hatpin which fastened her hat. There was nothing about her which marked her as one of the "four hundred." She did not even wear the gloves, but carried them in her hand, and threw them carelessly upon the table when she arrived in Flora Street. Long, soft white ones, they lay there in their costly elegance beside Lizzie's postcard album that the livery-stable man gave her on her birthday, all the long day while Elizabeth was at Willow Grove, and Lizzie sweltered around under her pink parasol in long white silk gloves.

Grandmother Brady surveyed Elizabeth with decided disapproval. It seemed too bad on this her day of triumph, and after she had given a hint, as it were, about Lizzie's fine clothes, that the girl should be so blind or stubborn or both as to come around in that plain rig. Just a common white dress, and an old hat that might have been worn about a livery-stable. It was mortifying in the extreme. She expected a light silk, and kid gloves, and a beflowered hat. Why, Lizzie looked a great deal finer. Did Mrs. Bailey rig her out this way for spite? she wondered.

But, as it was too late to send Elizabeth back for more fitting garments, the old lady resigned herself to her disappointment. The pink parasol was lovely, and Lizzie was wild over it. Even Aunt Nan seemed mollified. It gave her great satisfaction to look the two girls over. Her own outshone the one from Rittenhouse Square by many counts, so thought the mother; but all day long, as she walked behind them or viewed them from afar, she could not understand why it was that the people who passed them always looked twice at Elizabeth and only once at Lizzie. It seemed, after all, that clothes did not make the girl. It was disappointing.

The box of candy was all that could possibly be desired. It was ample for the needs of them all, including the two youths from the livery-stable who had attached themselves to their party from the early morning. In fact, it was two boxes, one of the most delectable chocolates of all imaginable kinds, and the other of mixed candies and candied fruit. Both boxes bore the magic name "Huyler's" on the covers. Lizzie had often passed Huyler's, taking her noon walk on Chestnut Street, and looked enviously at the girls who walked in and out with white square bundles tied with gold cord as if it were an everyday affair. And now she was actually eating all she pleased of those renowned candies. It was almost like belonging to the great elite.

It was a long day and a pleasant one even to Elizabeth. She had never been to Willow Grove before, and the strange blending of sweet nature and Vanity Fair charmed her. It was a rest after the winter's round of monotonous engagements. Even the loud-voiced awkward youths from the livery-stable did not annoy her extremely. She took them as a part of the whole, and did not pay much attention to them. They were rather shy of her, giving the most of their attention to Lizzie, much to the satisfaction of Aunt Nan.

They mounted the horses in the merry-go-rounds, and tried each one several times. Elizabeth wondered why anybody desired this sort of amusement, and after her first trip would have been glad to sit with her grandmother and watch the others, only that the old lady seemed so much to desire to have her get on with the rest. She would not do anything to spoil the pleasure of the others if she could help it; so she obediently seated herself in a great sea-shell drawn by a soiled plaster nymph, and whirled on till Lizzie declared it was time to go to something else.

They went into the Old Mill, and down into the Mimic Mine, and sailed through the painted Venice, eating candy and chewing gum and shouting. All but Elizabeth. Elizabeth would not chew gum nor talk loud. It was not her way. But she smiled serenely on the rest, and did not let it worry her that someone might recognize the popular Miss Bailey in so ill-bred a crowd. She knew that it was their way, and they could have no other. They were having a good time, and she was a part of it for to-day. They weighed one another on the scales with many jokes and much laughter, and went to see all the moving pictures in the place. They ate their lunch under the trees, and then at last the music began.

They seated themselves on the outskirts of the company, for Lizzie declared that was the only pleasant place to be. She did not want to go "way up front." She had a boy on either side of her, and she kept the seat shaking with laughter. Now and then a weary guard would look distressedly down the line, and motion for less noise; but they giggled on. Elizabeth was glad they were so far back that they might not annoy more people than was necessary.

But the music was good, and she watched the leader with great satisfaction. She noticed that there were many people given up to the pleasure of it. The melody went to her soul, and thrilled through it. She had not had much good music in her life. The last three years, of course, she had been occasionally to the Academy of Music; but, though her grandmother had a box there, she very seldom had time or cared to attend concerts. Sometimes, when Melba, or Caruso, or some world-renowned favorite was there, she would take Elizabeth for an hour, usually slipping out just after the favorite solo with noticeable loftiness, as if the orchestra were the common dust of the earth, and she only condescended to come for the soloist. So Elizabeth had scarcely known the delight of a whole concert of fine orchestral music.

She heard Lizzie talking.

"Yes, that's Walter Damrosh! Ain't that name fierce? Grandma thinks it's kind of wicked to pernounce it that way. They say he's fine, but I must say I liked the band they had last year better. It played a whole lot of lively things, and once they had a rattle-box and a squeaking thing that cried like a baby right out in the music, and everybody just roared laughing. I tell you that was great. I don't care much for this here kind of music myself. Do you?" And Jim and Joe both agreed that they didn't, either. Elizabeth smiled, and kept on enjoying it.

Peanuts were the order of the day, and their assertive crackle broke in upon the finest passages. Elizabeth wished her cousin would take a walk;

and by and by she did, politely inviting Elizabeth to go along; but she declined, and they were left to sit through the remainder of the afternoon concert.

After supper they watched the lights come out, Elizabeth thinking about the description of the heavenly city as one after another the buildings blazed out against the darkening blue of the June night. The music was about to begin. Indeed, it could be heard already in the distance, and drew the girl irresistibly. For the first time that day she made a move, and the others followed, half wearied of their dissipations, and not knowing exactly what do to next.

They stood the first half of the concert very well, but at the intermission they wandered out to view the electric fountain with its many-colored fluctuations, and to take a row on the tiny sheet of water. Elizabeth remained sitting where she was, and watched the fountain. Even her grandmother and aunt grew restless, and wanted to walk again. They said they had had enough music, and did not want to hear any more. They could hear it well enough, anyway, from further off. They believed they would have some ice-cream. Didn't Elizabeth want some?

She smiled sweetly. Would Grandmother mind if she sat right there and heard the second part of the concert? She loved music, and this was fine. She didn't feel like eating another thing to-night. So the two ladies, thinking the girl queer that she didn't want ice-cream, went off to enjoy theirs with a clear conscience; and Elizabeth drew a long breath, and sat back with her eyes closed, to rest and breathe in the sweet sounds that were beginning to float out delicately as if to feel whether the atmosphere were right for what was to come after.

It was just at the close of this wonderful music, which the programme said was Mendelssohn's "Spring Song," when Elizabeth looked up to meet the eyes of someone who stood near in the aisle watching her, and there beside her stood the man of the wilderness!

He was looking at her face, drinking in the beauty of the profile and wondering whether he was right. Could it be that this was his little brown friend, the maid of the wilderness? This girl with the lovely, refined face, the intellectual brow, the dainty fineness of manner? She looked like some white angel dropped down into that motley company of Sunday-school picnickers and city pleasure-seekers. The noise and clatter of the place seemed far away from her. She was absorbed utterly in the sweet sounds.

When she looked up and saw him, the smile that flashed out upon her face was like the sunshine upon a day that has hitherto been still and almost sad. The eyes said, "You are come at last!" The curve of the lips said, "I am glad you are here!"

He went to her like one who had been hungry for the sight of her for a long time, and after he had grasped her hand they stood so for a moment while the hum and gentle clatter of talk that always starts between numbers seethed around them and hid the few words they spoke at first.

"O, I have so longed to know if you were safe!" said the man as soon as he could speak.

Then straightway the girl forgot all her three years of training, and her success as a débutante, and became the grave, shy thing she had been to him when he first saw her, looking up with awed delight into the face she had seen in her dreams for so long, and yet might not long for.

The orchestra began again, and they sat in silence listening. But yet their souls seemed to speak to each other through the medium of the music, as if the intervening years were being bridged and brought together in the space of those few waves of melody.

"I have found out," said Elizabeth, looking up shyly with a great light in her eyes. "I have found what it all means. Have you? O, I have wanted so much to know whether you had found out too!"

"Found out what?" he asked half sadly that he did not understand.

"Found out how God hides us. Found what a friend Jesus Christ can be."

"You are just the same," said the man with satisfaction in his eyes. "You have not been changed nor spoiled. They could not spoil you."

"Have you found out too?" she asked softly. She looked up into his eyes with wistful longing. She wanted this thing so very much. It had been in her prayers for so long.

He could not withdraw his own glance. He did not wish to. He longed to be able to answer what she wished.

"A little, perhaps," he said doubtfully. "Not so much as I would like to. Will you help me?"

"*He* will help you. You will find Him if you search for Him with all your heart," she said earnestly. "It says so in His book."

Then came more music, wistful, searching, tender. Did it speak of the things of heaven to other souls there than those two?

He stooped down, and said in a low tone that somehow seemed to blend with the music like the words that fitted it:

"I will try with all my heart if you will help me."

She smiled her answer, brimming back with deep delight.

Into the final lingering notes of an andante from one of Beethoven's sublime symphonies clashed the loud voice of Lizzie:

"O Bess! Bess! B-es-see! I say, Bessie! Ma says we'll have to go over by the cars now if we want to get a seat. The concert's most out, and there'll be a fierce rush. Come on! And Grandma says, bring your friend along with you if you want." This last with a smirking recognition of the man, who had turned around wonderingly to see who was speaking.

With a quick, searching glance that took in bedraggled organdie, rose hat, and pink parasol, and set them aside for what they were worth, George Benedict observed and classified Lizzie.

"Will you excuse yourself, and let me take you home a little later?" he asked in a low tone. "The crowd will be very great, and I have my automobile here."

She looked at him gratefully, and assented. She had much to tell him. She leaned across the seats, and spoke in a clear tone to her cousin.

"I will come a little later," she said, smiling with her Rittenhouse Square look that always made Lizzie a little afraid of her. "Tell Grandmother I have found an old friend I have not seen for a long time. I will be there almost as soon as you are."

They waited while Lizzie explained, and the grandmother and aunt nodded a reluctant assent. Aunt Nan frowned. Elizabeth might have brought her friend along, and introduced him to Lizzie. Did Elizabeth think Lizzie wasn't good enough to be introduced?

He wrapped her in a great soft rug that was in the automobile, and tucked her in beside him; and she felt as if the long, hard days that had passed since they had met were all forgotten and obliterated in this night of delight. Not all the attentions of all the fine men she had met in society had ever been like his, so gentle, so perfect. She had forgotten the lady as completely as if she had never heard of her. She wanted now to tell her friend about her heavenly Father.

He let her talk, and watched her glowing, earnest face by the dim light of the sky; for the moon had come out to crown the night with beauty, and the unnatural brilliance of electric blaze, with all the glitter and noise of Willow Grove, died into the dim, sweet night as those two sped onward toward the city. The heart of the man kept singing, singing, singing: "I have found her at last! She is safe!"

"I have prayed for you always," he said in one of the pauses. It was just as they were coming into Flora Street. The urchins were all out on the sidewalk yet, for the night was hot; and they gathered about, and ran hooting after the car as it slowed up at the door. "I am sure He did hide you safely, and I shall thank Him for answering my prayer. And now I am coming to see you. May I come to-morrow?"

There was a great gladness in her eyes. "Yes," she said.

The Bradys had arrived from the corner trolley, and were hovering about the door self-assertively. It was almost apparent to an onlooker that this was a good opportunity for an introduction, but the two young people were entirely oblivious. The man touched his hat gravely, a look of great admiration in his eye, and said, "Good night" like a benediction. Then the girl turned and went into the plain little home and to her belligerent relatives with a light in her eyes and a joy in her steps that had not been there earlier in the day. The dreams that visited her hard pillow that night were heavenly and sweet.

Chapter 16
Alone Again

"Now we're goin' to see ef the paper says anythin' about our Bessie," said Grandmother Brady the next morning, settling her spectacles over her nose comfortably and crossing one fat gingham knee over the other. "I always read the society notes, Bess."

Elizabeth smiled, and her grandmother read down the column:

"Mr. George Trescott Benedict and his mother, Mrs. Vincent Benedict, have arrived home after an extended tour of Europe," read Mrs. Brady. "Mrs. Benedict is much improved in health. It is rumored they will spend the summer in their country seat on Wissahickon Heights."

"My!" interrupted Lizzie with her mouth full of fried potatoes. "That's the fellow that was engaged to that Miss What's-her-Name Loring. Don't you 'member? They had his picture in the papers, and her; and then all at once she threw him over for some dook or something, and this feller went off. I heard about it from Mame. Her sister works in a department-store, and she knows Miss Loring. She says she's an awfully handsome girl, and George Benedict was just gone on her. He had a fearful case. Mame says Miss Loring — what *is* her name? — O, Geraldine — Geraldine Loring bought some lace of her. She heard her say it was for the gown she was going to wear at the horse-show. They had her picture in the paper just after the horse-show, and it was all over lace. I saw it. It cost a whole lot. I forget how many dollars a yard. But there was something the matter with the dook. She didn't marry him, after all. In her picture she was driving four horses. Don't you remember it, Grandma? She sat up tall and high on a seat, holding a whole lot of ribbons and whips and things. She has an elegant figger. I guess mebbe the dook wasn't rich enough. She hasn't been engaged to anybody else, and I shouldn't wonder now but she'd take George Benedict back. He was so awful stuck on her!"

Lizzie rattled on, and the grandmother read more society notes, but Elizabeth heard no more. Her heart had suddenly frozen, and dropped down like lead into her being. She felt as if she never would be able to raise it again. The lady! Surely she had forgotten the lady. But Geraldine Loring! Of all women! Could it be possible! Geraldine Loring was

118

almost — well, fast, at least, as nearly so as one who was really of a fine old family, and still held her own in society, could be. She was beautiful as a picture; but her face, to Elizabeth's mind, was lacking in fine feeling and intellect. A great pity went out from her heart to the man whose fate was in that doll-girl's hands. True, she had heard that Miss Loring's family were unquestionable, and she knew her mother was a most charming woman. Perhaps she had misjudged her, for it could not be otherwise.

The joy had gone out of the morning when Elizabeth went home. She went up to her Grandmother Bailey at once, and after she had read her letters for her, and performed the little services that were her habit, she said:

"Grandmother, I'm expecting a man to call upon me to-day. I thought I had better tell you."

"A man!" said Madam Bailey, alarmed at once. She wanted to look over and portion out the right man when the time came. "What man?"

"Why, a man I met in Montana," said Elizabeth, wondering how much she ought to tell.

"A man you met in Montana! Horrors!" exclaimed the now thoroughly aroused grandmother. "Not that dreadful creature you ran away from?"

"O no!" said Elizabeth, smiling. "Not that man. A man who was very kind to me, and whom I like very much."

So much the worse. Immediate action was necessary.

"Well, Elizabeth," said Madam Bailey in her stiffest tones, "I really do not care to have any of your Montana friends visit you. You will have to excuse yourself. It will lead to embarrassing entanglements. You do not in the least realize your position in society. It is all well enough to please your relatives, although I think you often overdo that. You could just as well send them a present now and then, and please them more than to go yourself. But as for any outsiders, it is impossible. I draw the line there."

"But Grandmother —"

"Don't interrupt me, Elizabeth; I have something more to say. I had word this morning from the steamship company. They can give us our staterooms on the Deutschland on Saturday, and I have decided to take them. I have telegraphed, and we shall leave here to-day for New York. I have one or two matters of business I wish to attend to in New York. We shall go to the Waldorf for a few days, and you will have more opportunity to see New York than you have yet. It will not be too warm to enjoy going about a little, I fancy; and a number of our friends are going to be at the Waldorf, too. The Craigs sail on Saturday with us. You will have young company on the voyage."

Elizabeth's heart sank lower than she had know it could go, and she grew white to the lips. The observant grandmother decided that she had done well to be so prompt. The man from Montana was by no means to be admitted. She gave orders to that effect, unknown to Elizabeth.

The girl went slowly to her room. All at once it had dawned upon her that she had not given her address to the man the night before, nor told him by so much as a word what were her circumstances. An hour's meditation brought her to the unpleasant decision that perhaps even now in this hard spot God was only hiding her from worse trouble. Mr. George Benedict belonged to Geraldine Loring. He had declared as much when he was in Montana. It would not be well for her to renew the acquaintance. Her heart told her by its great ache that she would be crushed under a friendship that could not be lasting.

Very sadly she sat down to write a note.

"My dear Friend," she wrote on plain paper with no crest. It was like her to choose that. She would not flaunt her good fortune to his face. She was a plain Montana girl to him, and so she would remain.

"My grandmother has been very ill, and is obliged to go away for her health. Unexpectedly I find that we are to go to-day. I supposed it would not be for a week yet. I am so sorry not to see you again, but I send you a little book that has helped me to get acquainted with Jesus Christ. Perhaps it will help you too. It is called 'My Best Friend.' I shall not forget to pray always that you may find Him. He is so precious to me! I must thank you in words, though I never can say it as it should be said, for your very great kindness to me when I was in trouble. God sent you to me, I am sure. Always gratefully your friend,

"ELIZABETH."

That was all, no date, no address. He was not hers, and she would hang out no clues for him to find her, even if he wished. It was better so.

She sent the note and the little book to his address on Walnut Street; and then after writing a note to her Grandmother Brady, saying that she was going away for a long trip with Grandmother Bailey, she gave herself into the hands of the future like a submissive but weary child.

The noon train to New York carried in its drawing-room-car Madam Bailey, her granddaughter, her maid, and her dog, bound for Europe. The society columns so stated; and so read Grandmother Brady a few days afterward. So also read George Benedict, but it meant nothing to him.

When he received the note, his mind was almost as much excited as when he saw the little brown girl and the little brown horse vanishing behind the little brown station on the prairie. He went to the telephone, and reflected that he knew no names. He called up his automobile, and tore up to Flora Street; but in his bewilderment of the night before he had not noticed which block the house was in, nor which number. He thought he knew where to find it, but in broad daylight the houses were all alike for three blocks, and for the life of him he could not remember whether he had turned up to the right or the left when he came to Flora Street. He tried both, but saw no sign of the people he had but casually noticed at Willow Grove.

He could not ask where she lived, for he did not know her name. Nothing but Elizabeth, and they had called her Bessie. He could not go from house to house asking for a girl named Bessie. They would think him a fool, as he was, for not finding out her name, her precious name, at once. How could he let her slip from him again when he had just found her?

At last he hit upon a bright idea. He asked some children along the street whether they knew of any young woman named Bessie or Elizabeth living there, but they all with one accord shook their heads, though one volunteered the information that "Lizzie Smith lives there." It was most distracting and unsatisfying. There was nothing for it but for him to go home and wait in patience for her return. She would come back sometime probably. She had not said so, but she had not said she would not. He had found her once; he might find her again. And he could pray. She had found comfort in that; so would he. He would learn what her secret was. He would get acquainted with her "best Friend." Diligently did he study that little book, and then he went and hunted up the man of God who had written it, and who had been the one to lead Elizabeth into the path of light by his earnest preaching every Sabbath, though this fact he did not know.

The days passed, and the Saturday came. Elizabeth, heavy-hearted, stood on the deck of the Deutschland, and watched her native land disappear from view. So again George Benedict had lost her from sight.

It struck Elizabeth, as she stood straining her eyes to see the last of the shore through tears that would burn to the surface and fall down her white cheeks, that again she was running away from a man, only this time not of her own free will. She was being taken away. But perhaps it was better.

And it never once entered her mind that, if she had told her grandmother who the friend in Montana was, and where he lived in Philadelphia, it would have made all the difference in the world.

From the first of the voyage Grandmother Bailey grew steadily worse, and when they landed on the other side they went from one place to another seeking health. Carlsbad waters did not agree with her, and they went to the south of France to try the climate. At each move the little old lady grew weaker and more querulous. She finally made no further resistance, and gave up to the role of invalid. Then Elizabeth must be in constant attendance. Madam Bailey demanded reading, and no voice was so soothing as Elizabeth's.

Gradually Elizabeth substituted books of her own choice as her grandmother seemed not to mind, and now and then she would read a page of some book that told of the best Friend. At first because it was written by the dear pastor at home it commanded her attention, and finally because some dormant chord in her heart had been touched, she allowed Elizabeth to speak of these things. But it was not until they had been away from home for three months, and she had been growing daily weaker and weaker, that she allowed Elizabeth to read in the Bible.

The girl chose the fourteenth chapter of John, and over and over again, whenever the restless nerves tormented their victim, she would read those words, "Let not your heart be troubled" until the selfish soul, who had lived all her life to please the world and do her own pleasure, came at last to hear the words, and feel that perhaps she did believe in God, and might accept that invitation, "Believe also in me."

One day Elizabeth had been reading a psalm, and thought her grandmother was asleep. She was sitting back with weary heart, thinking what would happen if her grandmother should not get well. The old lady opened her eyes.

"Elizabeth," she said abruptly, just as when she was well, "you've been a good girl. I'm glad you came. I couldn't have died right without you. I never thought much about these things before, but it really is worth while. In my Father's house. He is my Father, Elizabeth."

She went to sleep then, and Elizabeth tiptoed out and left her with the nurse. By and by Marie came crying in, and told her that the Madam was dead.

Elizabeth was used to having people die. She was not shocked; only it seemed lonely again to find herself facing the world, in a foreign land. And when she came to face the arrangements that had to be made, which, after all, money and servants made easy, she found herself dreading her own land. What must she do after her grandmother was laid to rest? She could not live in the great house in Rittenhouse Square, and neither could she very well go and live in Flora Street. O, well, her Father would hide her. She need not plan; He would plan for her. The mansions on the earth were His too, as well as those in heaven.

And so resting she passed through the weary voyage and the day when the body was laid to rest in the Bailey lot in the cemetery, and she went back to the empty house alone. It was not until after the funeral that she went to see Grandmother Brady. She had not thought it wise or fitting to invite the hostile grandmother to the other one's funeral. She had thought Grandmother Bailey would not like it.

She rode to Flora Street in the carriage. She felt too weary to walk or go in the trolley. She was taking account of stock in the way of friends, thinking over whom she cared to see. One of the first bits of news she had heard on arriving in this country had been that Miss Loring's wedding was to come off in a few days. It seemed to strike her like a thunderbolt, and she was trying to arraign herself for this as she rode along. It was therefore not helpful to her state of mind to have her grandmother remark grimly:

"That feller o' yurs 'n his aughtymobble has been goin' up an' down this street, day in, day out, this whole blessed summer. Ain't been a day he didn't pass, sometimes once, sometimes twicet. I felt sorry fer him sometimes. Ef he hadn't been so high an' mighty stuck up that he couldn't recognize me, I'd 'a' spoke to him. It was plain ez the nose on your face he was lookin' fer you. Don't he know where you live?"

"I don't believe he does," said Elizabeth languidly. "Say, Grandmother, would you care to come up to Rittenhouse Square and live?"

"Me? In Rittenhouse Square? Fer the land sakes, child, no. That's flat. I've lived me days out in me own sp'ere, and I don't intend to change now at me time o' life. Ef you want to do somethin' nice for me, child, now you've got all that money, I'd like real well to live in a house that hed white marble steps. It's been me one aim all me life. There's some round on the next street that don't come high. There'd be plenty room for us all, an' a nice place fer Lizzie to get married when the time comes. The parlor's real big, and you could send her some roses, couldn't you?"

"All right, Grandmother. You shall have it," said Elizabeth with a relieved sigh, and in a few minutes she went home. Some day pretty soon she must think what to do, but there was no immediate hurry. She was glad that Grandmother Brady did not want to come to Rittenhouse Square. Things would be more congenial without her.

But the house seemed great and empty when she entered, and she was glad to hear the friendly telephone bell ringing. It was the wife of her pastor, asking her to come to them for a quiet dinner.

This was the one home in the great city where she felt like going in her loneliness. There would be no form nor ceremony. Just a friend with them. It was good. The doctor would give her some helpful words. She was glad they had asked her.

Chapter 17
A Final Flight and Pursuit

"George," said Mrs. Vincent Benedict, "I want you to do something for me."

"Certainly, Mother, anything I can."

"Well, it's only to go to dinner with me to-night. Our pastor's wife has telephoned me that she wants us very much. She especially emphasized you. She said she absolutely needed you. It was a case of charity, and she would be so grateful to you if you would come. She has a young friend with her who is very sad, and she wants to cheer her up. Now don't frown. I won't bother you again this week. I know you hate dinners and girls. But really, George, this is an unusual case. The girl is just home from Europe, and buried her grandmother yesterday. She hasn't a soul in the world belonging to her that can be with her, and the pastor's wife has asked her over to dinner quietly. Of course she isn't going out. She must be in mourning. And you know you're fond of the doctor."

"Yes, I'm fond of the doctor," said George, frowning discouragedly; "but I'd rather take him alone, and not with a girl flung at me everlastingly. I'm tired of it. I didn't think it of Christian people, though; I thought she was above such things."

"Now, George," said his mother severely, "that's a real insult to the girl, and to our friend too. She hasn't an idea of doing any such thing. It seems this girl is quite unusual, very religious, and our friend thought you would be just the one to cheer her. She apologized several times for presuming to ask you to help her. You really will have to go."

"Well, who is this paragon, anyway? Anyone I know? I suppose I've got to go."

"Why, she's a Miss Bailey," said the mother, relieved. "Mrs. Wilton Merrill Bailey's granddaughter. Did you ever happen to meet her? I never did."

"Never heard of her," growled George. "Wish I hadn't now."

"George!"

"Well, Mother, go on. I'll be good. What does she do? Dance, and play bridge, and sing?"

"I haven't heard anything that she does," said his mother, laughing.

124

"Well, of course she's a paragon; they all are, Mother. I'll be ready in half an hour. Let's go and get it done. We can come home early, can't we?"

Mrs. Benedict sighed. If only George would settle down on some suitable girl of good family! But he was so queer and restless. She was afraid for him. Ever since she had taken him away to Europe, when she was so ill, she had been afraid for him. He seemed so moody and absent-minded then and afterwards. Now this Miss Bailey was said to be as beautiful as she was good. If only George would take a notion to her!

Elizabeth was sitting in a great arm-chair by the open fire when he entered the room. He had not expected to find anyone there. He heard voices up-stairs, and supposed Miss Bailey was talking with her hostess. His mother followed the servant to remove her wraps, and he entered the drawing-room alone. She stirred, looked up, and saw him.

"Elizabeth!" he said, and came forward to grasp her hand. "I have found you again. How came you here?"

But she had no opportunity to answer, for the ladies entered almost at once, and there stood the two smiling at each other.

"Why, you have met before!" exclaimed the hostess. "How delighted I am! I knew you two would enjoy meeting. Elizabeth, child, you never told me you knew George."

George Benedict kept looking around for Miss Bailey to enter the room; but to his relief she did not come, and, when they went out to the dining-room, there was no place set for her. She must have preferred to remain at home. He forgot her, and settled down to the joy of having Elizabeth by his side. His mother, opposite, watched his face blossom into the old-time joy as he handed this new girl the olives, and had eyes for no one else.

It was to Elizabeth a blessed evening. They held sweet converse one with another as children of the King. For a little time under the old influence of the restful, helpful talk she forgot "the lady," and all the perplexing questions that had vexed her soul. She knew only that she had entered into an atmosphere of peace and love and joy.

It was not until the evening was over, and the guests were about to leave, that Mrs. Benedict addressed Elizabeth as Miss Bailey. Up to that moment it had not entered her son's mind that Miss Bailey was present at all. He turned with a start, and looked into Elizabeth's eyes; and she smiled back to him as if to acknowledge the name. Could she read his thoughts? he wondered.

It was only a few steps across the Square, and Mrs. Benedict and her son walked to Elizabeth's door with her. He had no opportunity to speak to

Elizabeth alone, but he said as he bade her good-night, "I shall see you tomorrow, then, in the morning."

The inflection was almost a question; but Elizabeth only said, "Good night," and vanished into the house.

"Then you have met her before, George?" asked his mother wonderingly.

"Yes," he answered hurriedly, as if to stop her further question. "Yes, I have met her before. She is very beautiful, Mother."

And because the mother was afraid she might say too much she assented, and held her peace. It was the first time in years that George had called a girl beautiful.

Meantime Elizabeth had gone to her own room and locked the door. She hardly knew what to think, her heart was so happy. Yet beneath it all was the troubled thought of the lady, the haunting lady for whom they had prayed together on the prairie. And as if to add to the thought she found a bit of newspaper lying on the floor beside her dressing-table. Marie must have dropped it as she came in to turn up the lights. It was nothing but the corner torn from a newspaper, and should be consigned to the waste-basket; yet her eye caught the words in large head-lines as she picked it up idly, "Miss Geraldine Loring's Wedding to Be an Elaborate Affair." There was nothing more readable. The paper was torn in a zigzag line just beneath. Yet that was enough. It reminded her of her duty.

Down beside the bed she knelt, and prayed: "O my Father, hide me now; hide me! I am in trouble; hide me!" Over and over she prayed till her heart grew calm and she could think.

Then she sat down quietly, and put the matter before her.

This man whom she loved with her whole soul was to be married in a few days. The world of society would be at the wedding. He was pledged to another, and he was not hers. Yet he was her old friend, and was coming to see her. If he came and looked into her face with those clear eyes of his, he might read in hers that she loved him. How dreadful that would be!

Yes, she must search yet deeper. She had heard the glad ring in his voice when he met her, and said, "Elizabeth!" She had seen his eyes. He was in danger himself. She knew it; she might not hide it from herself. She must help him to be true to the woman to whom he was pledged, whom now he would have to marry.

She must go away from it all. She would run away, now at once. It seemed that she was always running away from someone. She could go back to the mountains where she had started. She was not afraid now of the man from whom she had fled. Culture and education had done their work. Religion had set her upon a rock. She could go back with the protection that her money would put about her, with the companionship of some good, elderly woman, and be safe from harm in that way; but she could not stay here and meet George Benedict in the morning, nor face Geraldine Loring on her wedding-day. It would be all the same the facing whether she were in the wedding-party or not. Her days of mourning for her grandmother would of course protect her from this public facing. It was the thought she could not bear. She must get away from it all forever.

Her lawyers should arrange the business. They would purchase the house that Grandmother Brady desired, and then give her her money to build a church. She would go back, and teach among the lonely wastes of mountain and prairie what Jesus Christ longed to be to the people made in His image. She would go back and place above the graves of her father and mother and brothers stones that should bear the words of life to all who should pass by in that desolate region. And that should be her excuse to the world for going, if she needed any excuse — she had gone to see about placing a monument over her father's grave. But the monument should be a church somewhere where it was most needed. She was resolved about that.

That was a busy night. Marie was called upon to pack a few things for a hurried journey. The telephone rang, and the sleepy night-operator answered crossly. But Elizabeth found out all she wanted to know about the early Chicago trains, and then lay down to rest.

Early the next morning George Benedict telephoned for some flowers from the florist; and, when they arrived, he pleased himself by taking them to Elizabeth's door.

He did not expect to find her up, but it would be a pleasure to have them reach her by his own hand. They would be sent up to her room, and she would know in her first waking thought that he remembered her. He smiled as he touched the bell and stood waiting.

The old butler opened the door. He looked as if he had not fully finished his night's sleep. He listened mechanically to the message, "For Miss Bailey with Mr. Benedict's good-morning," and then his face took on a deprecatory expression.

"I'm sorry, Mr. Benedict," he said, as if in the matter he were personally to blame; "but she's just gone. Miss Elizabeth's mighty quick in her ways, and last night after she come home she decided to go to Chicago on the early train. She's just gone to the station not ten minutes ago. They was late, and had to hurry. I'm expecting the footman back every minute."

"Gone?" said George Benedict, standing blankly on the door-step and looking down the street as if that should bring her. "Gone? To Chicago, did you say?"

"Yes, sir, she's gone to Chicago. That is, she's going further, but she took the Chicago Limited. She's gone to see about a monument for Madam's son John, Miss 'Lizabuth's father. She said she must go at once, and she went."

"What time does that train leave?" asked the young man. It was a thread of hope. He was stung into a superhuman effort as he had been on the prairie when he had caught the flying vision of the girl and horse, and he had shouted, and she would not stop for him.

"Nine-fifty, sir," said the butler. He wished this excited young man would go after her. She needed someone. His heart had often stirred against fate that this pearl among young mistresses should have no intimate friend or lover now in her loneliness.

"Nine-fifty!" He looked at his watch. No chance! "Broad Street?" he asked sharply.

"Yes, sir."

Would there be a chance if he had his automobile? Possibly, but hardly unless the train was late. There would be a trifle more chance of catching the train at West Philadelphia. O for his automobile! He turned to the butler in despair.

"Telephone her!" he said. "Stop her if you possibly can on board the train, and I will try to get there. I must see her. It is important." He started down the steps, his mind in a whirl of trouble. How should he go? The trolley would be the only available way, and yet the trolley would be useless; it would take too long. Nevertheless, he sped down toward Chestnut Street blindly, and now in his despair his new habit came to him. "O my Father, help me! Help me! Save her for me!"

Up Walnut Street at a breakneck pace came a flaming red automobile, sounding its taunting menace, "Honk-honk! Honk-honk!" but George Benedict stopped not for automobiles. Straight into the jaws of death he rushed, and was saved only by the timely grasp of a policeman, who rolled him over on the ground. The machine came to a halt, and a familiar voice shouted: "Conscience alive, George, is that you? What are you trying to do? Say, but that was a close shave! Where you going in such a hurry, anyway? Hustle in, and I'll take you there."

The young man sprang into the seat, and gasped: "West Philadelphia station, Chicago Limited! Hurry! Train leaves Broad Street station at nine-fifty. Get me there if you can, Billy. I'll be your friend forever."

By this time they were speeding fast. Neither of the two had time to consider which station was the easier to make; and, as the machine was headed toward West Philadelphia, on they went, regardless of laws or vainly shouting policemen.

George Benedict sprang from the car before it had stopped, and nearly fell again. His nerves were not steady from his other fall yet. He tore into the station and out through the passageway past the beckoning hand of the ticket-man who sat in the booth at the staircase, and strode up three steps at a time. The guard shouted: "Hurry! You may get it; she's just starting!" and a friendly hand reached out, and hauled him up on the platform of the last car.

For an instant after he was safely in the car he was too dazed to think. It seemed as if he must keep on blindly rushing through that train all the way to Chicago, or she would get away from him. He sat down in an empty seat for a minute to get his senses. He was actually on the train! It had not gone without him!

Now the next question was, Was she on it herself, or had she in some way slipped from his grasp even yet? The old butler might have caught her by telephone. He doubted it. He knew her stubborn determination, and all at once he began to suspect that she was with intention running away from him, and perhaps had been doing so before! It was an astonishing thought and a grave one, yet, if it were true, what had meant that welcoming smile in her eyes that had been like dear sunshine to his heart?

But there was no time to consider such questions now. He had started on this quest, and he must continue it until he found her. Then she should be made to explain once and for all most fully. He would live through no more torturing agonies of separation without a full understanding of the matter. He got upon his shaking feet, and started to hunt for Elizabeth.

Then all at once he became aware that he was still carrying the box of flowers. Battered and out of shape it was, but he was holding it as if it held the very hope of life for him. He smiled grimly as he tottered shakily down the aisle, grasping his floral offering with determination. This was not exactly the morning call he had planned, nor the way he had expected to present his flowers; but it seemed to be the best he could do. Then, at last, in the very furthest car from the end, in the drawing-room he found her, sitting gray and sorrowful, looking at the fast-flying landscape.

"Elizabeth!" He stood in the open door and called to her; and she started as from a deep sleep, her face blazing into glad sunshine at sight of him. She put her hand to her heart, and smiled.

"I have brought you some flowers," he said grimly. "I am afraid there isn't much left of them now; but, such as they are, they are here. I hope you will accept them."

"Oh!" gasped Elizabeth, reaching out for the poor crushed roses as if they had been a little child in danger. She drew them from the battered box and to her arms with a delicious movement of caressing, as if she would make up to them for all they had come through. He watched her, half pleased, half savagely. Why should all that tenderness be wasted on mere fading flowers?

At last he spoke, interrupting her brooding over his roses.

"You are running away from me!" he charged.

"Well, and what if I am?" She looked at him with a loving defiance in her eye.

"Don't you know I love you?" he asked, sitting down beside her and talking low and almost fiercely. "Don't you know I've been torn away from you, or you from me, twice before now, and that I cannot stand it any more? Say, don't you know it? Answer, please!" The demand was kind, but peremptory.

"I was afraid so," she murmured with drooping eyes, and cheeks from which all color had fled.

"Well, why do you do it? Why did you run away? Don't you care for me? Tell me that. If you can't ever love me, you are excusable; but I must know it all now."

"Yes, I care as much as you," she faltered, "but —"

"But what?" sharply.

"But you are going to be married this week," she said in desperation, raising her miserable eyes to his.

He looked at her in astonishment.

"Am I?" said he. "Well, that's news to me; but it's the best news I've heard in a long time. When does the ceremony come off? I wish it was this morning. Make it this morning, will you? Let's stop this blessed old train and go back to the Doctor. He'll fix it so we can't ever run away from each other again. Elizabeth, look at me!"

But Elizabeth hid her eyes now. They were full of tears.

"But the lady —" she gasped out, struggling with the sobs. She was so weary, and the thought of what he had suggested was so precious.

"What lady? There is no lady but you, Elizabeth, and never has been. Haven't you known that for a long time? I have. That was all a hallucination of my foolish brain. I had to go out on the plains to get rid of it, but I left it there forever. She was nothing to me after I saw you."

"But — but people said — and it was in the paper. I saw it. You cannot desert her now; it would be dishonorable."

"Thunder!" ejaculated the distracted young man. "In the paper! What lady?"

"Why, Miss Loring! Geraldine Loring. I saw that the preparations were all made for her wedding, and I was told she was to marry you.''

In sheer relief he began to laugh.

At last he stopped, as the old hurt look spread over her face.

"Excuse me, dear," he said gently. "There was a little acquaintance between Miss Loring and myself. It only amounted to a flirtation on her part, one of many. It was a great distress to my mother, and I went out West, as you know, to get away from her. I knew she would only bring me unhappiness, and she was not willing to give up some of her ways that were impossible. I am glad and thankful that God saved me from her. I believe she is going to marry a distant relative of mine by the name of Benedict, but I thank the kind Father that *I* am not going to marry *her*. There is only one woman in the whole wide world that I am willing to marry, or ever will be; and she is sitting beside me now."

The train was going rapidly now. It would not be long before the conductor would reach them. The man leaned over, and clasped the little gloved hand that lay in the girl's lap; and Elizabeth felt the great joy that had tantalized her for these three years in dreams and visions settle down about her in beautiful reality. She was his now forever. She need never run away again.

The conductor was not long in coming to them, and the matter-of-fact world had to be faced once more. The young man produced his card, and said a few words to the conductor, mentioning the name of his uncle, who, by the way, happened to be a director of the road; and then he explained the situation. It was very necessary that the young lady be recalled at once to her home because of a change in the circumstances. He had caught the train at West Philadelphia by automobile, coming as he was in his morning clothes, without baggage and with little money. Would the conductor be so kind as to put them off that they might return to the city by the shortest possible route?

The conductor glared and scolded, and said people "didn't know their own minds," and "wanted to move the earth." Then he eyed Elizabeth, and she smiled. He let a grim glimmer of what might have been a sour smile years ago peep out for an instant, and — he let them off.

They wandered delightedly about from one trolley to another until they found an automobile garage, and soon were speeding back to Philadelphia.

They waited for no ceremony, those two who had met and loved by the way in the wilderness. They went straight to Mrs. Benedict for her blessing, and then to the minister to arrange for his services; and within the week a quiet wedding-party entered the arched doors of the placid brown church with the lofty spire, and Elizabeth Bailey and George Benedict were united in the sacred bonds of matrimony.

There were present Mrs. Benedict, and one or two intimate friends of the family, besides Grandmother Brady, Aunt Nan, and Lizzie.

Lizzie brought a dozen bread-and-butter plates from the ten-cent store. They were adorned with cupids and roses and much gilt. But Lizzie was disappointed. No display, no pomp and ceremony. Just a simple white dress and white veil. Lizzie did not understand that the veil had been in the Bailey family for generations, and that the dress was an heirloom also. It was worn because Grandmother Bailey had given it to her, and told her she wanted her to wear it on her wedding-day. Sweet and beautiful she looked as she turned to walk down the aisle on her husband's arm, and she smiled at Grandmother Brady in a way that filled the grandmother's heart with pride and triumph. Elizabeth was not ashamed of the Bradys even among her fine friends. But Lizzie grumbled all the way home at the plainness of the ceremony, and the lack of bridesmaids and fuss and feathers.

The social column of the daily papers stated that young Mr. and Mrs. George Benedict were spending their honeymoon in an extended tour of the West, and Grandmother Brady so read it aloud at the breakfast table to the admiring family. Only Lizzie looked discontented:

"She just wore a dark blue tricotine one-piece dress and a little plain dark hat. She ain't got a bit of taste. Oh *Boy!* If I just had her pocket book wouldn't I show the world? But anyhow I'm glad she went in a private car. There was a *little* class to her, though if t'had been mine I'd uv preferred ridin' in the parlor coach an' havin' folks see me and my fine husband. He's some looker, George Benedict is! Everybody turns to watch 'em as they go by, and they sail along and never seem to notice. It's all perfectly throwed away on 'em. Gosh! I'd hate to be such a nut!"

"Now, Lizzie, you know you hadn't oughtta talk like that!" reproved her grandmother. "After her giving you all that money fer your own wedding. A thousand dollars just to spend as you please on your cloes and a blowout, and house linens. Jest because she don't care for gewgaws like you do, you think she's a fool. But she's no fool. She's got a good head on her, and she'll get more in the long run out of life than you will. She's been real loving and kind to us all, and she didn't have any reason to neither. We never did much fer her. And look at how nice and common she's been with us all, not a bit high headed. I declare, Lizzie, I should think you'd be ashamed!"

"Oh, well," said Lizzie shrugging her shoulders indifferently. "She's all right in her way, only 'taint my way. And I'm thankful t'goodness that I had the nerve to speak up when she offered to give me my trousseau. She askt me would I druther hav her buy it for me, or have the money to pick it out m'self, and I spoke up right quick and says, 'Oh, cousin Bessie, I wouldn't *think* of givin' ya all that trouble. I'd take the *money* ef it's all the same t'you,' and she jest smiled and said all right, she expected I knew what I wanted better'n she did. So yes'teddy when I went down to the station to see her off she handed me a bank book. And — Oh, say, I fergot! She said there was a good-bye note inside. I ain't had time to look at it since. I went right to the movies on the dead run to get there 'fore the first show begun, and it's in my coat pocket. Wait 'till I get it. I s'pose it's some of her old *religion!* She's always preaching at me. It ain't that she says so much as that she's always *meanin'* it underneath everything, that gets my goat! It's sorta like having a piece of God round with you all the time watching you. You kinda hate to be enjoyin' yerself fer fear she won't think yer doin' it accordin' to the Bible.''

Lizzie hurtled into the hall and brought back her coat, fumbling in the pocket.

"Yes, here 'tis Ma! Wanta see the figgers? You never had a whole thousand dollars in the bank t'woncet yerself, did ya?''

Mrs. Brady put on her spectacles and reached for the book, while Lizzie's mother got up and came behind her mother's chair to look over at the magic figures. Lizzie stooped for the little white note that had fluttered to her feet as she opened the book, but she had little interest to see what it said. She was more intent upon the new bank book.

It was Grandmother Brady that discovered it:

"Why, Lizzie! It ain't *one* thousand, it's *five* thousand, the book says! You don't s'pose she's made a mistake, do you?''

Lizzie seized the book and gazed, her jaw dropping open in amaze. "Let me have it!'' demanded Lizzie's mother, reaching for the book.

"Where's yer note, Lizzie, mebbe it'll explain,'' said the excited grandmother.

Lizzie recovered the note which again had fluttered to the floor in the confusion and opening it began to read:

"Dear Lizzie," it read,

"I've made it five thousand so you will have some over for furnishing your home, and if you still think you want the little bungalow out on the Pike you will find the deed at my lawyer's, all made out in your name. It's my wedding gift to you, so you can go to work and buy your furniture at once, and not wait till Dan gets a raise. And here's wishing you a great deal of happiness,

"Your loving cousin,

"ELIZABETH.''

"There!" said Grandmother Brady sitting back with satisfaction and holding her hands composedly, "Whadd' I tell ya?"

"Mercy!" said Lizzie's mother. "Let me see that note! The idea of her *giving* all that money when she didn't have to!"

But Lizzie's face was a picture of joy. For once she lost her hard little worldly screwed-up expression and was wreathed in smiles of genuine eagerness:

"Oh *Boy!*" she exclaimed delightedly, dancing around the room. "Now we can have a victrola, an' a player-piano, and Dan'll get a Ford, one o' those limousine-kind! Won't I be some swell? What'll the girls at the store think now?"

"H'm! You'd much better get a washing machine and a 'lectric iron!" grumbled Grandmother Brady practically.

"Well, all I got to say about it is, she was an awful fool to trust *you* with so much money," said Lizzie's mother discontentedly, albeit with a pleased pride as she watched her giddy daughter fling on hat and coat to go down and tell Dan.

"I sh'll work in the store fer the rest of the week, jest to 'commodate 'em," she announced putting her head back in the door as she went out, "but not a day longer. I got a lot t'do. Say, won't I be some lady in the five-an'-ten the rest o' the week? Oh *Boy! I'll tell the world!*"

Meantime in their own private car the bride and groom were whirling on their way to the west, but they saw little of the scenery, being engaged in the all-absorbing story of each other's lives since they had parted.

And one bright morning, they stepped down from the train at Malta and gazed about them.

The sun was shining clear and wonderful, and the little brown station stood drearily against the brightness of the day like a picture that has long hung on the wall of one's memory and is suddenly brought out and the dust wiped away.

They purchased a couple of horses, and with camp accoutrements following began their real wedding trip, over the road they had come together when they first met. Elizabeth had to show her husband where she had hidden while the men went by, and he drew her close in his arms and thanked God that she had escaped so miraculously.

It seemed so wonderful to be in the same places again, for nothing out here in the wilderness seemed much to have changed, and yet they two were so changed that the people they met did not seem to recognize them as ever having been that way before.

They dined sumptuously in the same coulee, and recalled little things they had said and done, and Elizabeth now worldly wise, laughed at her own former ignorance as her husband reminded her of some questions she had asked him on that memorable journey. And ever through the beautiful journey he was telling her how wonderful she seemed to him, both then and now.

Not however, till they reached the old ranchhouse, where the woman had tried to persuade her to stay, did they stop for long.

Elizabeth had a tender feeling in her heart for that motherly woman who had sought to protect her, and felt a longing to let her know how safely she had been kept through the long journey and how good the Lord had been to her through the years. Also they both desired to reward these kind people for their hospitality in the time of need. So, in the early evening they rode up just as they did before to the little old log house. But no friendly door flung open wide as they came near, and at first they thought the cabin deserted, till a candle flare suddenly shone forth in the bedroom, and then Benedict dismounted and knocked.

After some waiting the old man came to the door holding a candle high above his head. His face was haggard and worn, and the whole place looked dishevelled. His eyes had a weary look as he peered into the night and it was evident that he had no thought of ever having seen them before:

"I can't do much fer ya, strangers," he said, his voice sounding tired and discouraged. "If it's a woman ye have with ye, ye better ride on to the next ranch. My woman is sick. Very sick. There's nobody here with her but me, and I have all I can tend to. The house ain't kept very tidy. It's six weeks since she took to bed."

Elizabeth had sprung lightly to the ground and was now at the threshold:

"Oh, is she sick? I'm so sorry? Couldn't I do something for her? She was good to me once several years ago!"

The old man peered at her blinkingly, noting her slender beauty, the exquisite eager face, the dress that showed her of another world — and shook his head:

"I guess you made a mistake, lady. I don't remember ever seeing you before —"

"But I remember you," she said eagerly stepping into the room. "Won't you please let me go to her?"

"Why, shore, lady, go right in ef you want to. She's layin' there in the bed. She ain't likely to get out of it again I'm feared. The doctor says nothin' but a 'noperation will ever get her up, and we can't pay fer 'noperations. It's a long ways to the hospital in Chicago where he wants her sent, and M'ria and I, we ain't allowin' to part. It can't be many years —"

But Elizabeth was not waiting to hear. She had slipped into the old bedroom that she remembered now so well and was kneeling beside the bed talking to the white faced woman on the thin pillow:

"Don't you remember me?" she asked. "I'm the girl you tried to get to stay with you once. The girl that came here with a man she had met in the wilderness. You told me things that I didn't know, and you were kind and wanted me to stay here with you? Don't you remember me? I'm Elizabeth!"

The woman reached out a bony hand and touched the fair young face that she could see but dimly in the flare of the candle that the old man now brought into the room:

"Why, yes, I remember," the woman said, her voice sounded alive yet in spite of her illness. "Yes, I remember you. You were a dear little girl, and I was so worried about you. I would have kept you for my own — but you wouldn't stay. And he was a nice looking young man, but I was afraid for you — You can't always tell about them — You *mostly* can't —!"

"But he was all right, Mother!" Elizabeth's voice rang joyously through the cabin. "He took care of me and got me safely started toward my people, and now he's my husband. I want you to see him. George come here!"

The old woman half raised herself from the pillow and looked toward the young man in the doorway:

"You don't say! He's your *husband!* Well, now isn't that grand! Well, I certainly am glad! I was that worried —!"

They sat around the bed talking, Elizabeth telling briefly of her own experiences and her wedding trip which they were taking back over the old trail, and the old man and woman speaking of their trouble, the woman's break-down and how the doctor at Malta said there was a chance she could get well if she went to a great doctor in Chicago, but how they had no money unless they sold the ranch and that nobody wanted to buy it.

"Oh, but we have money," laughed Elizabeth joyously, "and it is our turn now to help you. You helped us when we were in trouble. How soon can you start? I'm going to play you are my own father and mother. We can send them both, can't we George?"

It was a long time before they settled themselves to sleep that night because there was so much planning to be done, and then Elizabeth and her husband had to get out their stores and cook a good supper for the two old people who had been living mostly on corn meal mush for several weeks.

And after the others were all asleep the old woman lay praying and thanking God for the two angels who had dropped down to help them in their distress.

The next morning George Benedict with one of the men who looked after their camping outfit went to Malta and got in touch with the Chicago doctor and hospital, and before he came back to the ranch that night everything was arranged for the immediate start of the two old people. He had even planned for an automobile and the Malta doctor to be in attendance in a couple of days to get the invalid to the station.

Meantime Elizabeth had been going over the old woman's wardrobe which was scanty and coarse, and selecting garments from her own baggage that would do for the journey.

The old woman looked glorified as she touched the delicate white garments with their embroidery and ribbons:

"Oh, dear child! Why, I couldn't wear a thing like that on my old worn-out body. Those look like angels' clothes." She put a work-worn finger on the delicate tracery of embroidery and smoothed a pink satin ribbon bow.

But Elizabeth overruled her. It was nothing but a plain little garment she had bought for the trip. If the friend thought it was pretty she was glad, but nothing was too pretty for the woman who had taken her in in her distress and tried to help her and keep her safe.

The invalid was thin with her illness, and it was found that she could easily wear the girl's simple dress of dark blue with a white collar, and little dark hat, and Elizabeth donned a khaki shirt and brown cap and sweater herself and gladly arrayed her old friend in her own bridal travelling gown for her journey. She had not brought a lot of things for her journey because she did not want to be bothered, but she could easily get more when she got to a large city, and what was money for but to clothe the naked and feed the hungry? She rejoiced in her ability to help this woman of the wilderness.

On the third day, garbed in Elizabeth's clothes, her husband fitted out for the East in some of George Benedict's extra things, they started. They carried a bag containing some necessary changes, and some wonderful toilet accessories with silver monograms, enough to puzzle the most snobbish nurse, also there was a luscious silk kimona of Elizabeth's in the bag. The two old people were settled in the Benedict private car, and in due time hitched onto the Chicago Express and hurried on their way. Before the younger pair went back to their pilgrimage they sent a series of telegrams arranging for every detail of the journey for the old couple, so that they would be met with cars and nurses and looked after most carefully.

And the thanksgiving and praise of the old people seemed to follow them like music as they rode happily on their way.

They paused at the little old schoolhouse where they had attended the Christian Endeavor meeting, and Elizabeth looked half fearfully up the road where her evil pursuers had ridden by, and rode closer to her husband's side. So they passed on the way as nearly as Elizabeth could remember every step back as she had come, telling her husband all the details of the journey.

That night they camped in the little shelter where Benedict had come upon the girl that first time they met, and under the clear stars that seemed so near they knelt together and thanked God for His leading.

They went to the lonely cabin on the mountain, shut up and going to ruin now, and Benedict gazing at the surroundings and then looking at the delicate face of his lovely wife was reminded of a white flower he had once seen growing out of the blackness down in a coal mine, pure and clean without a smirch of soil.

They visited the seven graves in the wilderness, and standing reverently beside the sand-blown mounds she told him much of her early life that she had not told him before, and introduced him to her family, telling a bit about each that would make him see the loveable side of them. And then they planned for seven simple white stones to be set up, bearing words from the book they both loved. Over the care worn mother was to be written "Come unto me all ye that labor and are heavy laden and I will give you rest."

It was on that trip that they planned what came to pass in due time. The little cabin was made over into a simple, pretty home, with vines planted about the garden, and a garage with a sturdy little car; and not far away a church nestled into the side of the hill, built out of the stones that were native, with many sunny windows and a belfry in which bells rang out to the whole region round.

At first it had seemed impractical to put a church out there away from the town, but Elizabeth said that it was centrally located, and high up where it could be seen from the settlements in the valleys, and was moreover on a main trail that was much travelled. She longed to have some such spot in the wilderness that could be a refuge for any who longed for better things.

When they went back they sent out two consecrated missionaries to occupy the new house and use the sturdy little car. They were to ring the bells, preach the gospel and play the organ and piano in the little church.

Over the pulpit there was a beautiful window bearing a picture of Christ, the Good Shepherd, and in clear letters above were the words: "And thou shalt remember all the way which the Lord thy God led thee these forty years in the wilderness, to humble thee, and to prove thee, to know what was in thine heart, whether thou wouldst keep his commandments, or no."

And underneath the picture were the words:

" 'In the time of trouble He shall hide me in His pavilion; in the secret of His tabernacle shall He hide me.' In memory of His hidings,

>   "George and Elizabeth Benedict."

But in the beautiful home in Philadelphia, in an inner intimate room these words are exquisitely graven on the wall, "Let not your heart be troubled."

THE STORY
OF A
WHIM

Chapter 1

Five Girls, an Organ, and the Whim

"How cold it is! Let's walk up and down the platform, girls. Why doesn't that train come?"

"I'm going in to see if the agent knows anything about it," said one with determined mouth and big brown eyes.

They waited shivering in a group until she returned, five girls just entering womanhood. They were part of a small house-party, spending Thanksgiving week at the old stone house on the hill above the station, and they had come down to meet another girl who was expected on the train.

"He says the train is half an hour late," said Hazel Winship, the hostess, coming down the stone steps of the station.

"What shall we do? There is not time to make it worth while to go back to the house. Shall we go inside, or walk?"

"O, walk by all means," said Victoria Landis. "It is so stuffy and hot in there I feel as if I was a turkey half-roasted now from the little time we stayed there."

"Let us walk up this long platform to that freight-house and see the men unload that car," proposed Esther Wakefield. And so it was agreed.

"Tra la la!" hummed Victoria. "O girls, why didn't we stay and finish singing that glee? It was so pretty! Listen. Is this right?" and she hummed it over again.

"Yes, it was too bad to have to tear ourselves away from that dear piano," said Ruth Summers. "Say, Hazel, what are you going to do with your poor despised organ? Send it to a home missionary?"

"I'll send it somewhere, I suppose. I don't know anyone around here to give it to. I wish I could send it where it would give pleasure to someone."

"There are probably plenty of people who would be delighted with it if you only knew them. The owner of this forlorn furniture, for instance," said Victoria as they separated to thread their way between boxes and chairs that had been shoved out on the platform from a half-emptied freight-car. "Girls, just look at that funny old stove and those uncomfortable chairs! How would you like to set up housekeeping with that?"

1

"The couch isn't so bad if it were covered," said Hazel, poking it in a gingerly way with her gloved finger. "It looks as though it might have been comfortable once."

"That's Hazel all over!" said Esther. "If it were possible, she would just enjoy having that couch stay over a train or two while she re-covered it with some bright denim, and make a pillow for it;" and clear girlish laughter rang out, while Hazel's cheeks grew pink as she joined in.

"Well, girls, wouldn't that be interesting? Just think how pleased the dear old lady who owns it would be when she found the new cover, and how entirely mystified."

"You might send her your organ," suggested Ruth Summers. "Perhaps she would like that just as well."

"What a lovely idea!" said Hazel, her eyes shining with enthusiasm. "I'll just do it. Come, let's look for the address."

"You romantic little goose!" exclaimed her friends. "Take her away! The perfect idea! I just believe she would!"

"Of course I would," said Hazel; "why shouldn't I? Papa said I might do as I please with it. Here; this is a card behind here. Read it. 'Christie W. Bailey, Pine Ridge, Fla.' Girls, I shall *do* it. Who has a pencil? I want to write it down. Do all these things belong to the same person? Look on their cards. She must be very poor."

"Poor as a church mouse," said Victoria, "if this is all she has."

"I should like to inquire how you are so sure it is a 'she,' " said Emily Whitten; " 'Christie' sounds as though it might belong to a man or a boy. Don't you think so, Victoria?"

"It's an old colored mammy, I'm positive," said Victoria.

"I don't care," said Hazel of the firm mouth. "If they are black people they will enjoy it all the more. Black people are fond of music, and it will be a real help for the little children. But I don't believe Christie is an old mammy at all. She is a girl about our own age. She has had to go to Florida on account of her health, and she is poor, too poor to board; so she will keep house in a room or two," — waving her hand toward the unpretentious huddling of furniture about them, — "and perhaps she teaches school. She will put the organ in the schoolroom, or have a Sunday school in her own home, and I shall write her a note and send some music for the children to learn. She can do lots of nice things with that organ."

"Now, Hazel," protested five voices, but just then the shriek of a whistle brought them all about face and flying down the platform to reach the station before the train drew up. In the bustle of welcoming the newcomer Hazel's scheme was forgotten, and not until when in the evening they were seated about the great open fire did it again come into the conversation. It was Victoria Landis who told the newcomer about it, beginning with: "O Marion, you can't think what Hazel's latest wild scheme of philanthropy is."

But Marion, a girl after Hazel's own heart, listened with glowing eyes.

"Really, Hazel?" she said when the tale was finished, looking at her hostess with sympathy. "Won't that be just lovely! You must send it in time for Christmas, you know; and why not pack a box to go with it? We could all help. It would be great fun, and give us something to do not entirely selfish while we are enjoying ourselves here."

"Do you mean it?" said Victoria. "Well, I will not be outdone. I will give a covering for that old couch, and Ruth shall make a most bewildering sofa pillow for it, the like of which was never seen in any house in Florida. What color shall it be, blue or red? And will denim be fine enough, or do you prefer tapestry or brocatelle? Speak out, Hazel; we're with you hand and heart, no matter how wildly you soar this time."

And so amid laughter and jokes the plan grew.

"I have a lot of singing-books, if you think there is really a chance of a Sunday school," said Esther.

"There must be something pretty for the house, a good picture perhaps," mused Ruth Summers; and Hazel's eyes grew bright with joy as she looked from one face to another and saw that they really meant what they said.

Six pairs of hands can do much in four days; and, when the guests left for their various homes or schools, there stood on the back porch of the old stone house on the hill a well-packed box marked and labelled, an organ securely boxed, and a large roll, all bearing the magic sentence, "Christie W. Bailey, Pine Ridge, Fla."

There had been much discussion and argument on the part of Mrs. Winship and her husband. They were inclined to think Hazel had outdone herself in romance this time, though they were well used to such unprecedented escapades from her babyhood; but she had finally won them all over, had explained how the goods had been put off at that particular freight-station from up the branch road, to be put on the through freight at the Junction, had enlarged upon the desolateness of the life of that young girl who was moving to Florida alone, until every member of the party became infected with pity for her, and vied with the others to make that Christmas box the nicest ever sent to a girl.

They began to believe in "Christie," and to wonder whether her name was Christine or Christiana, or simply Christie after some family name;

and gradually all thought of her being other than a young girl faded from their minds.

Mother Winship had so far forgotten her doubts as to contribute a good Smyrna rug no more in use in the stone house, after the party had gone down to the freight-house and watched the goods repacked in another freight-car for the Junction, and come back with the report that there was not a sign of a carpet in the lot. They also told how they had peeked through the crack of a box of books and distinctly seen the worn cover of an arithmetic, which proved the "school-ma'am theory," while an old blue-checked apron, visible through another crack, settled the sex of Christie irrevocably.

Hazel Winship had written a long letter in her delicate tracery on her finest paper, and sealed it with a prayer, and had gone back to her college duties a hundred miles away, and Christmas was fast coming on as the three freight pieces started on their way.

On the edge of a clearing, where the tall pines thinned against the sky, and tossed their garlands of gray moss from bough to bough, there stood a little cabin built of logs. It was set up on stilts out of the hot white sand, and, underneath, a few chickens wandered aimlessly, as unaware of the home over their heads as mortals are of the heaven above them. Some sickly orange-trees, apparently just set out, gave the excuse for the clearing, and beyond the distance stretched away into desolateness and black-jack oaks.

A touch of whitewash here and there and a bit of grass — which in that part of the world is so scarce that it is usually used for a path instead of being a setting for that path — would have done wonders for the place, but there was nothing but the white, neglected, "mushy" sand, discouraging alike to wheel and foot.

Inside the cabin there was a rusty cook-stove, and a sulky tea-kettle at the back and the remains of a meal in a greasy frying-pan still over the dead fire. An old table was drawn out with one leaf up and piled with un-washed dishes, boxes of crackers, and papers of various eatables. The couch in the corner was evidently the only bed, and the red and gray blankets still lay in the heap where they had been tossed when the occupant arose that morning. From some nails in the corner hung several articles of clothing and a hat. The corner by the door was given over to tools and a few garden implements which were considered too good to leave out-of-doors. Every chair but one was occupied by books or papers or clothing.

Outside the back door a dry-goods box by the pump with a tin basin and a cake of soap did duty as a wash-stand. On the whole, it was not an attractive home, even though sky and air were more than perfect.

The occupant of this residence was driving dully along the sand road at the will of a stubborn little Florida pony, which wriggled his whole body with a motion intended to convey to his driver the idea that he was trotting as fast as any reasonable being could expect a horse to go, while in reality the monotonous sand and scrub-oaks were moving past as slowly as was possible.

It was the day before Christmas, but the driver did not care. What was Christmas to one whose friends were all gone, and who never gave or received a Christmas gift?

The pony, like all slow things, got there at last, and came trotting up to the post-office in good style. The driver got out of the shackly wagon, and went into the post-office, which served also as general store.

"Hollo Chris!" called a sickly looking man from the group on the counter. "Bin a-wonderin' when you was comin.' Got some moh freight fer yoh oveh to the station."

The newcomer turned his broad shoulders about, and faced the speaker.

"I haven't any more freight coming," he said. "It's all come three weeks ago."

"Well, but it's oveh theh," insisted the other, "three pieces. Your name mahked plain same like the otheh."

"Somebody sent you a Christmas gift, Chris," said a tall young fellow, slapping him on the shoulder, "better go and get it."

Chapter 2

A Christmas Box That Didn't Match

The young man, still insisting that the freight was not his, followed the agent reluctantly over to the station, accompanied by several of his companions, who had nothing better to do than to see the joke out.

There it was, a box, a bundle, and a packing-case, all labelled plainly and most mysteriously, "Christie W. Bailey, Pine Ridge, Fla."

The man who owned the name could scarcely believe his eyes. He knew of no one who would send him anything. An old neighbor had forwarded the few things he had saved from the sale of the old farm after his father and mother died, and the neighbor had since died himself; so this could not be something forgotten.

He felt annoyed at the arrival of the mystery, and did not know what to do with the things, but at last brought over the wagon and reluctant pony, and with the help of the other men got them loaded on, the pony meanwhile eying his load with dislike and meditating how slow he could make his gait on account of his burden.

Christie Bailey did not wait at the store that night as long as he usually did. He had intended going home by moonlight, but decided to try to make it before the sun went down. He wanted to understand about the freight at once. He found when he went back to the post-office that he could not sit with the same pleasure on a nail-keg and talk as usual. His mind was on the wagon-load. He bought a few things, and started home.

The sun had brought the short winter day suddenly to a close, as it has a habit of doing in Florida, by dropping out of sight and leaving utter darkness with no twilight.

Christie lighted an old lantern, and got the things into the cabin at once. Then he took his hatchet and screw-driver, and set to work.

First the packing-case, for he instinctively felt that herein lay the heart of the matter. But not until he had taken the entire front off the case and taken out the handsome organ did he fully realize what had come to him.

More puzzled than ever, he stood back with his arms folded, and whistled. He saw the key attached to a card, and, unlocking the organ, touched gently one of the ivory keys with his rough finger, as one might touch a being from another world.

6

Then he glanced about to see where he should put it; and suddenly, even in the dull, smoky lamplight, the utter gloom and neglect of the place burst upon him. Without more ado he selected the freest side of the room, and shoved everything out of the way.

Then he brought a broom and swept it clean. After that he set the organ against the wall, and stood back to survey the effect. The disorderly table and the rusty stove were behind him, and the organ gave the spot a strange, cleared-up appearance.

He did not feel at home. He turned to the confusion behind him. Something must be done before he opened anything more. He felt somehow as if the organ was a visitor, and must not see his poor housekeeping.

He seized the frying-pan, scraped the contents into the yard, and called the dog. The dishes he put into a wooden tub outside the door, and pumped water over them. Then the mass of papers and boxes on table and chairs he piled into the darkest corner on the floor, straightened the row of boots and shoes, and, having done all that he could, he came back to the roll and box still unopened.

The roll came first. He undid the strings with awkward fingers, and stood back in admiration once more when he brought to light a thick, bright rug and a Japanese screen.

He spread the rug down, and puzzled some time over the screen, as to its use, but finally stood it up in front of the worst end of the room and began on his box.

There, at last, on the top was a letter in a fine, unknown hand. He opened it slowly, the blood mounting into his face, he knew not why, and read:

"Dear Christie: — You see I am so sure you are a girl of my own age that I have concluded to begin my letter informally, and wish you a very merry Christmas and a glad, bright New Year. Of course you may be an old lady or a nice, comfortable, middle-aged one; and then perhaps you will think we are very silly; but we hope and believe you are a girl like ourselves, and so our hearts have opened to you, and we are sending you some things for Christmas."

There followed an account of the afternoon at the freight-station, written in Hazel's most winning way, in which the words and ways and almost the voices and faces of Victoria Landis and Ruth and Esther and Marion and all the rest were shadowed forth.

The color on the young man's face deepened as he read, and he glanced up uneasily at his few poor chairs and miserable couch; then before he read further he went and pulled the screen along to hide more of the confusion.

He read the letter through, his heart waking up to the world and to long-ings he had never known he possessed before, — to the world in which Christmas has a place and in which young, bright life gives forth glad im-pulses; read to the end even, where Hazel inscribed her bit of a sermon full of good wishes and a little tender prayer that the spirit of Christmas might reign in that home and that the organ might be a help and a blessing to all around.

There was a pitiful look of almost helpless misery on the young man's face when he had finished. The good old times when God had been a re-ality were suddenly brought into his reckless, isolated life, and he knew that God was God, even though he had neglected Him so long, and that to-morrow was Christmas Day.

As a refuge from his own thoughts he turned back to the brimming box.

The first article he took out was a pair of dainty knit lavender bedroom slippers with black and white ermine edges and delicate satin bows. Emily Whitten's aunt had knit them for her to take to college with her; and, Emily's feet being many sizes smaller than her aunt supposed, she had never worn them, and had tucked them in at the last minute to make a safe resting-place for a delicate glass vase, which she said would be lovely to hold flowers, on the organ, Sundays.

They had written their nonsense thoughts on bits of labels all over the things, these gay young girls; and the young man read and smiled, and finally laughed aloud. He felt like a little boy just opening his first Christmas stocking.

He unpinned the paper on the couch-cover, and read in Victoria's large, stylish, angular hand full directions for putting it on the couch. He glanced with a twinge of shame at the old lounge, and realized that these gay girls had seen all his shabby belongings and pitied him, and he half-resented the whole thing, until the delight of being pitied and cared for overcame his bitterness, and he laughed again.

Green, soft and restful, had been chosen for the couch-cover; and it could not have fitted better if Victoria Landis had secretly had a tape-measure in her pocket and measured the couch, which perhaps she did on her second trip to the freight-house.

Ruth Summers had made the pillows — there were two of them, and they were large and comfortable and sensible, of harmonizing greens and browns and a gleam of gold here and there.

With careful attention to the directions, the new owner arrayed his old lounge, and placed the pillows as directed, "with a throw and a pat, not *laid* stiffly," from a postscript in Ruth's clear feminine hand. Then he stood back in awe that a thing so familiar and so ugly could suddenly assume such an air of ease and elegance. Would he ever be able to bring the rest of the room up to the same standard?

But the box invited further investigation. There was a bureau set of dainty blue and white, a cover for the top and a pincushion to match. There were also a few yards of the material and a rough sketch with directions for a possible dressing-table, to be made of a wooden box in case Christie had no bureau.

It was from Emily Whitten, and she said she could not remember seeing a bureau among the things, but she was sure any girl would know how to fix one up, and perhaps be glad of some new fixings for it.

At these things the young man looked helplessly, and finally went out into the moonlight, and hunted up an old box which he brushed off with the broom and brought inside, where he clumsily spread out the blue and white frills over its splintery top, and then solemnly tried to stick a pin into the cushion, fumbling in the lapel of his coat for one.

He was growing more and more bewildered with his new possessions, and as each came to light he began to wonder how he was going to be able to entertain and keep up to such a lot of fineries.

Mother Winship had put in a gay knit afghan which looked well over the couch, and next came a layer of Sunday-school singing-books, a Bible, and some lesson leaves. A card said that Esther Wakefield had sent these and she hoped they would be a help in the new Sunday school.

There followed a roll of blackboard cloth, a large cloth map of Palestine, and a box of chalk; and the young man grew more and more helpless. This was worse than the bureau set and the slippers. What was he to do with them all? *He* start a Sunday school! He would be much more likely to start children in the opposite way from heaven if he went on as he had been going the last two years.

His face hardened, and he was almost ready to sweep the whole lot back into the box, nail them up, and send them back where they came from. What did he want of a lot of trash with a set of such burdensome obligations attached?

But curiosity made him go back to see what there was left in the box, and a glance around his room made him unwilling to give up all this luxury.

He looked curiously at the box of fluffy lace things with Marion Halstead's card lying atop. He could only guess that they were some girl's fixings, and he wondered vaguely what he should do with them. Then he unwrapped a photograph of the six girls which had been hurriedly taken and was inscribed, "Guess which is which," with a list of their names written on a circle of paper like spokes to a wheel.

He studied each face with interest, and somehow it was for the writer of the letter that he sought, Hazel Winship. And he thought he should know her at once.

This was going to be very interesting. It would while away some of the long hours when there was nothing worth while to do, and keep him from thinking how long it took orange groves to pay, and what hard luck he had always had.

He decided at first glance that the one in the centre with the clear eyes and firm, sweet mouth was the instigator of all this bounty; and, as his eyes travelled from one face to another and came back to hers each time, he felt more sure of it. There was something frank and pleasant in her gaze. Somehow it would not do to send that girl back her things and tell her he was in no need of her charity. He liked to think she had thought of him, even though she did think of him as a poor discouraged girl or an old mammy.

He stood the picture up against the lace of the pincushion, and forever gave up the idea of trying to send those things back.

There seemed to be one thing more in the bottom of the box, and it was fastened inside another protecting board. He took it at last from its wrappings — a large picture, Hofmann's head of Christ, framed in broad dark Flemish oak to match the tint of the etching.

Dimly he understood who was the subject of the picture, although he had never seen it before. Silently he found a nail and drove it deep into the log of the wall. Just over the organ he hung it, without the slightest hesitation. He had recognized at once where this picture belonged, and knew that it, and not the bright rug, nor the restful couch, nor the gilded screen, nor even the organ itself, was to set the standard henceforth for his home and his life.

He knew this all in an undertone, without its quite coming to the surface of his consciousness. He was weary by this time, with the unusual excitement of the occasion, and much bewildered. He felt like a person suddenly lifted up a little way from the earth and obliged against his will to walk along unsupported in the air.

His mind was in a perfect whirl. He looked from one new thing to another, wondering more and more what they expected of him. The ribbons and lace of the bureau fixings worried him, and the lace collars and pincushion. What had he to do with such? Those foolish little slippers mocked him with a something that was not in his life, a something for which he was not even trying to fit himself. The organ and the books and, above all, the picture seemed to dominate him and demanded of him things which he could never give. A Sunday school! Whan an absurdity! He!

And the eyes in the picture seemed to look into his soul, and to say, all quietly enough, that He had come here now to live, to take command of his home and its occupant.

He rebelled against it, and turned away from the picture. He seemed to hate all the things, and yet the comfort of them drew him irresistibly.

In sheer weariness at last he put out his light, and, wrapping his old blankets about him, lay down upon the rug; for he would not disturb the couch lest the morning should dawn and his new dream of comfort look as if it had fled away. Besides, how was he ever to get it together again? And, when the morning broke and Christie awoke to the splendor of his things by daylight, the wonder of it all dawned, too, and he went about his work with the same spell still upon him.

Now and again he would raise his eyes to the pictured Christ and drop them again, reverently. It seemed to him this morning as if that Presence were living and had come to him in spite of all his railings at fate, his bitterness and scoffing, and his feckless life. It seemed to say with that steady gaze: "What will you do with me? I am here, and you cannot get away from my drawing."

It was not as if his life had been filled formerly with tradition and teaching; for his mother had died when he was a little fellow, and the thin-lipped, hard-working maiden aunt who had cared for him in her place, whatever religion she might have had in her heart, never thought it necessary to speak it out beyond requiring a certain amount of decorum on Sunday and regular attendance at Sunday school.

In Sunday school it had been his lot to be under a good elder who read the questions from a lesson leaf and looked helplessly at the boys who were employing their time in more pleasurable things the while. The very small amount of holy things he had absorbed from his days at Sunday schools had failed to leave him with a strong idea of the love of God or any adequate knowledge of the way to be saved.

In later years, of course, he had listened listlessly to preaching; and, when he went to college — a small, insignificant one, — he had come in contact with religious people; but here, too, he had heard as one hears a thing in which one has not the slightest interest.

He had gathered and held this much, that the God in whom the Christian world believed was holy and powerful, and that most of the world were culprits. Heretofore God's love had passed him by unaware.

Now the pictured eyes of the Son of God seemed to breathe out tenderness and yearning. For the first time in his life a thought of the possibility of love between his soul and God came to him.

His work that morning was much more complicated than usual. He wasted little time in getting breakfast. He had to clean house. He could not bear the idea that the old regime and the new should touch shoulders as they did behind that screen. So with broom and scrubbing-brush he went to work.

He had things in pretty good shape at last, and was just coming in from giving the horse a belated breakfast when a strange impulse seized him.

At his feet, creeping all over the white sand in delicate tracery, were wild pea blossoms, crimson, white, and pink. He had never noticed them before. What were they but weeds? But with a new insight into possibilities in art, he stooped and gathered a few of them, and, holding them awkwardly, went into the house to put them into his new vase. He felt half-ashamed of them, and held them behind him as he entered; but with the shame there mingled an eagerness to see how they would look in the vase on the "blue bureau thing."

   " 'Will you walk into my parlor?'
    Said the spider to the fly,
    'Tis the prettiest little parlor
    That ever you did spy,' "

sang out a rich tenor voice in greeting.

"I say, Chris! What are you setting up for? What does it all mean? Ain't going to get married or nothing, are you, man? because I'll be obliged to go to town and get my best coat out of pawn if you are."

"Aw, now that is gweat!" drawled another voice, English in its accents. "Got anything good to dwink? Twot it out, and we'll be better able to appweciate all this lugshuwy!"

Chapter 3
"And What
Are You Going to Say to Her?"

The young man felt a rising tendency to swear. He had forgotten all about the fellows and their agreement to meet and have the day out in jollification. So great had been the spell upon him that he had forgotten to put the little feminine things away from curious eyes.

There he stood foolishly in the middle of his own floor, a bunch of "weeds" in his hand which he had not the sense to drop, while afar the sound of a cracked church bell gave a soft reminder, which the distant popping of firecrackers at a cabin down the road confirmed, that this was Christmas Day. Christmas Day, and the face of the Christ looking down at him tenderly from his own wall.

The oath that was rising to his lips at his foolish plight was stayed. He could not take that name in vain with those eyes upon him. The spell was not broken even yet.

With a sudden quick settling of his lips, he threw back his head, daring in his eyes, and walked over to the glass vase to fill it with water. It was like him to brave it out and tell the whole story now that he was caught.

He was a broad-shouldered young man, firmly knit, with a head well set on his shoulders, and but for a certain careless slouch in his gait might have been fine to look upon. His face was not handsome, but he had good brown eyes with deep hazel lights in them that kindled when he looked at you.

His hair was red, deep and rich, and decidedly curly. His gestures were strong and regular. If there had not been a certain hardness about his face he would have been interesting, but that look made one turn away disappointed.

His companions were both big men like himself. The Englishman — one of that large class of second or third sons with a good education and a poor fortune, and very little practical knowledge how to better it, so many of whom come to Florida to try orange-growing — was loose-jointed and awkward, with pale blue eyes, hay-colored hair, and a large jaw with loose lips. The other was handsome and dark, with a weak mouth and daring black eyes which continually warred with one another.

13

Both were dressed in rough clothes, trousers tucked into boots with spurs, dark flannel shirts, and soft riding-hats. The Englishman wore gloves and affected a certain loud style in dress. They carried their riding-whips, and walked undismayed upon the bright colors of the rug.

"O, I say now, get off there with those great clods of boots, can't you?" exclaimed Christie, with a sudden descent of housewifely carefulness. "Anybody'd think you'd been brought up in a barn, Armstrong."

Armstrong put on his eye-glasses, — he always wore them as if they were a monocle, — and examined the rug carefully.

"Aw, I beg pawdon! Awfully nice, ain't it? Sorry I didn't bwing my patent leathers along. Wemind me next time, please, Maw-timer."

Christie told the story of his Christmas gifts in as few words as possible. Somehow he did not feel like elaborating it.

The guests seized upon the photograph of the girls, and became hilarious over it.

"Takes you for a girl, does she?" said Mortimer. "That's great! Which one is she? I choose that fine one with snapping black eyes and handsome teeth. She knew her best point, or she wouldn't have laughed when her picture was taken."

Victoria Landis's eyes would have snapped indeed, could she have heard the comments upon herself and the others; but she was safe out of hearing, far up in the North.

The comments went on most freely. Christie found himself disgusted with his friends. Only yesterday he would have laughed at all they said, and now what made the difference? Was it that letter? Would the other fellows feel the same if he should read it to them?

But he never would! The red blood stole up in his face. He could hear their shouts of laughter now over the tender little girlish phrases. It should not be desecrated. He was glad indeed that he had put it in his coat pocket the night before.

There seemed to be a sacredness about the letter and the pictures and all the things, and it went against the grain to hear the coarse laughter of his friends.

At last they began to speak about the girl in the centre of the group, the clear-eyed, firm-mouthed one whom he had selected for Hazel. His blood boiled. He could stand it no longer. With one sweep of his long, strong arm he struck the picture from them with "Aw, shut up! You make me tired!" and, picking it up, put it in his pocket.

Whereat the fun of his companions took a new turn. It suited their fancy to examine the toilet-table decked out in blue and lace. The man named

Mortimer knew the lace collars and handkerchiefs for woman's attire, and they turned upon their most unwilling host and decked him in fine array.

He sat helpless and mad, with a large lace collar over his shoulders, and another hanging down in front arranged over the bureau-cover, which was spread across him as a background, while a couple of lace-bordered handkerchiefs adorned his head.

"And what are you going to say to her for all these pretty presents, Christie, my girl?" laughed Mortimer.

"Say to her!" gasped Christie.

It had not occurred to him before that it would be necessary to say anything. A horrible oppression seemed to be settling down upon his chest. He wished that the whole array of things were back in their boxes and on their way to their ridiculous owners. He got up, and kicked at the rug, and tore the lace finery from his neck, stumbling on the lavender bedroom slippers which his tormentors had stuck on the toes of his shoes.

"Why, certainly, man, — I beg your pardon, — *my dear girl* —" went on Mortimer. "You don't intend to be so rude as not to reply, or say, 'I thank you very kindly'!"

Christie's thick auburn brows settled into a scowl, and the attention of the others was drawn to the side of the room where the organ stood.

"That's awfully fine, don't you know?" remarked Armstrong, levelling his eye-glasses at the picture. "It's by somebody gweat, I dawn just wemembah who."

"Fine frame," said Mortimer tersely as he opened the organ and sat down before it.

And the new owner of the picture felt for the first time in his acquaintance with those two men that they were somehow out of harmony with him.

He glanced up at the picture with the color mounting in his face, half pained for the friendly gaze that had been so lightly treated. He did not in the least understand himself.

But the fingers touching the keys now were not altogether unaccustomed. A soft, sweet strain broke through the room, and swelled louder and fuller until it seemed to fill the little log house and be wafted through the open windows to the world outside.

Christie stopped in his walk across the room, held by the music. It seemed the full expression of all he had thought and felt during the last few hours.

A few chords, and the player abruptly reached out to the pile of singing-books above him, and, dashing the book open at random, began playing, and in a moment in a rich, sweet tenor sang. The others drew near, and each took a book and joined in.

> "He holds the key of all unknown,
>   And I am glad;
> If other hands should hold the key,
> Or if He trusted it to me,
>   I might be sad."

The song was a new creed spoken to Christie's soul by a voice that seemed to fit the eyes in the picture. What was the matter with him? He did not at all know. His whole life seemed suddenly shaken.

It may be that the fact of his long residence alone in that desolate land, with but few acquaintances, had made him more ready to be swayed by this sudden stirring of new thoughts and feelings. Certain it was that Christie Bailey was not acting like himself.

But the others were interested in the singing. It had been long since they had had an instrument to accompany them, and they enjoyed the sound of their own voices. They would have preferred, perhaps, a book of college songs, or, better still, the latest street songs; but, as they were not at hand, and "Gospel Hymns" were, they found pleasure even in these.

On and on they sang, through hymn after hymn, their voices growing stronger as they found pieces which had in them some hint of familiarity.

The music filled the house, and floated out into the bright summer Christmas world outside; and presently Christie felt rather than saw a movement at the window, and, looking up, beheld it dark with little, eager faces of the black children. Their supply of firecrackers having given out, they had sought for further celebration, and had been drawn with delight by the unusual sounds. Christie dropped into a chair and gazed at them in wonder, his eyes growing troubled and the frown deepening. He could not make it out. Here he had been for some time, and these little children had never ventured to his premises. Now here they were in full force, their faces fairly shining with delight, their eyes rolling with wonder and joy over the music.

It seemed a fulfilment of the prophecy of the letter that had come with the organ. He began to tremble at the thought of the possibilities that might be entailed upon him with his newly acquired and unsought-for property. And yet he could not help a feeling of pride that all these things were his and that a girl of such evident refinement and cultivation had taken the trouble to send them. To be sure, she wouldn't have done it at all if she had had any idea who or what he was, but that did not matter. She did not know, and she never would know.

He saw the children's curious eyes wander over the room and rest here and there delighted, and his own eyes followed theirs. How altogether nice it was! What a desolate hole it had been before! How was it he had not noticed?

Amid all these thoughts the concert came suddenly to a close. The organist turned upon his stool, and, addressing the audience in the window, remarked, with a good many flourishes: "That finishes the programme for to-day, dear friends. Allow me to announce that a Sunday school will be held in this place on next Sunday afternoon at half-past two o'clock, at which you are all invited to be present. Do you understand? Half-past two. And bring your friends. Now will you all come?"

Amid many a giggle and a bobbing of round black heads they answered as one boy and one girl, "Yes, sah!" and went rollicking down the road in haste to spread the news, their bare feet flying through the sand, and vanished as they had come.

Chapter 4

"A Letter That Wrote Itself"

"What did you do that for?" thundered Christie, suddenly realizing what would be the outcome of this performance.

"Don't speak so loud, Christie, dear; it isn't ladylike, you know. I was merely saving you the trouble of announcing the services. You'll have a good attendance, I'm sure, and we'll come and help you out with the music," said Mortimer in a sweetly unconscious tone.

Christie came at him with clenched fist, which he laughingly dodged, and went on bantering. But the two young men soon left, for Christie was angry and was not good company. They tried to coax him off to meet some of their other boon companions, but he answered shortly, "No," and they left him to himself.

Left alone, he was in no happy frame of mind. He had intended to go with them. There would be something good to eat, and of course something to drink, and cards, and a jolly good time all around. He could forget for a little while his hard luck, and the slowness of the oranges, and his own wasted life, and feel some of the joy of living. But he had the temper that went with his hair, and now nothing would induce him to go.

Was it possible there was something else, too, holding him back? A subtle something which he did not understand, somehow connected with the letter and the picture and the organ?

Well, if there was, he did not stop to puzzle it out. Instead, he threw himself down on the newly arrayed couch, and let his head sink on one of those delightfully soft pillows, and tried to think.

He took out the letter, and read it over again.

When he read the sentences about praying for him, there came a choking sensation in his throat such as he had not felt since the time he nearly drowned, and realized that there was no mother any more to go to. This girl wrote as a mother might perhaps talk, if one had a mother.

He folded the letter, and put it back in his pocket; and then, closing and locking the door, he sat down at the organ and tried to play it.

As he knew nothing whatever about music, he did not succeed very well, and he turned from it with a sigh to look up at those pictured eyes once more and find them following his every movement. Some pictures have that power of seeming to follow one around the room.

Christie got up and walked away, still looking at the picture, and turned and came back again.

Still the eyes seemed to remain upon his face with that strong, compelling gaze. He wondered what it meant, and yet he was glad it had come. It seemed like a new friend.

Finally he sat down and faced the question that was troubling him. He must write a letter to that girl — to those girls, and he might as well have done with it at once and get it out of the way. After that he could feel he had paid the required amount, and could enjoy his things. But it simply was not decent not to acknowledge their receipt. But the tug of war was to know how to do it.

Should he confess that he was a young man and not the Christie they had thought, and offer to send back the things for them to confer upon a more worthy subject?

He glanced hastily about on his new belongings with sudden dismay. Could he give up all this? No. He would not.

His eyes caught the pictured eyes once more. He had found a friend and a little comfort. It had come to him unbidden. He would not bid it depart.

Besides, it would only make those kind people most uncomfortable. They would think they had been doing something dreadful to send a young man presents, especially one whom they had never seen. He knew the ways of the world, a little. And that Hazel Winship who had written the letter, she was a charming person. He would not like to spoil her pretty dream of his being a friendless girl. Let her keep her fancies; they could do no harm.

He would write and thank her as if he were the girl they all supposed him. He had always been good at playing a part or imitating any one; he would just write the letter in a girlish hand — it would not be hard to do — and thank them as they expected to be thanked by another girl. That would be the end of it. Then, when his oranges came into bearing, — if they ever did, — he would send them each a box of oranges anonymously, and all would be right.

As for that miserable business Mortimer had got him into, he would fix that up by shutting up the house and riding away early Sunday morning, and the children might come to Sunday school to their hearts' content. He would not be there to be bothered or bantered.

In something like a good humor he settled to his task.

He wrote one or two formal notes, and tore them up. As he looked about on the glories of his room, he began to feel that such thanks were inadequate to express his feelings. Then he settled to work once more, and began to be interested.

"My dear unknown Friend," he wrote, "I scarcely know how to begin to thank you for the kindness you have showered upon me."

He read the sentence over, and decided it sounded very well and not at all as if a man had written it. The spirit of fun took possession of him, and he made up his mind to write those girls a good long letter, and tell them all about his life, only tell it just as if he were a girl. It would while away this long, unoccupied day. He wrote on:

"You wanted to know all about me; so I am going to tell you. I do not, as you suppose, teach school. I had a little money from the sale of father's farm after he died, and I put it into some land down here planted to young orange-trees. I had heard a great deal about how much money was to be made in orange-growing, and thought I would like to try it. I am all alone in the world — not a soul who cares in the least about me, and so there was no one to advise me against it.

"I came down here and boarded at first, but found it would be a good thing for me to live among my trees, so I could look after things better; so I had a little cabin built of logs right in the grove, and sent for all the old furniture that had been saved from the old home, which was not much, as most things had been sold with the house. You saw how few and poor they were.

"It seems so strange to think that you, who evidently have all the good things of the world to make you happy, should have stopped to think and take notice of poor, insignificant me. It is wonderful, more wonderful than anything that ever happened to me in all my life. I look about on my beautified room, and cannot believe it is I.

"I live all alone in my log cabin, surrounded by a lot of young trees which seem to me very slow in doing anything to make me rich. If I had known all I know now, I never would have come here; but one has to learn by experience, and I'll just have to stick now until something comes of it.

"I am not exactly a girl just like yourselves as you say; for I am twenty-eight years old, and, to judge by your pictures, there isn't one of you as old as that. You are none of you over twenty-two, I am sure, if you are that.

"Besides, you are all beautiful girls, while I most certainly am not. To begin with, my hair is red, and I am brown and freckled from the sun and wind and rain; and, in fact, I am what is called homely. So you see it is not as serious a matter for me to live all alone down here in an orange-grove as it would be for one of you. I have a strong little pony who carries me on his back or in my old buckboard, and does the ploughing. What work I cannot do myself about the grove, I hire done, of course. I also have a few chickens and a dog.

"If you could have seen my little house the night your boxes arrived and were unpacked, you would appreciate the difference the things you have sent make in my surroundings. But you can never know what a difference they will make in my life."

Here the rapid pen halted, and the writer wondered whether that might be a prophecy. So far, he reflected, he had written nothing but what was strictly true; and yet he had not made known his identity.

This last sentence seemed to be writing itself, for he really had no idea that the change in his room would make much difference in his life, except to add a little comfort. He raised his eyes; and, as they met those in the picture, it seemed to be forced upon him that there was to be a difference, and somehow he was not sorry. The old life was not attractive, but he wondered what it would be. He felt as if he were standing off watching the developments in his own life as one might watch the life of the hero in a story.

There was one more theme in Hazel Winship's letter which he had not touched upon, he found, after he had gone over each article by name and said nice things about them all and what a lot of comfort he would have from them.

He was especially pleased with his sentence about the bedroom slippers and lace collars. "They are much too fine and pretty to be worn," he had written, "especially by such a large, awkward person as I am; but I like to feel them and see them, and think how pretty they would look on some of the dainty, pretty girls who sent them to me."

But all the time he was reading his letter over he felt that something would have to be said on that other subject. At last he started it again:

"There is a cabin down the road a little way, and this morning a friend of mine came in and played a little while on the organ — I can't play myself, but I am going to learn" — he had not thought about learning before, but now he knew he should — "and we all got to singing out of the books you sent. By and by I looked up, and saw the doorway full of little ragamuffins listening for all they were worth. I presume I shall be able to give them a good deal of pleasure listening to that organ sometimes, though I am afraid I wouldn't be much of a hand at starting a Sunday school" — that sentence sounded rather mannish for a girl of twenty-eight; but he had to let it stand, as he could think of nothing better to say — "as I never knew much about such things. Though I'm obliged for your praying, I'm sure. It will give me a pleasant feeling at night when I'm all alone to know some one in the world is thinking about me, and I'm sure if prayers can do any good yours ought to.

"But about the Sunday school, I don't want to disappoint you after you've been so kind to send all the papers and books. Maybe I could give the black children some of the papers, and let them study the lessons out for themselves; and I used to be quite a hand at drawing once. I might practise up and draw them some pictures to amuse them sometime when they come around again. I'll do my best.

"I like to think of you all at college having a good time. My school days were the best of my life. I wish I could go over them again. I have a lot of books; but, when I come in tired at night, it seems so lonely here, and I'm so tired I just go to sleep. It doesn't seem to make much difference about my reading any more, anyway. The oranges won't know it. They grow just as soon for me as if I kept up with the procession.

"I appreciate your kindness, though I don't know how to tell you how deeply it has touched me. I have picked out the one in the middle, the girl with the laughing eyes, and a sweet, firm mouth, and the loveliest expression I ever saw on any face, to be Miss Hazel Winship, the one who thought of this whole beautiful plan. Am I right? I'll study the others up later.

"Yours very truly —" here he paused, and, carefully erasing the last word, wrote "lovingly,"

                                                    "Christie W. Bailey."

He sat back, and covered his face with his hands. A queer, glad feeling had come over him while he was writing those things about Hazel Winship. He wondered what it was. He actually enjoyed saying those things to her and knowing she would be pleased to read them, and not think him impertinent.

And he had written a good many promises, after all. What led him on to that? Did he mean to keep them? Yes, he believed he did; only those fellows, Armstrong and Mortimer, should not know anything about it. He would carry out his plan of going away Sundays until those ridiculous fellows forgot their nonsense. And, so thinking, he folded and addressed his letter.

A little more than a week later six girls gathered in a cosy college room — Hazel's — to hear the letter read.

"You see," said Hazel, with triumphant light in her eyes, "I was right; she is a girl like us. It doesn't matter in the least little bit that she is twenty-eight. That isn't old. And for once I am glad you see that my impulses are not always crazy. I am going to send this letter home at once to father and mother. They were really quite troublesome about this. They thought it was the wildest thing I ever did, and I've been hearing from it all vacation. Now listen!"

And Hazel read the letter amid many interruptions.

"I'll tell you what it is, girls," she said, as she finished the letter; "we must keep track of her now we've found her. I'm so glad we did it. She isn't a Christian, that's evident; and we must try to make her into one, and work through her a Sunday school. That would be a work worth while. Then maybe sometime we can have her up here for a winter, and give her a change. Wouldn't she enjoy it? It can't be this winter, because we'll have to work so hard here in college we'd have no time for anything else; but after we have all graduated wouldn't it be nice? I'll tell you what I'd like to do; I'd like the pleasure of taking Christie Bailey to Europe. I know she would enjoy it. Just think what fun it would be to watch her eyes shine over new things. I don't mind her red hair one bit. Red-haired people are lovely if they know how to dress to harmonize with their complexions."

"How fortunate we used green for that couch-cover! Christie's hair will be lovely against it," murmured Victoria, in a serio-comic tone, while all the girls set up a shout at Hazel's wild flights of fancy.

"Take Christie Bailey to Europe! O, Hazel! I'm afraid you will be simply dreadful, now you have succeeded in one wild scheme. You will make us do all sorts of things, and never stop at reason."

Hazel's cheeks flushed. It always hurt her a little that these girls did not go quite as far in her philanthropic ideas as she did herself. She had quite taken this Christie girl into her heart, and she wanted them all to do the same.

"Well, girls, you must all write to her, anyway, and encourage her. Think what it would be to be down there, a girl, all alone, and raising oranges. I think she is a hero!"

"O, we'll all write, of course," said Victoria, with mischief in her eye; "but call her a heroine, do, Hazel."

And they all did write, letters full of bright nonsense, and sweet, tender, chatty letters, and letters full of girlish pity, attempts to make life more bearable to the poor girl all alone down in Florida. But a girl who confesses to being homely and red-haired and twenty-eight cannot long hold a prominent place in the life of any but an enthusiast such as Hazel was, and very soon the other five letters dropped off, and Christie Bailey was favored with but one correspondent from that Northern college.

But to return to Florida. That first Sunday morning after Christmas, everything did not go just as was planned by Christie.

In the first place, he overslept. He had discovered some miserable scales on some of his most cherished trees, and he had had to trudge to town Saturday morning, — the man was using the pony ploughing, — and get some whale-oil soap, and then spend the rest of the day until dark spraying his trees. It was no wonder that he was too tired to wake early the next day.

Then, when he finally went out to the pony, he discovered that he was suffering from a badly cut foot, probably the result of the careless hired man and a barbed-wire fence. The swollen foot needed attention.

The pony made comfortable, he reflected on what he would do next. To ride on that pony away anywhere was impossible. To walk he was not inclined. The sun was warm for that time of year, and he still felt stiff from his exertions of the day before. He concluded he would shut up the house, and lie down, and keep still when any one came to call, and they would think him away.

With this purpose in view he gave the pony and the chickens a liberal supply of food, that he need not come out again till evening, and went into the house; but he had no more than reached there when he heard a loud knocking at the front door, evidently with the butt end of a whip; and before he could decide what to do it was thrown open, and Mortimer and Armstrong entered, another young Englishman following close behind. Armstrong wore shiny patent-leather shoes, and seemed anxious to make them apparent.

"Good mawning, Miss Bailey," he said, affably. "Glad to see you looking so fresh and sweet. We just called round to help you pwepare for your little Sunday school."

Chapter 5
A Sunday School in Spite of Itself

Christie was angry. He stood still, looking from one to another of his three guests like a wild animal at bay. They knew he was angry, and that fact contributed not a little to their enjoyment. They meant to carry out the joke to the end.

The third man, Rushforth by name, stood grinning at the rear of the other two. The joke had been so thoroughly explained to him that he could fully appreciate it. He was not noted for being quick at a joke. Armstrong, however, seemed to have a full sense of the ridiculous.

Firmly and cheerfully they took their way with Christie; and he, knowing that resistance was futile, sat down upon his couch in glum silence, and let them work their will.

"I stopped on the way over, and reminded our friends in the cabin below that the hour was two-thirty," remarked Mortimer, as he took a large dinner-bell from his side pocket and rang a note or two. "That's to let them know the time when we are ready to 'take up.' "

Christie scowled, and the others laughed uproariously.

"Now, Armstrong, you and I will go out and reconnoitre for seats, while Rushforth stays here and helps this dear girl dust her parlor ornaments and brickbats. We'll need plenty of seats, for we'll have quite a congregation if all I've asked turn out."

They came back in a few minutes laden with boxes and boards which they ranged in three rows across the end of the cabin facing the organ.

Christie sat and glared at them.

He was very angry, and was trying to think whether to bear it out and see what they would do next, or run away to the woods. He had little doubt that if he should attempt the latter they would all three follow him, and perhaps bind him to a seat to witness the performances they had planned; for they were evidently "taking it out of him" for having all this luxury and not taking them into the innermost confidences of his heart about it.

He shut his teeth and wondered what Hazel would say if she knew how outrageously her idea of a Sunday school was going to be burlesqued.

Armstrong tacked up the blackboard, and got out the chalk. Then,

25

discovering the folded cloth map of the Holy Land, he tacked that up at the end wall where all could see it. Mortimer mapped out the programme.

"Now, Rushforth, you pass the books and the lesson leaves, and I'll stay at the organ and preside. Miss Christie's a little shy about speaking out to-day, you see, and we'll have to help her along before we put her in the superintendent's place. Christie, you can make some pictures on the blackboard. Anything'll do. This is near Christmas — you can make Santa Claus coming down the chimney if you like. I'll run the music, and we'll have quite a time of it. We'll be able to tell the fellows all about it down at the lake next week, and I shouldn't wonder if we'd have a delegation over from Mulberry Creek next Sunday to hear Elder Bailey speak — I beg pardon; I mean Miss Bailey. You must excuse me, dear; on account of your freckles I sometimes take you for a man."

Mortimer spread open a Bible that had come with the singing-books, and actually found the place in the lesson leaf, and made them listen while he read, and declared that Christie ought to give a talk on the lesson. And thus they carried on their banter the whole morning long.

Christie sat glowering in the corner.

He could not make up his mind what to do. For some strange reason he did not want a Sunday school caricatured in his house and with that picture looking down upon it all, and yet he did not know why he didn't want it. He had never been squeamish before about such things. The fellows would not understand it, and he did not understand it himself. But it went against the grain.

Now as it came on about dinner-time he thought they would perhaps go if he offered no refreshments; but no; they seemed to have no such idea. Instead, they sent Armstrong outside to their light wagon they had tied at the tree by the roadside, and he came back laden with a large basket which they proceeded to unpack.

There were canned meats and jellies and pickles and baked beans and all sorts of canned goods that have to be substituted for the genuine article in Florida, where fresh meat and vegetables are not always to be had.

Armstrong went out again, and this time came back with a large case of bottles.

He set it down with a thump on the floor just opposite the picture, while he shut the door. The clink of the bottles bespoke a hilarious hour, and carried memories of many a time of feasting in which Christie had participated before.

His face crimsoned as if some honored friend had suddenly been brought to look upon the worst of his hard, careless life, and he suddenly rose with determination. Here was something which he could not stand.

He drank sometimes, it is true. The fellows all knew it. But both he and they knew that the worst things they had ever done in their lives had been done and said under the influence of liquor. They all had memories of wild debauches of several days' duration, when they had been off together and had not restrained themselves. Each one knew his own heart's shame after such a spree as this. Each knew the other's shame. They never spoke about it, but it was one of the bonds that bound them together, these drunken riots of theirs, when they put their senses at the service of cards and wine, and never stopped until the liquor had given out. At such times each knew that he would have sold his soul for one more penny to stake at the game, or one more drink, had the devil been about in human form to bid for it.

They were none of them drunkards, few of them even constant drinkers, partly because they had little money to spend in such a habit. They all had strong bodies able to endure much, and their life out-of-doors did not tend to create unnatural cravings of appetite. Rather had they forced themselves into these revelries as a means of amusing themselves in a land where there was little but work to fill up the long months and years of waiting.

This case of liquor was not the first that had been in Christie's cabin. He had never felt before that it was out of place in entering there; but now the picture hung there, and the case of liquor, representing the denial of God, seemed to Christie a direct insult to the One whose presence had in a mysterious way crept into the cabin with the picture.

Also he saw in a flash what the fellows were planning to do. They knew his weakness. They remembered how skilled his tongue was in turning phrases when loosened by intoxicants. They were planning to get him drunk — perhaps had even drugged some of the bottles slightly — and then to make him talk, and even pray, it might be!

At another time this might have seemed funny to him. He had not realized before how far he had been going in the way from truth and righteousness. But now his whole soul rose up in loathing of himself, his ways, and his companions.

A sentence of his mother's prayer for him when he was but a little child that had not been in his mind for years now came as clear as if a voice had spoken in his ear, "God make my little Chris a good man!"

And this was how it had been answered. Poor mother!

What Hazel Winship would think of the scene also flashed into his mind. He strode across that room in his angry strength before his astonished companions could stop him; and, taking that case of liquor in his muscular arms, he dashed it far out the open door across the road and into the woods. Then he turned back to the three amazed men.

"You won't have any of that stuff in here!" he said firmly. "If you're bound to have a Sunday school, a Sunday school we'll have; but we won't have any drunken men at it. Perhaps you enjoy mixing things up that way, but I'm not quite a devil yet."

They had not known there was such strength in him. He looked fairly splendid as he stood there in the might of right, his deep eyes glowing darker brown and every mahogany curl a-tremble with determination.

"Aw! Certainly! Beg pawdon!" said Armstrong, settling his eye-glasses that he might observe his former friend more closely. "I meant no hawm, I'm suah." Armstrong was always polite. If an earthquake had thrown him to the ground, he would have arisen and said, "Aw! I beg pawdon!"

But Christie was master in his own house. The others exclaimed a little, and tried to joke him upon his newly acquired temperance principles; but he would not open his lips further on the subject, and they ate their canned meats and jellies and bread moistened only by water from Christie's pump in the yard.

They had scarcely finished when the first instalment of the Sunday school arrived in faded but freshly starched calicoes laundered especially for the occasion. They pattered to the door barefooted, clean, and shining, followed by some of their elders, who lingered smiling and shy at the gateway, uncertain whether to credit the invitation to "Mr. Christie's" cabin. Mr. Christie had never been so hospitable before. But the children, spying the rudely improvised benches, crept in, and the others followed.

Christie stood scowling in the back end of the cabin. Sunday school was on his hands. He could not help it any more than he could help the coming of the organ and the picture. It was a part of his new possessions.

He felt determined that it should not be a farce. How he was going to prevent it he did not know, but he meant to do it.

He looked up at the picture again. It seemed to give him strength. Of course it was but fancy that it had seemed to smile approval after he had flung that liquor out the door; but in spite of his own reason he could not but feel that the Man of the picture was enduring insult here in his house, and that he must fight for His sake.

Added to that was Hazel Winship's faith in him and her desire for a Sunday school. His honor was at stake. He would never have gone out and gathered up a Sunday school to nurse into life, even for Hazel Winship. Neither would he have consented to help in one if his permission had been asked; but now, when it was, as it were, thrust upon him, like a little foundling child all smiling and innocent of possible danger to it, what could he do but help it out?

They were all seated now, and a hush of expectancy pervaded the room.

The three conspirators over by the organ were consulting and laughing in low tones.

Christie knew that the time had come for action. He raised his eyes to the picture once more. To his fancy the eyes seemed to smile assurance to him as he went forward to the organ.

Christie quietly took up a singing-book, and, opening at random, said, "Let us sing number one hundred and thirty-four." He was surprised when they began to sing to find it was the same song that Mortimer had sung first on Christmas morning.

His three friends turned in astonishment toward him. They began to think he was entering into the joke like his own old self, but instead there was a grave, earnest look on his face they had never seen there before.

Mortimer put his fingers on the keys, and began at once. Christie seemed to have taken the play out of their hands and turned the tables upon them. They began to wonder what he would do next. This was fine acting on his part, they felt, for him to take the predicament in which they had placed him and work it out in earnest.

The song was almost finished, and still Christie did not know what to do next.

He announced another hymn at random, and watched old Aunt Tildy settle her steel-bowed spectacles over her nose and fumble among the numbers. The Sunday school was entering into the music with zest. The male trio who led were singing with might and main, but with an amused smile on their faces as if they expected developments soon.

Just then an aged black man came hobbling in. His hair and whiskers were white, and his worn Prince Albert coat ill fitted his bent figure; but there was a clerical manner which clung to the old coat and gave Christie hope. When the song was finished, he raised his eyes without any hesitation and spoke clearly.

"Uncle Moses," he said, "we want to begin right, and you know all about Sunday schools; can't you give us a start?"

Uncle Moses slowly took off his spectacles, and put them carefully away in his pocket while he cleared his throat.

"I ain't much on speechifyin', Mistah Bailey," said he; "but I kin pray. 'Kase you see when I's talkin' to God den I ain't thinkin' of my own sinful, stumblin' speech."

The choir did not attempt to restrain their risibles, but Christie was all gravity.

"That's it, Uncle. That's what we need. You pray." It came to him to wonder for an instant whether Hazel Winship was praying for her Sunday school then, too.

All during the prayer Christie wondered at himself. He conducting a religious service in his own house and asking somebody to pray! And yet, as the trembling, pathetic sentences rolled out, he felt glad that homage was being rendered to the Presence that seemed to have been in the room ever since the picture came.

"O our Father in heaven, we is all poh sinnahs!" said Uncle Moses, earnestly, and Christie felt it was true, himself among the number. It was the first prayer that the young man ever remembered to have felt all the way through. "We is all sick and miserable with the disease of sin. We's got it *bad,* Lord" — here Christie felt the seat behind him shake. Mortimer was behaving very badly. "But, Lord," went on the quavering old voice, "we know dere's a remedy. Away down in Palestine, in de Holy Land, in an Irish shanty, was where de fust medicine-shop of de world was set up, an' we been gettin' de good ob it eber sence. O Lord, we praise thee to-day for de little chile dat lay in dat manger a long time ago, dat brung de fust chance of healing to us poh sinners —"

Mortimer could scarcely contain himself, and the two Englishmen were laughing on general principles. Christie raised his bowed head, and gave Mortimer a warning shove, and they subsided somewhat; but the remarkable prayer went on to its close, and to Christie it seemed to speak a new gospel, familiar, and yet never comprehended before. Could it be that these poor, ignorant people were to teach him a new way?

By the time the prayer was over, he had lost his trepidation. The spirit of it had put a determination into him to make this gathering a success, not merely for the sake of foiling his tormentors, but for the sake of the trusting, childlike children who had come there in good faith.

He felt a little exultant thrill as he thought of Hazel Winship and her commission. He would try to do his best for her sake to-day at least, whatever came of it in future. Neither should those idiots behind him have a grand tale of his breaking down in embarrassment to take away to the fellows over at the lake.

Summoning all his daring, he gave out another hymn, which happened fortunately to be familiar to the audience, and to have many verses; and he reached for a lesson leaf.

O, if his curiosity had but led him to examine the lesson for to-day, or any lesson, in fact! He must say something to carry things off, and he must have a moment to consider. The words swam before his eyes.

He could make nothing out of it all.

Dared he ask one of the fellows to read the Scripture lesson while he prepared his next line of action?

He looked at them. They were an uncertain quantity, but he must have time to think a minute. Armstrong was the safest. His politeness would hold him within bounds.

When the song finished, he handed the leaflet to Armstrong, saying, briefly, "You read the verses, Armstrong."

Armstrong in surprise answered, "Aw, certainly," and adjusting his eye-glasses, began, "Now when Jesus was bawn in Bethlehem —"

"Hallelujah!" interjected Uncle Moses, with his head thrown back and his eyes closed. He was so happy to be in a meeting once more.

"Aw! I beg pahdon, suh! What did you say?" said Armstrong, looking up innocently.

This came near to breaking up the meeting, at least, the white portion of it; but Christie, a gleam of determination in his eye because he had caught a little thread of a thought, said gruffly: "Go on, Armstrong. Don't mind Uncle Moses."

When the reading was over, Christie, annoyed by the actions of his supposed helpers, seized a riding-whip from the corner of the room and came forward to where the map of Palestine hung. As he passed his three friends, he gave them such a glare that instinctively they crouched away from the whip, wondering whether he were going to inflict instant punishment upon them. But Christie was only bent on teaching the lesson.

"This is a map," he said. "How many of you have ever seen a map of Florida?"

Several children raised their hands.

"Well, this isn't a map of Florida; it's a map of Palestine, that place that Uncle Moses spoke about when he prayed. And Bethlehem is on it somewhere. See if you can find it anywhere. Because that's the place that the verses that were just read tell about."

Rushforth suddenly roused to helpfulness. He espied Bethlehem, and at the risk of a cut with the whip from the angry Sunday-school superintendent he came forward and put his finger on Bethlehem.

Christie's face cleared. He felt that the waters were not quite so deep, after all. With Bethlehem in sight and Aunt Tildy putting on her spectacles, he felt he had his audience. He turned to the blackboard.

"Now," said he, taking up a piece of yellow chalk, "I'm going to draw a star. That was one of the first Christmas things that happened about that time. While I'm drawing it, I want you to think of some of the other things the lesson tells about; and, if I can, I'll draw them."

The little heads bobbed eagerly this side and that to see the wonder of a star appear on the smooth black surface with those few quick strokes.

"I reckon you bettah put a rainbow up 'bove de stah, fer a promise," put in old Uncle Moses, " 'cause the Scripture say somewhere, 'Where is de promise of His comin'?' An' de rainbow is His promise in de heavens."

"All right," said Christie, breathing more freely, though he did not quite see the connection. And soon a rainbow arch glowed at the top over the star. Then began to grow desire to see this and that thing drawn, and the scholars, interested beyond their leader's wildest expectations, called out: "Manger, wise men! King!"

Christie stopped at nothing from a sheep to an angel. He made some attempt to draw everything they asked for.

And his audience did not laugh. They were hushed into silence. Part of them were held in thrall by overwhelming admiration for his genius, and the other part by sheer astonishment. The young men, his companions, looked at Christie with a new respect, and gazed gravely from him to a shackly cow, which was intended to represent the oxen that usually fed from the Bethlehem manger, and wondered. A new Christie Bailey was before them, and they knew not what to make of him.

For Christie was getting interested in his work. The blackboard was almost full, and the perspiration was standing out on his brow and making little damp, dark rings of the curls about his forehead.

"There's just room for one more thing. What shall it be, Uncle Moses?" he said as he paused. His face was eager and his voice was interested.

"Better write a cross down, sah, 'cause dat's de reason for dat baby's comin' into dis world. He came to die to save us all."

"Amen!" said Aunt Tildy, wiping her eyes and settling her spectacles for the last picture, and Christie turned with relief back to his almost finished task. A cross was an easy thing to make.

He built it of stone, massive and strong; and, as its arms grew, stretched out to save, something of its grandeur and purpose seemed to enter his mind and stay.

"Now let's sing 'Rock of Ages,' " said Uncle Moses, closing his eyes in a happy smile, and the choir hastily found it and began.

As the Sunday school rose to depart, and shuffled out with many a scrape and bow and admiring glance backward at the glowing blackboard, Christie felt a hand touch his arm; and, glancing down, he saw a small girl with great, dark eyes set in black fringes gazing up at the picture above the organ, her little bony hand on his sleeve.

"Is dat man yoh all's fader?" she asked him, timidly.

A great wave of color stole up into Christie's face.

"No," he answered. "That is a picture of Jesus when He grew up to be a man."

"O!" gasped the little girl, in admiration, "did you done draw dat? Did you all evah see Jesus?"

The color deepened.

"No, I did not draw that picture," said Christie; "it was sent a present to me."

"O," said the child, disappointed, "I thought you'd maybe seed Him sometime. But He look like you, He do. I thought He was you all's fader."

The little girl turned away, but her words lingered in Christie's heart. His Father! How that stirred some memory! His Father in heaven! Had he perhaps spoken wrong when he claimed no relationship with Jesus, the Christ?

Chapter 6
"My Father!"

The three young men who had come to play a practical joke had stayed to clear up. Gravely and courteously they had gone about the work, had piled the hymn-books neatly on top of the organ, and placed the boards and boxes away under the house for further use if needed, for the entire Sunday school had declared, upon leaving the house with a bow and a smile, "I'll come again next Sunday, Mistah Christie; I'll come *every* Sunday." And Christie had not said them nay.

The young men had bade a quite good evening to their host, not once calling him "Miss Christie," had voted the afternoon a genuine success, and were actually gone.

Christie sank to the couch, and looked into the eyes looking down upon him.

He was tired. O, he was more tired than he had ever been in his life before! He was so tired he would like to cry. And the pictured eyes seemed yearning to comfort him.

He thought of the words of the little black girl. "Is dat man you's fader?"

"My Father!" he said aloud. "My Father!" The words echoed with a pleasant ring in the little silent, lonely room. He did not know why he said it, but he repeated it again.

And now if the traditions of his childhood had been filled with the Bible, a host of verses would have flocked about him; but, as his mind had not been filled with holy things, he had it all to learn, and his ideas of the Man, Christ Jesus, were of the vaguest and crudest. And perhaps, as to the children of old, God was speaking directly to his heart.

Christie lay still and thought. Went over all his useless life, and hated it; went over the past week with its surprises, and then over the strange afternoon. His own conduct seemed to him the most surprising, after all. Now why, just *why,* had he thrown that case of liquor out of the door, and why had he gone ahead with that Sunday school? There was a mysterious power at work within him. Was the secret the presence of the Man of the picture?

The sun dropped over the rim of the flat, low horizon, and left the pines looming dark against a starry sky. All the earth went dark with night. And Christie lay there in the quiet darkness, yet not alone. He kept thinking over what the little girl had said to him, and once again he said it out loud in the hush of the room, "My Father!"

But, as the darkness grew deeper, there seemed to be a luminous halo up where he knew the picture hung, and while he rested there with closed eyes he felt that presence growing brighter. Those kind eyes were looking down upon him out of the dark of the room.

This time he called, "My Father!" with recognition in his voice, and out from the shadows of his life the Christ stepped nearer till He stood beside the couch, and, stooping, blessed him, breathed His love upon him, while he looked up in wonder and joy. And, perhaps because he was not familiar with the words of Christ, the young man was unable to recall in what form those precious words of blessing had fallen upon his ear during the dream, or trance, or whatever it might be, that had come upon him.

When the morning broke about him, Christie, waking, sat up and remembered, and decided that it must have been a dream induced by the unusual excitement of the day before; yet there lingered with him a wondrous joy for which he could not account.

Again and again he looked at the picture reverently, and said under his breath, "My Father."

He began to wonder whether he was growing daft. Perhaps his long loneliness was enfeebling his mind that he was so susceptible to what he had always considered superstition; nevertheless, it gave him joy, and he finally decided to humor himself in this fancy. This was the permission of his old self toward the new self that was being born within him.

He went about his work singing.

> "He holds the key of all unknown,
>   And I am glad —"

"Well, I *am* glad!" he announced aloud, as if some one had disputed the fact he had just stated. "About the safest person to hold the key, after all, I guess;" and even as a maiden might steal a glance to the eyes of her lover, so the soul in him glanced up to the eyes of the picture.

The dog and the pony rejoiced as they heard their master's cheery whistle, and Christie felt happier that day than he had since he was a little boy.

Towards night he grew quieter. He was revolving a scheme. It would be rather interesting to write out an account of the Sunday school, not, of course, the part the fellows had in it, for that must not be known, but just the pleasant part, about Uncle Moses and Aunt Tildy. He would write it to Hazel Winship, — not that it was likely he would ever send it, but it would be pleasant work to pretend to himself he was writing her another letter. He had not enjoyed anything for a long time as much as he enjoyed writing that letter to her the other day.

Perhaps after a long time, if she ever answered his letter, — and here he suddenly realized he was cherishing a faint hope in his heart that she would answer it, — he might revise this letter and send it to her. It would please her to know he was trying to do his best with a Sunday school for her, and she would be likely to appreciate some of the things that had happened. He would do it; he would do it this very evening.

He hurried through his day's work with a zest. There was something to look forward to in the evening. It was foolish, perhaps, but surely no more foolish than his amusements the last four years had been. It was innocent, at least, and could do no one any harm.

Then, as he sat down to write, he glanced instinctively to the picture. It still wove its spell of the eyes about him, and he had not lost the feeling that Christ had come to him, though he had never made the slightest attempt or desired to come to Christ. And under the new influence he wrote his thoughts, as one might wing a prayer, scarce believing it would ever reach a listening ear, yet taking comfort in the sending. And so he wrote:

"*My dear new Friend:* — I did not expect to write to you again; at least, not so soon; for it seems impossible that one so blessed with this world's good things should have time to care to think twice of one like me. I do not even know now whether I shall ever send this when it is written, but it will while away my lonely evening to write, and give me the pleasure of a little talk with a companion whom I much appreciate, and if I never send it, it can do no harm.

"It is about the Sunday school. You know I told you I could never do anything like that; I did not know how; and I never dreamed that I could — or would, perhaps I ought to say — more than to give the negroes the papers you sent and let them hear the organ sometimes. But a very strange thing has happened. A Sunday school has come to me in spite of myself.

"The friend who was playing the organ this Christmas morning, when the black children stood at the door listening, in jest invited them to a Sunday school, and they came. I was vexed because I did not know what to do with them. Then, too, the friend came, bringing two others; and they all thought it was a huge joke. I saw they were going to act out a farce; and, while I never had much conscience about these things before, I seemed to know that it would not be what you would like. Then, too, that wonderful picture that you sent disturbed me. I did not like to laugh at religion with that picture looking on.

"You may perhaps wonder at me. I do not understand myself, but that picture has had a strange effect upon me. It made me do a lot of things Sunday that I did not want to do. It made me take hold and do something to make that Sunday school go right. I didn't know how in the least. Of course I've been to Sunday school; I did not mean that; but I never took much notice of things, how they were done; and I was not one to do it, anyway. I felt my unfitness dreadfully, and all the more because those friends of mine were here, and I knew they were making fun. I made them sing a lot, and then I asked old Uncle Moses to help us out. I wish I could show you Uncle Moses."

Here the writer paused, and seemed to be debating a point a moment, and then rapidly wrote:

"I'll try to sketch him roughly."

There followed a spirited sketch of Uncle Moses with both hands crossed atop his heavy cane, his benign chin leaning forward interestedly. One could fairly see how yellow with age were his whitened locks, how green with age his ancient coat. Christie had his talents, though there were few outlets for them.

It is of interest to note just here that, when this letter reached the Northern college, as it did one day, those six girls clubbed together, and laughed and cried over the pictures, and finally, after due council, Christie Bailey was offered a full course in a famous woman's college of art. This he smiled over and quitely declined, saying he was much too old to begin anything like that, which required that one should begin at babyhood to accomplish anything by it. This the girls sighed over and argued over, but finally gave up, as they found Christie wouldn't.

But to return to the letter. Christie gave a full account of the prayer, which had touched his own heart deeply. Then he described and sketched Aunt Tildy with her spectacles. He had a secret longing to put in Armstrong with his glasses and the incident of his interruption with the Bible-reading; but, as that would reflect somewhat upon his character as an elderly maiden, to be found consorting with three such young men, he restrained himself. But he put an extra vigor into the front row of little black heads, bobbing this way and that, singing with might and main.

"I knew they ought to have a lesson next, but I didn't know how to teach it any better than I know how to make an orange-tree bear in a hurry. However, I determined to do my best. I happened to remember there had been something said in what was read about a star; so I made one, and told them each to think of something they had heard about in that lesson that they wanted me to draw. That worked first-rate. They tried everything, pretty near, in the encyclopaedia, and I did my best at each till the whole big blackboard was full. I wish you could see it. It looks like a Noah's ark hanging up there on the wall now, for I have not cleaned it off yet. I keep it there to remind me that I really did teach a Sunday-school class once.

"When they went away, they all said they were coming again, and I don't doubt they'll do it. I'm sure I don't know what to do with them if they do, for I've drawn all there is to draw; and, as for teaching them anything, they can teach me more in a minute than I could teach them in a century. Why, one little child looked up at me with her big, round, soft eyes, for all the world like my faithful dog's eyes, so wistful and pretty, and asked me if that picture on the wall was my father.

"I wish I knew more about that picture. I know it must be meant for Jesus Christ. I am not quite so ignorant of all religion as not to see that. There is the halo with the shadow of the cross above His head. And, when the sun has almost set, it touches there, and the halo seems to glow and glow almost with phosphorescent light until the sun is gone and leaves us all in darkness; and then I fancy I can see it yet glow out between the three arms of the cross.

"And now I do not know why I am writing this. I did not mean to do so when I began, but I feel as if I must tell of the strange experience I had last night."

And then Christie told his dream. Told it till one reading could but feel as he felt, see the vision with him, yearn for the blessing, and be glad and wonder always after.

"Tell me what it means," he wrote. "It seems as if there was something in this presence for me. I cannot believe that it is all imagination, for it would leave me when day comes. It has set me longing for something, I know not what. I never longed before, except for my oranges to bring me money. When I wanted something I could not have, heretofore, I went and did something I knew I ought not, just for pleasure of doing wrong, a sort of defiant pleasure. Now I feel as if I wanted to do right, to be good, like a little child coming to its father. I feel as if I wanted to ask you, as that little soul asked me yesterday, 'Do you all's know that Man?' "

Christie folded his letter, and flung it down upon the table with his head upon his hands. With the writing of that experience the strength seemed to have gone out of him. He felt abashed in its presence. He seemed to have avowed something, to have made a declaration of desire and intention for which he was hardly ready yet; and still he did not want to go back. He was like a man groping in the dark, not knowing where he was, or whether there was light, or whether indeed he wanted the light if there was any to be had.

But before he retired that night he dropped upon his knees beside his couch, with bowed and reverent head, and after waiting silently awhile he said aloud, "My Father!" as if he were testing a call. He repeated it again, more eagerly, and a third time, with a ring in his voice, "My Father!"

That was all. He did not know how to pray. His soul had grown no farther than just to know how to call to his Father, but it was enough. A kind of peace seemed to settle down upon him, a feeling that he had been heard.

Once more there came to him a knowledge that he was acting out of all reason, and he wondered whether he could be losing his mind. He, a redhaired, hard-featured orange-grower, who but yesterday had carried curses so easily upon his lips, and might again to-morrow, to be allowing his emotions thus to carry him away! It was simply childish!

But so deep was the feeling that a Friend was near, that he might really say, "My Father," if only to the dark, that he determined to keep up the hallucination, if indeed hallucination it was, as long as it would last. And so he fell asleep again to dream of benediction.

And on the morrow a sudden desire took him to mail that letter he had written the night before. And what harm, since he would never see the girl, and since she thought him a poor, forlorn creature — half daft this letter might prove him; but even so she might write him again, which result he found he wanted very much when he came to think about it; and so without giving himself a chance to repent by rereading it he drove the limping pony to town and mailed it.

Now, as it came on toward the middle of the week, a conviction suddenly seized Superintendent Christie Bailey that another Sunday was about to dawn and another time of trial would perhaps be his. He had virtually bound himself to that Sunday school by the mailing of that foolish letter. He could have run away if it had not been for that, and those girls up North would never have bothered their heads any more about their old Sunday school. What if Mortimer should bring the fellows over from the lake? What if! Oh, horror! His blood froze in his veins.

Chapter 7
"I Love You"

After his supper that night he doggedly seized the lesson leaf, and began to study. He read the whole thing through, hints and suggestions and elucidations and illustrations and all, and then began over again.

At last it struck him that the hints for the infant class would about suit his needs, and without further ado he set himself to master them. Before long he was interested as a child in his plans, and the next evening was spent in cutting out paper crosses as suggested in the lesson, one for every scholar he expected to be present, and lettering them with the golden text.

He spent another evening still in making an elaborate picture on the reverse side of the blackboard, to be used at the close of his lesson after he had led up to it by more simple work on the other side.

He even went so far as to take the hymn-book and select the hymns, and to write out a regular programme. No one should catch him napping this time. Neither should the prayer be forgotten. Uncle Moses would be there, and they could trust him to pray.

Christie was a little anxious about his music, for upon that he depended principally for success. He felt surprised over himself that he so much wished to succeed, when a week ago he had not cared. What would he do, though, if Mortimer did not turn up, or, worse still, if he had planned more mischief?

But the three friends appeared promptly on the hour, gravity on their faces and helpfulness in the very atmosphere that surrounded them. They had no more practical jokes to play. They had recognized that for some hidden reason Christie meant to play this thing out in earnest, and their liking and respect for him were such that they wanted to assist in the same spirit.

They liked him none the less for his prompt handling of the case of liquors. They carried a code of honor in that colony that respected moral courage when they saw it. Besides, everybody liked Christie.

They listened gravely to Christie's lesson, even with interest. They took their little paper crosses, and studied them curiously, and folded them away in their breast pockets, — Armstrong had passed them about, being careful to reserve three for himself, Mortimer, and Rushforth, — and they sang with a right good will.

40

And, when the time came to leave, they shook hands with Christie like the rest, and without the least mocking in their voices said they had had a pleasant time and they would come again. Then each man took up a box and a board, and stowed them away as he passed out.

And thus was Christie set up above the rest to a position of honor and respect. This work that he had taken up — that they had partly forced him to take up — separated him from them somewhat, and perhaps it was this fact that Christie had to thank afterward for his freedom from temptation during those first few weeks of the young man's acquaintance with his heavenly Father.

For how would it have been possible for him to grow into the life of Christ if he had been constantly meeting and drinking liquor with these boon companions?

The new life could not have grown with the old.

Christie's action that first Sunday afternoon had made a difference between him and the rest. They could but recognize it, and they admired it in him; therefore they set him up. What was there for Christie but to try to act up to his position?

Before the end of another week there arrived from the North a package of books and papers and Sunday-school cards and helps such as would have delighted the heart of the most advanced Sunday-school teacher of the day. What those girls could not think of, the head of the large religious bookstore to which they had gone thought of for them, and Christie had food for thought and action during many a long, lonely evening.

And always these evenings ended in his kneeling in the dark, where he fancied the light of Christ's halo in the picture could send its glow upon him, and saying aloud in a clear voice, "My Father," while outside in the summer-winter night was only the wailing of the tall pines as they waved weird fingers dripping with gray moss, or the plaintive call of the tit-willow, through the night.

There had come with the package, too, a letter for Christie. He put it in his breast pocket with glad anticipation, and hustled that pony home at a most unmerciful trot; at least, so thought the pony.

When Hazel Winship read that second letter aloud to the other girls, she did not read the whole of it. The pages which contained the sketches she passed about freely, and they read and laughed over the Sunday school, and talked enthusiastically of its future; but the pages which told of the Sabbath-evening vision and of Christie's feeling toward the picture Hazel kept to herself.

She felt instinctively that Christie would rather not have it shown. It seemed so sacred to her and so wonderful. Her heart went out to the other soul seeking its Father.

When they were all gone out of her room that night, she locked her door and knelt a long time praying, praying for the soul of Christie Bailey. Something in the longing of that letter from the South had reproached her, that she, with all her helps to enlightenment, was not appreciating to its full the love and care of her heavenly Father. And so Christie unknowingly helped Hazel Winship nearer to her Master.

And then Hazel wrote the letter, in spite of a Greek thesis, THE thesis in fact, that was waiting and calling to her with urgency — the letter that Christie carried home in his breast pocket.

He did not wait to eat his supper, though he gave the pony his. Indeed, it was not a very attractive function at its best.

Christie was really handsome that night, with the lamplight bringing out all the copper tints and garnet shadows in his hair. His finely cut lips curled in a smile of anticipation. He had not realized before how much, how very much, he wanted to hear from Hazel Winship again.

His heart was thumping like a girl's as he tore open the delicately perfumed envelope and took out the many closely written pages of the letter; and his heart rejoiced that it was long and closely written. He resolved to read it slowly and make it last a good while.

"My dear, dear Christie," it began, "your second letter has come, and first I want to tell you that I *love* you."

Christie gasped, and dropped the sheets upon the table, his arms and face upon them. His heart was throbbing painfully, and his breath felt like great sobs.

When he raised his eyes by and by, as he was growing to have a habit of doing, to the picture, they were full of tears; and they fell and blurred the delicate writing of the pages on the table, and the Christ knew and pitied him, and seemed almost to smile.

No one had ever told Christie Bailey of loving him, not since his mother those long years ago had held him to her breast and whispered to God to make her little Chris a good man.

He had grown up without expecting love. He scarcely thought he knew the meaning of the word. He scorned it in the only sense he ever heard it spoken of. And now, in all his loneliness, when he had almost ceased to care what the world gave him, to have this free, sweet love of a pure-hearted girl rushed upon him without stint and without cause overpowered him.

Of course he knew it was not his, this love she gave so freely and so frankly. It was meant for a person who never existed, a nice, homely old maid, whose throne in Hazel's imagination had come to be located in his cabin for some strange wonderful reason; but yet it was his, too, his to enjoy, for it certainly belonged to no one else. He was robbing no one else to let his hungry heart be filled a little while with the fulness of it.

One resolve he made instantly, without hesitation, and that was that he would be worthy of such love if so be in him it lay to be. He would cherish it as a tender flower that had been meant for another, but had fallen instead into his rough keeping; and no thought or word or action of his should ever stain it.

Then with true knighthood in his heart to help him onward he raised his head and read on, a great joy upon him which almost engulfed him.

"And I believe you love me a little, too."

Christie caught his breath again. He saw that it was true, although he had not known it before.

"Shall I tell you why I think so? Because you have written me this little piece out of your heart-life, this story of your vision of Jesus Christ, for I believe it was such.

"I have not read that part of your letter to the other girls. I could not. It seemed sacred; and, while I know they would have sympathized and understood, yet I felt perhaps you wrote it just to me, and I would keep it sacred for you.

"And so I am sending you this little letter just to speak of that to you. I shall write in my other letter with the rest of the girls, all about the Sunday school, how glad we are, and all about the pictures how fine they are; and you will understand. But this letter is all about your own self.

"I have stopped most urgent work upon my thesis to write this, too; so you may know how important I consider you, Christie. I could not sleep last night, for praying about you."

It was a wonderful revelation to Christie, that story of the longing of another soul that his might be saved. To the lonely young fellow, grown used as he was to thinking that not another one in all the world cared for him, it seemed almost unbelievable.

He forgot for the time that she considered him another girl like herself. He forgot everything save her pleading that he would give himself to Jesus. She wrote of Jesus Christ as one would write of a much-loved friend, met often face to face, consulted about everything in life, and trusted beyond all others.

A few weeks ago this would indeed have been wonderful to the young man, but that it could have any relation to himself — impossible! Now, with the remembrance of his dream, and the joy his heart had felt from the presence of a picture in his room, it seemed it might be true that Christ would love even him, and with so great a love.

The pleading took hold upon him. Jesus was real to this one girl; He might become real to him.

The thought of that girlish figure kneeling beside her bed in the solemn night hours praying for him was almost more than he could bear. It filled him with awe and a great joy. He drew his breath in sobs, and did not try to keep the tears from flowing. It seemed that the fountains of the years were broken up in him, and he was weeping out his cry for the lonely, unloved childhood he had lost, and the bitter years of mistakes that had followed.

It appeared that the Bible had a great part to play in this new life put before him. Verses which he recognized as from the Scripture abounded in the letter, which he did not remember ever to have heard before, but which came to him with a rich sweetness as if spoken just for him.

Did the Bible contain all that? And why had he not known it before? He had gone to other books for respite from his loneliness. Why had he never known that here was deeper comfort than all else could give?

"Think of it, Christie," the letter said; "Jesus Christ would have come to this earth and lived and died to save you if you had been the only one out of the whole earth that was going to accept Him."

He turned his longing eyes to the picture. Was that true? And the eyes seemed to answer, "Yes, Christie, I would."

Before he turned out his light that night he took the Bible from the organ, and, opening at random, read, "For I have loved thee with an ever-lasting love; therefore with loving-kindness have I drawn thee." And a light of belief overspread his face. He could not sleep for many hours, for thinking of it all.

There was no question in his mind of whether he would or not. He felt he was the Lord's in spite of everything else. The loving-kindness that had drawn him had been too great for any human resistance.

Then with the realization of the loving-kindness had come self-reproach for his so long denial and worse than indifference. He did not understand the meaning of repentance and faith, but he was learning them in his life.

Christie was never the same after that night. Something had changed in him. It may have been growing all those days since the things first came, but that letter from Hazel Winship marked a decided epoch in his life. All his manhood rose to meet the sweetness of the girl's unasked prayer for him.

It mattered not that she thought not of him as a man. She had prayed, and the prayer had reached up to heaven and back to him again.

The only touch of sadness about it was that he should never be able to see her and thank her face to face for the good she had done to him. He thought of her as some far-away angel who had stooped to earth for a little while, and in some of his reveries dreamed that perhaps in heaven, where all things were made right, he should know her. For the present it was enough that he had her sweet friendship, and her companionship in writing.

Not for worlds now would he reveal his identity. And the thought that this might be wrong did not enter his mind. What harm could it possibly do? and what infinite good to himself! — and perhaps through himself to a few of those little black children. He let this thought come timidly to the front.

This was the beginning of the friendship that made life a new thing to Christie Bailey. Long letters he wrote, telling the thoughts of his inmost heart as he had never told them to any one on earth, as he would never have been able to tell them to one whom he hoped to meet sometime, as he would have told them to God.

And the college student found time amid her essays and her fraternities to answer them promptly.

Her companions wondered why she wasted so much valuable time on that poor "cracker" girl, as they sometimes spoke of Christie, and how she could have patience to write so long letters; but their curiosity did not go so far as to wonder what she found to say; else they might have noticed that less and less often did Hazel offer to read aloud her letters from the Southland. But they were busy, and only occasionally inquired about Christie now, or sent a message.

Hazel herself sometimes wondered why this stranger girl had taken so deep a hold upon her; but the days went by and the letters came frequently, and she never found herself willing to put one by unanswered. There was always some question that needed answering, some point on which her young convert to Jesus Christ needed enlightenment.

Then, too, she found herself growing nearer to Jesus because of this friendship with one who was just learning to trust Him in so childlike and earnest a way.

"Do you know," she said confidingly to Ruth Summers one day, "I cannot make myself see Christie Bailey as homely? It doesn't seem possible to me. I think she is mistaken. I know I shall find something handsome about her when I see her, which I shall some day."

And Ruth smiled mockingly. "O Hazel, Hazel, it will be better, then, for you never to see poor Christie, I am sure; for you will surely find your ideal different from the reality."

But Hazel's eyes grew dreamy, and she shook her head.

"No, Ruth, I'm sure, sure. A girl couldn't have all the beautiful thoughts Christie has, and not be fine in expression. There will be some beauty in her, I am sure. Her eyes, now, I know are magnificent. I wish she would send me a picture; but she won't have one taken, though I've coaxed and coaxed."

Chapter 8
Sad News From the North

In his own heart-life Christie was changing day by day. The picture of Christ was his constant companion. At first shyly and then openly he grew to make a confidant of it. He studied the lines of the face, and fitted them to the lines of the life depicted in the New Testament, and without his knowing it his own face was changing. The lines of recklessness and hardness about his mouth were gone. The dullness of discontent was gone from his eyes. They could light now from within in a flash with a joy that no discouragement could quite quench.

By common consent Christie's companions respected his new way of life, and perhaps after the first few weeks if he had shown a disposition to go back to the old way of doing might have even attempted to keep him to his new course.

They every one knew that their way was a bad way. Each man was glad at heart when Christie made an innovation. They came to the Sunday school and helped, controlling their laughter admirably whenever Uncle Moses gave occasion; and they listened to Christie's lessons, which, to say the least, were original, with a courteous deference, mingled with a kind of pride that one of their number could do this.

They also refrained from urging him to go with them on any more revellings. Always he was asked, but in a tone that he came to feel meant that they did not expect him to accept, and would perhaps have been disappointed if he had done so.

Once, when Christie, unthinkingly, half-assented to go on an all-day's ride with some of them, Mortimer put his hand kindly on Christie's shoulder, and said in a tone Christie had never heard him use before: "I wouldn't, Chris. It might be a bore."

Christie turned, and looked earnestly into his eyes for a minute, and then said, "Thank you, Mort!"

As he stood watching them ride away, a sudden instinct made him reach his hand to Mortimer, and say, "Stay with me this time, old fellow"; but the other shook his head, smiling somewhat sadly, Christie thought, and said as he rode off after the others, "Too late, Chris; it isn't any use."

Christie thought about it a good deal that day as he went about his grove without his customary whistle, and at night, before he began his evening's reading and writing, he knelt and breathed his first prayer for the soul of another.

The winter blossomed into spring, and the soft wind blew the breath of yellow jessamine and bay blossoms from the swamps. Christie's wire fence bloomed out into a mass of Cherokee roses, and among the glossy orange-leaves there gleamed many a white, starry blossom, earnest of the golden fruit to come.

Christie with throbbing heart and shining eyes picked his first orange-blossoms, a goodly handful, and, packing them after the most approved methods for long journeys, sent them to Hazel Winship.

Never any oranges, be they numbered by thousands of boxes, could give him the pleasure that those first white waxen blossoms gave as he laid his face gently among them and breathed a blessing on the one to whom they went, before he packed them tenderly in their box.

Christie was deriving daily joy now from Hazel Winship's friendship. Sometimes when he remembered the tender little sentences in her letters his heart fairly stood still with longing that she might know who he was and yet be ready to say them to him. Then he would crush this wish down, and grind his heel upon it, and tell his better self that only on condition of never thinking such a thought again would he allow another letter written her, another thought sent toward her.

Then would he remember the joy she had already brought into his life, and go smiling about his work, singing,

> "He holds the key of all unknown,
>   And I am glad."

Hazel Winship spent that first summer after her graduation, most of it, visiting among her college friends at various summer resorts at seaside or on mountain-top. But she did not forget to cheer Christie's lonely summer days — more lonely now because some of his friends had gone North for a while — with bits of letters written from shady nooks on porch or lawn, or sitting in a hammock.

"Christie, you are my safety-valve," she wrote once. "I think you take the place with me of a diary. Most girls use a diary for that. If I was at home with mother, I might use her sometimes; but there are a good many things that if I should write her she would worry, and there really isn't any need, but I could not make her sure. So you see I have to bother you. For instance, there is a young man here —" Christie drew his brows together fiercely. This was a new aspect. There were other young men, then. Of course — and he drew a deep sigh.

It was during the reading of that letter that Christie began to wish there were some way for him to make his real self known to Hazel Winship. He began to see some reasons why what he had done was not just all right.

But there was a satisfaction in being the safety-valve, and there was delight in their trysting-hour when they met before the throne of God. Hazel had suggested this when she first began to try to help Christie Christward; and they had kept it up, praying for this one and that one and for the Sunday school.

Once Christie had dared to think what joy it would be to kneel beside her and hear her voice praying for him. Would he ever hear her voice? The thought had almost taken his breath away. He had not dared to think of it again.

The summer deepened into autumn; and the oranges, a goodly number for the first crop, green disks unseen amid their background of green leaves, blushed golden day by day. And then, just as Christie was beginning to be hopeful about how much he would get for his fruit, there came a sadness into his life that shadowed all the sunshine, and made the price of oranges a very small affair. For Hazel Winship fell ill.

At first it did not seem to be much — a little indisposition, a headache and loss of appetite. She wrote Christie she did not feel well and could not write a long letter.

Then there came a silence of unusual length, followed by a letter from Ruth Summers, at whose home Hazel had been staying when taken ill. It was brief and hurried, and carried with it a hint of anxiety, which, as the days of silence grew into weeks, made Christie's heart heavy.

"Hazel is very ill indeed," she wrote, "but she has worried so that I promised to write and tell you why she had not answered your letter."

The poor fellow comforted himself day after day with the thought that she had thought of him in all her pain and suffering.

He wrote to Ruth Summers, asking for news of his dear friend; but, whether from the anxiety over the sick one, or from being busy about other things, or it may be from indifference, — he could not tell, — there came no answer for weeks.

During this sad time he ceased to whistle. There grew a sadness in his eyes that told of hidden pain, and his cheery ways with the Sunday school were gone.

One day when his heart had been particularly heavy, and he had found the Sabbath-school lesson almost an impossibility, the little dusky girl who had spoken to him before touched him gently on the arm.

"Mistah Christie feel bad? Is somebody you all love, sick?"

Almost the tears filled Christie's eyes as he looked at her in surprise, and nodded his head.

"Youm 'fraid they die?"

Again Christie nodded. He could not speak; something was choking him. The sympathetic voice of the little girl was breaking down his self-control.

The little black fingers touched his hand sorrowfully, and there was in her eyes a longing to comfort, as she lifted them first to her beloved superintendent's face and then to the picture above them.

"But you all's fathah's not dead," she pleaded, shyly.

Christie caught her meaning in a flash, and marvelled afterwards that a child should have gone so directly to the point, where he, so many years beyond her, had missed it. He had not learned yet how God has revealed the wise things of this world unto the babes.

"No, Sylvie," he said quickly, grasping the timid little fingers; "my Father is not dead. I will take my trouble to Him. Thank you."

The smile that broke over the little girl's face as she said good-night was the first ray of the light that began to shine over Christie Bailey's soul as he realized that God was not dead and God was his Father.

When they were all gone, he locked his doors, and knelt before his heavenly Father, pouring out his anguish, praying for his friend and for himself, yielding up his will, and feeling the return of peace, and surety that God doeth all things well. Again as he slept he saw the vision of the Christ bending over him in benediction, and when he woke he found himself singing softly,

> "He holds the key to all unknown,
> And I am glad."

He wondered whether it was just a happening — and then knew that it was not — that Ruth Summer's second letter reached him that day, saying that Hazel was at last past all danger and had spoken about Christie Bailey, and so she, Ruth, had hastened to send the message on, hoping the far-away friend would forgive her for the delay in answering.

After that Christie believed with his whole soul in prayer.

He set himself the pleasant task of writing to Hazel all he had felt and experienced during her illness and long silence. When she grew well enough to write him again, he might send it. He was not sure.

One paragraph he allowed himself, in which to pour out the pent-up feelings of his heart. But even in this he weighed every word. He began to long to be perfectly true before her, and to wish there were a way to tell her all the truth about himself without losing her friendship. This was the paragraph.

"I did not know until you were silent how much of my life was bound up with yours. I can never tell you how much I love you, but I can tell God about it, the God you taught me to love."

The very next day there came a note from Ruth Summers saying that Hazel was longing to hear from Florida again and that she was now permitted to read her own letters. Then with joy he took his letter to the office, and not long after received a little note in Hazel's own familiar hand, closing with the words: "Who knows? perhaps you will be able to tell me all about it some day, after all." And Christie, when he read it, held his hand on his heart to still the tumult of pain and joy.

"Have you written to Christie Bailey that you are coming?" said Victoria Landis, turning her eyes from the window of the drawing-room car, where she was studying the changing landscape, so new and strange to her Northern eyes.

"No," said Hazel, leaning back among her pillows; "I thought it would be more fun to surprise her. Besides, I want to see things just exactly as they are, as she has described them to me, you know. I don't want her to go and get fussed up to meet me. She wouldn't be natural at all if she did. I'm positive she's shy, and I must take her unawares. After I have put my arms around her neck in regular girl fashion and kissed her she will realize that it is just I, the one she has written to for a year, and everything will be all right; but if she has a long time to think about it, and conjure up all sorts of nonsense about her dress and mine, and the differences in our stations, she wouldn't be at all the same Christie. I love her just as she is, and that's the way I mean to see her first."

"I am afraid, Hazel, you'll be dreadfully disappointed," said Ruth Summers. "Things on paper are never exactly like the real things. Now look out that window. Is this the land of flowers? Look at all that blackened ground where it's been burnt over, and see those ridiculous green tufts sticking up every little way, varied by a stiff green palm-leaf, as if children had stuck crazy old fans in a play garden. You know the real is never as good as the ideal, Hazel."

"It's a great deal better," said Hazel positively. "Those green tufts, as you call them, are young pines. Some day they'll be magnificent. Those little fans are miniature palms. That's the way they grow down here. Christie has told me all about it. It looks exactly to a dot as I expected, and I'm sure Christie will be even better."

The two travelling companions looked lovingly at her, and remembered how near they had come to losing their friend only a little while before, and said no more to dampen her high spirits. This trip was for Hazel, to bring back the roses to her cheeks; and father, mother, brother, and friends were determined to do all they could to make it a success.

It was the morning after they arrived at the hotel that Hazel asked to be taken at once to see Christie. She wanted to go alone; but, as that was not to be thought of in her convalescent state, she consented to take Ruth and Victoria with her.

"You'll go out in the orange-grove and visit with the chickens while I have a little heart-to-heart talk with Christie, won't you, you dears?" she said, as she gracefully gave up her idea of going alone.

The old man who drove the carriage that took them there was exceedingly talkative. Yes, he knew Christie Bailey; most everybody did. They imparted to him the fact that this visit was to be a surprise party, and arranged with him to leave them for an hour while he went on another errand and returned for them. These matters planned, they settled down to gleeful talk.

Victoria Landis on the front seat with the interested driver — who felt exceedingly curious about this party of pretty girls going to visit Christie Bailey thus secretly — began to question him.

"Is Christie Bailey a very large person?" she asked mischievously. "Is she as large as I am? You see we have never seen her."

The old man looked at her quizzically. "Never seen her? Aw! *O,*" he said dryly. "Wall, yas, fer a *girl,* I should say she *was* ruther *big.* Yas, I should say she was fully as big as you be — if not bigger."

"Has she very red hair?" went on Victoria. There was purpose in her mischief. She did not want Hazel to be too much disappointed.

"Ruther," responded the driver. Then he chuckled unduly, it seemed to Hazel, and added, "Ruther red."

"Isn't she at all pretty?" asked Ruth Summers, leaning forward with a troubled air, as if to snatch one ray of hope.

"Purty!" chuckled the driver. "Wall, no, I shouldn't eggzactly call her purty. She's got nice eyes," he added, as an afterthought.

"There!" said Hazel, sitting up triumphantly. "I knew her eyes were magnificent. Now *please* don't say any more."

The driver turned his twinkly little eyes around, and stared at Hazel, and then clucked the horse over the deep sandy road.

He set them down at Christie's gateway, telling them to knock at the cabin door, and they would be sure to be answered by the owner, and he would return within the hour. Then he drove his horse reluctantly away, turning his head back as far as he could see, hoping Christie would come to the door. He would like to see what happened. For half a mile down the road he laughed to the black-jacks, and occasionally ejaculated: "No, she ain't just to say *purty!* But she's *good.* I might 'a' told 'em she was good."

This was the driver's tribute to Christie.

Chapter 9
The Discovery

Hazel walked up to the door of the cabin in a dream of anticipation realized. Here were the periwinkles nodding their bright eyes along the border of the path, and there the chickens stood on one kid foot of yellow, as Christie had described.

She could almost have found the way here alone, from the letters she had received. She drank in the air, and felt it give new life to her, and thought of the pleasant hours she would spend with Christie during the weeks that were to follow, and of the secret plan she had of taking Christie back home with her for the winter.

They knocked at the door, which was open, and, stepping in, stood surrounded by the familiar things; and all three felt the delight of giving these few simple gifts, which had been so little to them when they were given.

Then a merry whistle sounded from the back yard and heavy steps on the board path at the back door, and Christie walked in from the barn with the frying-pan in one hand and a dish-pan in the other. He had been out to scrape some scraps from his table to the chickens in the yard.

The blood came quickly to his cheeks at sight of his three elegant visitors. He put the cooking-utensils down on the stove with a thud, and drew off his old straw hat, revealing his garnet-tinted hair in all its glory against the sunshine of a Florida sky in the doorway behind him.

"Is Christie Bailey at home?" questioned Victoria Landis, who seemed the natural spokesman for the three.

"*I* am Christie Bailey," said the young man gravely, looking from one to another questioningly. "Won't you sit down?"

There was a moment's pause before the tension broke, and then a pained, sweet voice, the voice of Christie's dreams, spoke forth.

"But Christie Bailey is a young woman."

Christie looked at Hazel, and knew his hour had come.

"No, *I* am Christie Bailey," he said once more, his great, honest eyes pleading for forgiveness.

"Do you really mean it?" said Victoria, amusement growing in her eyes as she noted his every fine point, noted the broad shoulders and the

54

way he had of carrying his head up, noted the flash of his eyes and the toss of rich waves from his forehead.

"And you're not a girl, after all?" questioned Ruth Summers in a frightened tone, looking with troubled eyes from Christie to Hazel, who had turned quite white.

But Christie was looking straight at Hazel, all his soul come to judgment before her, his mouth closed, unable to plead his own cause.

"Evidently not!" remarked Victoria dryly. "What extremely self-evident facts you find to remark upon, Ruth!"

But the others did not hear them. They were facing one another, these two who had held communion of soul for so many months, and who, now that they were face to face, were suddenly cut asunder by an insurmountable wall of a composition known as truth.

Hazel's dark eyes burned wide and deep from her white face. The enthusiasm that could make her love an unseen, unlovely woman, could also glow with the extreme of scorn for one whom she despised. The firm little mouth he had admired was set and stern. Her lips were pallid as her cheeks, while the light of truth and righteousness fairly scintillated from her countenance.

"Then you have been deceiving me all this time!" Her voice was high and clear, tempered by her late illness, and keen with pain. Her whole alert, graceful body expressed the utmost scorn. She would have done for a model of the figure of Retribution.

And yet in that awful minute, as Christie met her eye for eye, and saw the judgment of "Guilty" pronounced upon him, and could but acknowledge it just, and saw before him the blankness of the punishment that was to be his, he had time to think with a thrill of delight that Hazel was all and more than he had dreamed of her as being. He had time to be glad that she was as she was. He would not have her changed one whit, retribution and all.

It was all over in a minute; the sentence gone forth, the girl turned and marched with stately step out of the door down the white path to the road. But the little ripples of air she swept by in passing rolled back upon the culprit a knowledge of her disappointment, chagrin, and humiliation.

Christie bowed his head in acceptance of his sentence, and looked at his other two visitors, his eyes beseeching that they would go and leave him to endure what had come upon him. Ruth was clinging to Victoria's arm, frightened. She had seen the delicate white of Hazel's cheek as she went out the door. But Victoria's eyes were dancing with fun.

"Why didn't you *say* something?" she demanded of Christie. "Go out and stop her before she gets away! See, she is out there by the hedge. You can make it all right with her." There was pity in her voice. She liked the honest eyes and fine bearing of the young man. Besides, she loved fun, and did not like to see this most enticing situation spoiled at the climax.

A light of hope sprang into Christie's eyes as he turned to follow her suggestion. It did not take him long to overtake Hazel's slow step in the deep, sandy way.

"I must tell you how sorry I am —" he began before he had quite caught up to her.

But she turned and faced him with her hand lifted in protest.

"If you are sorry, then please do not say another word. I will forgive you, of course, because I am a Christian; but don't ever speak to me again. I HATE deceit!" Then she turned and sped down the road like a flash, in spite of her weakness.

And Christie stood in the road where she left him, his head bared to the winter's sunshine, looking as if he had been struck in the face by a loved hand, his whole strong body trembling.

Victoria meanwhile was taking in the situation. She espied Hazel's photograph framed in a delicate tracery of Florida moss. Then she frowned. Hazel would never permit that to stay here now, and her instinct told her that it would be missed by its present owner, and that he had the kind of honor that would not keep it if it were demanded.

"This must not be in sight when Hazel comes back," she whispered softly, disengaging herself from Ruth's clinging hand, and going vigorously to work. She took down the photograph, slipped off the moss, and, looking about for a place of concealment, hid it in the breast pocket of an old coat lying on a chair near by. Then, going to the door, she watched for developments; but, as she perceived that Hazel had fled and Christie was dazed, she made up her mind that she was needed elsewhere, and, calling Ruth, hurried down the road.

"If you miss anything, look in your coat pocket for it," she said as she passed Christie in the road. But Christie was too much overcome to take in what she meant.

He went back to his cabin. The light of the world seemed crushed out for him. Even the organ and the couch and the various pretty touches that had entered his home through these Northern friends of a year ago seemed suddenly to have withdrawn themselves from him, as if they had discovered the mistake in his identity, and were frowning their disapproval and letting him know that he was holding property under false pretenses. Only the loving eyes of the pictured Christ looked tenderly at him, and with a leap of his heart Christie realized that Hazel had given him one thing that she could never take away.

With something almost like a sob he threw himself on his knees before the picture and cried out in anguish, "My Father!"

Christie did not get supper that night. He forgot that there was any need for anything but comfort and forgiveness in the world. He knelt there, praying, sometimes, but most of the time just letting his heart lie bleeding and open before his Father's eyes.

The night came on, and still he knelt.

By and by there came a kind of comfort in remembering the little black girl's words, "You all's Fathah's not dead." He was not cut off from his Father. Something like peace settled upon him, a resignation and a strength to bear.

To think the situation over clearly and see whether there was aught he could do was beyond him. His rebuke had come. He could not justify himself. He had done wrong, though without intention. Besides, it was too late to do anything now. He had been turned out of Eden. The angel with the flaming sword had bidden him no more think to enter. He must go forth and labor, but God was not dead.

The days after that passed slowly and dully. Christie hardly took account of time. He was like one laden with a heavy burden and made to draw it on a long road. He had started, and was plodding his best every day, knowing that there would be an end sometime; but it was to be hard and long.

Gradually he came out of the daze that Hazel's words had put upon him. Gradually he felt himself forgiven by God for his deceit. But he would not discuss even with his own heart the possibility of forgiveness from Hazel. She was right, of course. He had known from the first that her friendship did not belong to him. He would keep the memory of it safe; and by and by, when he could bear to think it over, it would be a precious treasure. At least, he could prove himself worthy of the year of her friendship he had enjoyed.

But, thinking his sad thoughts and going about the hardest work he could find, he avoided the public road as much as possible, taking to the little by-paths when he went out from his own grove. And thus one morning, emerging from a tangle of hummock land where the live-oaks arched high above him, and the wild grape and jessamine snarled themselves from magnolia to bay-tree in exquisite patterns, and rare orchids defied the world of fashion to find their hidden lofty homes, Christie heard voices near and the soft footfalls of well-shod horses on the rich, rooty earth of the bridle-path.

He stepped to one side to let the riders pass, for the way was narrow. Just where a ray of sunlight came through a clearing he stood, and the light fell all about him, on his bared head, for he held his hat in his hand, making his head look like one from a painting of an old master, all the copper tints shining above the clear depths of his eyes.

He knew who was coming. It was for this he had removed his hat. His forehead shone white in the shadowed road, where the hat had kept off the sunburn; and about his face had come a sadness and a dignity that glorified his plainness.

Hazel rode the forward horse. She looked weary, and the flush in her cheeks was not altogether one of health. She was controlling herself wonderfully, but her strength was not what they had hoped it would be when they brought her to the Southland. The long walk she had taken under pressure of excitement had almost worn her out, and she had been unable to go out since, until this afternoon, when with the sudden wilfulness of the convalescent she had insisted upon a horseback ride. She had gone much further than her two faithful friends had thought wise, and then suddenly turned toward home, too weary to ride rapidly.

And now she came, at this quick turn, upon Christie standing, sun-glorified, his head inclined in deference, his eyes pleading, his whole bearing one of reverence.

She looked at him, and started, and knew him. That was plain. Then, her face a deadly white, her eyes straight ahead, she rode by magnificently, a steady, unknowing gaze that cut him like a knife just glinting by from her in passing.

He bowed his head, acknowledging her right to do thus with him; but all the blood in his body surged into his face, and then, receding, left him as white as the girl who had just passed by him.

Victoria and Ruth, behind, saw and grieved. They bowed graciously to him as if to try to make up for Hazel's act, but he scarcely seemed to see them, for he was gazing down the narrow shadowed way after the straight little figure sitting her horse so resolutely and riding now so fast.

"I did not know you could be so cruel, Hazel," said Victoria, riding forward beside her. "That fellow was just magnificent, and you have stabbed him to the heart."

But Hazel had stopped her horse, dropped her bridle, and was slipping white and limp from her saddle to the ground. She had not heard.

It was Sunday morning before they had time to think or talk more about it. Hazel had made them very anxious. But Sunday morning she felt a little better, and they were able to slip into her darkened room, one at a time, and say a few words to her.

"Something must be done," said Victoria decidedly, scowling out the window at the ripples of the blue lake below the hotel lawn. "I cannot understand how this thing has taken so great a hold upon her. But I feel sure it is that and nothing else that is making her so ill. Don't you feel so, Ruth?"

"It is the disappointment," said Ruth with troubled eyes. "She told me this morning that it almost shook her faith in prayer and God to think that she should have prayed so for the conversion of that girl's soul —"

"And then found out it was a creature, after all, without a soul?" laughed Victoria. She never could refrain from saying something funny whenever she happened to think of it.

But Ruth went on.

"It wasn't his being a man, at all, instead of a girl. She wouldn't have minded who he or she was, if it had not been for the deceit. She says he went through the whole thing with her, professed to be converted and to be a very earnest Christian, and pray for other people, and talked about Christ in a wonderful way — and now to think he did it all for a joke, it just crushes her. She thinks he deceived her of course in those things, too. She says a man who would deceive in one thing would do so in another. She does not believe now even in his Sunday school. And then you know she is so enthusiastic that she must have said a lot of loving things to him. She is just horrified to think she has been carrying on a first-class low-down flirtation with an unknown stranger. I think the sooner she gets away from this country, the better. She ought to forget all about it."

"But she wouldn't forget. You know Hazel. And, besides, the doctor says it might be death to her to go back into the cold now in the present state of her health. No, Ruth, something else has got to be done."

"What can be done, Victoria? You always talk as if *you* could do *any*thing if you only set about it."

"I'm not sure but I could," said Victoria, laughing. "Wait and see. This thing has got to be reduced to plain, commonplace terms, and have all the heroics and tragics taken out of it. I may need your help; so hold yourself in readiness."

After that Victoria went to her room, whence she emerged about an hour later, and took her way by back halls and by-paths, and finally unseen, down the road.

She was not quite sure of her way, but by retracing her steps occasionally she brought up in front of Christie's cabin just as Aunt Tildy was settling her spectacles for the opening hymn.

She reconnoitred a few minutes till the singing was well under way, and then slipped noiselessly through the sand to the side of the house, where after a few experiments she discovered a crevice through which she could get a limited view of the Sunday school.

A smile of satisfaction hovered about her lips. At least, the Sunday school was a fact. So much she learned from her trip. Then she settled herself to listen.

Christie was praying.

It was the first time Christie's voice had been heard by any one but his Master in prayer. It had happened simply enough. Uncle Moses had been sent away to the village for a doctor for a sick child, and there was no one else to pray. To Christie it was not such a trial as it would have been a year ago. He had talked with his heavenly Father many times since that first cry in the night. But he was not an orator. His words were simple.

"Jesus Christ, we make so many mistakes, and we sin so often. Forgive us. We are not worth saving, but we thank Thee that Thou dost love us, even though all the world turn against us, and though we hate our own selves."

Victoria found her eyes filling with tears. If Hazel could but hear that prayer!

Chapter 10
Victoria Has a Finger in the Pie

During the singing of the next hymn the organist came within range of the watcher's eye, and she noted with surprise the young man to whom she had been introduced in the hotel parlor a few evenings before, Mr. Mortimer. He was a cousin of those Mortimers from Boston who roomed next to Ruth. He would be at the hotel again. He would be another link in the evidence. For Victoria had set out to sift the character of Christie Bailey through and through.

She was chained to the spot by her interest during the blackboard lesson, which by shifting her position a trifle she could see as well as hear; but during the singing of the closing hymn she left in a panic, and when the dusky crowd flowed out into the road she was well on her way toward home, and no one save the yellow-footed chickens that had clucked about her feet were the wiser.

Victoria did not immediately make known to Ruth the events of the afternoon. She had other evidence to gather before she presented it before the court. She wanted to be altogether sure of Christie before she put her finger in the pie at all. Therefore she was on the lookout for young Mr. Mortimer.

She had hoped he would visit his aunt Sunday evening, but if he did he was not in evidence. All day Monday she haunted the piazzas and entrances, but he did not come until Tuesday evening.

Victoria in the meanwhile had made herself agreeable to Mrs. Mortimer, and it did not take her long to monopolize the young man when he finally came. Indeed, he had been attracted to her from the first.

They were soon seated comfortably in two large piazza chairs, watching the moon rise out of the little lake and frame itself in wreaths of long gray moss which reached out lace-like fingers and seemed to try to snare it; but always it slipped through until it sailed high above, serene. So great a moon, and so different from a Northern moon!

Victoria had done justice to the scene with a fine supply of adjectives, and then addressed herself to her self-set task.

"Mr. Mortimer, I wonder if you know a man by the name of Bailey down here, Christie Bailey. Tell me about him, please. Who is he, and how did he come by such a queer name? Is it a diminutive of Christopher?"

She settled her fluffy draperies about her in the moonlight, and fastened her fine eyes on Mortimer interestedly; and he felt he had a pleasant task before him to speak of his friend to this charming girl.

"Certainly, I know Chris well. He's one of the best fellows in the world. Yes, his name is an odd one, a family name, I believe, his mother's family name, I think he told me once. No, no Christopher about it, just plain Christie. But how in the world do you happen to know anything about him? He told me once he hadn't a friend left in the North."

Victoria was prepared for this.

"O, I heard some one talking about a Sunday school he had started, and I am interested in Sunday schools myself. Did he come down here as a sort of missionary, do you know?"

She asked the question innocently enough, and Mortimer waxed earnest in his story.

"No, indeed! No missionary about Christie. Why, Miss Landis, a year ago Christie was one of the toughest fellows in Florida. He could play a fine hand at cards, and could drink as much whiskey as the next one; and there wasn't one of us with a readier tongue when it was loosened up with plenty of drinks —"

"I hope you're not one of that kind?" said Victoria, earnestly, looking at the fine, restless eyes and handsome profile outlined in the moonlight.

A shade of sadness crossed his face. No one had spoken to him like that in many a long day. He turned and looked into her eyes earnestly.

"It's kind of you to care, Miss Landis. Perhaps if I had met some one like you a few years ago, I should have been a better fellow." Then he sighed and went on:

"A strange change came over Christie about a year ago. Some one sent him an organ and some fixings for his room, supposing he was a girl — from his name, I believe. They got hold of his name at the freight-station where his goods were shipped. They must have been an uncommon sort of people to send so much to a stranger. There was a fine picture, too, which he keeps on his wall, some religious work of a great artist, I think. He treasures it above his orange-grove, I believe.

"Well, those things made the most marvellous change in that man. You wouldn't have known him. Some of us fellows went to see him soon after it happened, and we thought it would be a joke to carry out the suggestion that had come with the organ that Christie start a Sunday school; so we went and invited neighbors from all round, and went up there Sunday, and fixed seats all over his cabin.

"He was as mad as could be, but he couldn't help himself; so, instead of knocking us all out and sending the audience home, he just pitched in and had a Sunday school. He wouldn't allow any laughing, either. We fellows had taken lunch and a case of bottles over to make the day a success; and, when Armstrong — he's the second son of an earl — came in with the case of liquor, Chris rose in his might. Perhaps you don't know Christie has red hair. Well, he has a temper just like it, — and he suddenly rose up and fairly blazed at us, eyes and hair and face. He looked like a strong avenging angel. I declare, he was magnificent. We never knew he had it in him before.

"Well, from that day forth he took hold of that Sunday school, and he changed all his ways. He didn't go to any more 'gatherings of the clan,' as we called them. We were all so proud of him we wouldn't have let him if he had tried.

"The fellows, some of them, come to the Sunday school and help every Sunday — sing, you know, and play. We all stand by him. He's good as gold. There's not many could live alone in a Florida orange-grove from one year's end to another and keep themselves from evil the way Christie Bailey has. Wouldn't you like to see the Sunday school sometime? I'll get Chris to let me bring you if you say so."

Victoria smilingly said she would enjoy it; and then, her interest in Christie Bailey satisfied, she turned her attention to the young man before her.

"You didn't answer my question a while ago, about yourself." There was pleading in Victoria's voice, and the young man before her was visibly embarrassed. The tones grew more earnest. The moon looked down upon the two sitting there quietly. The voices of the night were all about them, but they heard not. Victoria had found a mission of her own while trying to straighten out another's.

But the next morning early Victoria laid out her campaign. She took Ruth out for a walk, and on the way she told her what she intended to do.

"And you propose to go to Christie Bailey's house this morning, Victoria, without telling Hazel anything about it? Indeed, Vic, I'm not going to do any such thing. What would Mrs. Winship say?"

"Mrs. Winship will say nothing about it, for she will never know anything about it. Besides, I don't care what she says so long as we straighten things out for Hazel. Don't you see Hazel must be made to understand that she hasn't failed, after all, that the young man was in earnest, and really meant to be a Christian, and that the only thing he failed in was in not having courage to speak out and tell her she had made a mistake? He didn't intend any harm, and after it had gone on for a while of course it was all the harder to tell. Now, Ruth, there's no use in your saying you won't go; for I've *got* to have a chaperone, you know; I couldn't go alone, and I *shall* go with or without you; so you may as well come."

Reluctantly Ruth went, half fearful of the result of this daring girl's plan, and only half understanding what it was she meant to do.

Christie came to the door when they knocked. He looked eagerly beyond them into the sunshine, hunting for another face, but none appeared. Victoria's eyes were dancing.

"She isn't here," she said mockingly, rightly interpreting his searching gaze. "So you'd better ask us in, or you won't find out what we came for. It is very warm out here in the sun."

Christie smiled a sad smile, and asked them in. He could not conjecture what they had come for. He stood gravely waiting for them to speak.

"Now, sir," said Victoria with decision, "I want you to understand that you have been the cause of a great deal of suffering and disappointment."

Christie's face took on at once a look of haggard misery as he listened anxiously, not taking his eyes from the speaker's face. Victoria was enjoying her task immensely. The young man looked handsomer with that abject expression on. It would do him no harm to suffer a little longer. Anyway, he deserved it, she thought.

"You were aware, I think, from a letter Miss Summers wrote you, that Miss Winship has been very ill indeed before she came down here — that she almost died."

Here Ruth nodded her head severely. She felt like meting out judgment to this false-hearted young man.

"You do not know perhaps that the long walk she took from your house last week, after the startling revelation she received here, was enough to have killed her in her weak state of health."

Christie's white, anxious face gave Victoria a flitting twinge of conscience as she began to realize that possibly the young man had suffered enough already without anything added by her, but she went on with her prepared programme.

"You probably do not know that, after she had controlled herself the other day when she was riding horseback until she had passed you by, she was utterly overcome by the humiliation of the sight of you, and slipped from her horse in the road, unconscious, since which time she has been hovering between life and death —"

Victoria had carefully weighed that sentence, and decided that, while it might be a trifle overdrawn, the circumstances nevertheless justified the statement, for truly they had held grave fears for Hazel's life several times during the last two or three days.

But a groan escaped the young man's white lips, and Victoria, springing to her feet, realized that his punishment had been enough. She went toward him involuntarily, a glance of pity in her face.

"Don't look like that!" she said. "I think she will get well; but I think, as you're to blame for a good deal of the trouble, it is time you offered to do something."

"What could I do?" said Christie in hoarse eagerness.

"Well, I think perhaps if you were to explain to her how it all happened it might change the situation somewhat."

"She has forbidden me to say a word," answered Christie in white misery.

"O, she has, has she?" said Victoria, surveying him with dissatisfaction. "Well, you ought to have done it anyway! You should have *insisted!* That's a man's part. She's got to know the truth somehow, and get some of the tragic taken out of this affair, or she will suffer for it, that's all; and there's no one to explain but you. You see it isn't the pleasantest thing to find one has written all sorts of confidences to a strange young man. Hazel is blaming herself as any common flirt might do if she had a conscience. But that, of course, though extremely humiliating to her pride, isn't the worst. She feels terribly about your having deceived her and pretending that you were a Christian, and she all the time praying out her life for you, while you were having a good joke out of it. It has hurt her self-respect a good deal, but it has hurt her religion more."

Christie raised his head in protest, but Victoria went on.

"Wait a minute, please. I want to tell you that I believe she is mistaken. I don't believe you were playing a part in telling her you had become a Christian, were you? Or that you were making fun of her enthusiasm and trying to see how far she would go, just for fun?"

"I have never written anything in joke to Miss Winship. I honor and respect her beyond any one else on earth. I have never deceived her in anything except that I did not tell her who I was. I thought there was no harm in it when I did it, but now I see it was a terrible mistake. And I feel that I owe my salvation to Miss Winship. She introduced me to Jesus Christ. I am trying to make Him my guide."

The young man raised his head, and turned his eyes with acknowledgment toward the pictured Christ as he made his declaration of faith.

Victoria and Ruth were awed into admiration.

"I almost expected to see a halo spring up behind his aureole of copper hair," said Victoria to Ruth on the way home.

Victoria had arranged to send him word when he could see Hazel, and the two girls went away, leaving Christie in a state of conflicting emotions. He could do nothing. He sat and thought and thought, going over all his acquaintance with Hazel, singling out what he had told her of his own feelings toward Christ. And she had thought he had done it all in joke! He began to see how hideous had been his action in her eyes. Knowing her pure, lovely soul as he did through her letters, he felt keenly for her. How could he blame her for her saintly condemning of him? And it was that day that he found in the breast pocket of his old working-coat the photograph of Hazel so much prized and so sadly missed since the day of her visit. He had supposed Victoria took it, but now he recalled her words about it as she ran after Hazel; and, smiling into the sweet, girlish face, he wondered whether she would ever forgive him.

The next day there came a note from Victoria, saying he might call at seven o'clock on Saturday evening, and Hazel would likely be able to see him a few minutes. A postscript in the writer's original style added: "And I *hope* you'll have sense enough to know what to say! If you don't, I'm sure I can't do anything more for you."

And Christie echoed the cry too deeply to be able to smile over it.

Victoria had laid her plans carefully. She arranged to spend more time with Hazel than she had been doing, pleading a headache as an excuse from going out for a ride in the hot sun, and sending Mrs. Winship in her place more than once. She found that Hazel had no intention of opening her heart to her; so she determined to make a move herself.

Hazel had been very quiet for a long time. Victoria thought she was asleep until at last she noticed a little quiver of her lip and the tiniest glisten of a tear rolling down the thin white cheek.

Without seeming to see she got up and moved around the room a moment, and then in a cheery tone began to tell her story.

"Hazel, dear, I'm going to tell you where I went last Sunday. It was so interesting! I wandered off alone out into the country, and by and by I heard some singing in a little log cabin by the road, and I slipped into the yard behind some crape myrtle bushes all in lovely bloom, where I was entirely hidden.

"I looked through a crack between the logs, and there I saw three rows of black children, and some older people, too, and at the organ — for there was a nice organ standing against the wall — sat Mr. Mortimer, that young man we met in the parlor the other evening, Mrs. Boston Mortimer's nephew, you know. There were some other white young men, too; and they were all singing.

"And after the singing there was a prayer. One of the young men prayed. It was all about being forgiven for mistakes and sins, and not being worth Christ's saving. It was a beautiful prayer! And, Hazel, it was Christie Bailey who prayed!"

Chapter 11
A Daring Manoeuvre

Hazel caught her breath, when she heard of Christie's prayer, and a bright flush glowed on her cheek; but Victoria went on:

"Then he taught the lesson, and he did it well. Those little children never stirred, they were so interested; and just as they were singing the closing hymn I came away in a hurry so they would not see me."

Victoria had timed her story from the window. She knew the carriage had returned and that Mother Winship would soon appear at the door-way. There would be no chance for Hazel to speak until she thought about the Sunday school a little while. The footsteps were coming along the hall now, and she could hear Ruth calling to Hazel's brother. She had one more thing to say. She came quite near to the couch, and whispered in Hazel's ear:

"Hazel, I don't believe he has deceived you about everything. I believe you have done him a great deal of good. Don't fret about it, dear."

Hazel was brighter that evening, and often Victoria caught her looking thoughtfully at her. The next day when they were left alone she said, "Tell me what sort of lesson they had at the Sunday school, Vic, dear."

And Victoria launched into a full account of the blackboard lesson and the queer-shaped little cards, which she could not quite see through the crack, that were passed around at the close, and treasured, she could see. Then cautiously she told of the interview with Mr. Mortimer and his account of Christie's throwing the bottles out the door. The story lost none of its color from Victoria's repetition of it; and, when she finished, Hazel's eyes were bright and she was sitting up and smiling.

"Wasn't that splendid, Vic?" she said, and then remembered and sank back thoughtfully upon the couch.

Victoria was glad the others came in just then and she could slip away. She had said all she wished to say at present, and would let things rest now until Saturday evening when Christie came.

Victoria had arranged with Mrs. Winship to stay up-stairs and have dinner with Hazel on Saturday evening while the family with Ruth Summers went down to the dining-room. She also arranged with the head waiter to send up Hazel's dinner early. And so by dint of much manoeuvring the coast was clear at seven, Hazel's dinner and her own disposed of, and the family just gone down to the dining-room, where they would be safe for at least an hour.

It was no part of Victoria's plan that Mother Winship or Tom or the Judge should come in at an inopportune moment and complicate affairs until Hazel had had everything fully explained to her. After that Victoria felt that she would wash her hands of the whole thing.

Mother Winship had just rustled down the hall, and Victoria, who had been standing by the hall door, waiting until she should be gone, came over to where Hazel sat in a great soft chair by an open fire of pine-knots.

"Hazel," she said in her matter-of-fact, everyday tone, "Christie Bailey has come to know if he may see you for a few minutes. He wants to say a few words of explanation to you. He has really suffered very much, and perhaps you will feel less humiliated by this whole thing if you let him explain. Do you feel able to see him now?"

Hazel looked up, a bright flush on her cheeks.

Victoria betrayed by not so much as the wavering of an eyelash that she was anxious as to the outcome of this simple proposal. Hazel's clear eyes searched her face, and she bore the scrutiny well.

Then Hazel sighed a troubled little breath, and said: "Yes, I will see him, Vic. I feel quite strong to-night, and — I guess it will be better, after all, for me to see him."

Then Victoria felt sure that it was a relief to have him come, and that Hazel had been longing for it for several days.

Christie came in gravely with the tread of one who entered a sacred place, and yet with the quiet dignity of a "gentleman unafraid." Indeed, so far had the object of his visit dominated him that he forgot to shrink from contact with the fashionable world from which he had been so entirely shut away for so long.

He was going to see Hazel. It was the opportunity of his life. As to what came after, it mattered not, now that the great privilege of entering her presence had been accorded him. He had not permitted himself to believe that she would see him even after he had sent up his card, as directed, to Miss Landis.

Victoria shut the door gently behind him, and left them together. She had prepared a chair not far away, where she might sit and guard the door against intrusion; and so she sat and listened to the far-away hum of voices in the dining-room, the tinkle of silver and glass, and the occasional burst from the orchestra in the balcony above the dining-room. But her heart stood still outside the closed door, and wondered whether she had done well or ill, and feared — now that she had done it — all evil things that can pass in review at such a time for judgment on one's own deeds.

Christie stood still before Hazel. The sight of her so thin and white, changed even from a week ago, startled him, — condemned him again, took away his power of speech for the moment.

She was all in soft white cashmere draperies, with delicate lace that fell over the little white wrists as petals of a flower. Her soft brown hair made a halo for her face, and was drawn simply and carelessly together at the back. Christie had never seen any one half so lovely. He caught his breath in admiration of her. He stood and did her reverence.

For one long minute they looked at each other, and then Hazel, who felt it hers to speak first, as she had silenced him before, said, as a young queen might have said, with just the shadow of a smile flickering over her face, "You may sit down."

The gracious permission, accompanied by a slight indication of the chair facing her own by the fire, broke the spell that bound Christie's tongue, and with a heart beating high over what he had come to say he began.

And the words he spoke were not the carefully planned words he had arranged to set before her. They had fled and left his soul bare before her gaze. He had nothing to tell but the story of himself.

"You think I have deceived you," he said, speaking rapidly because his heart was going in great, quick bounds; "and because I owe to you all the good that I have in life I have come to tell you the whole truth about myself. I thank you for having given me a few minutes to speak to you, and I will try not to weary you. I have been too much trouble to you already.

"I was a little lonely boy when my mother died —" Christie lowered his head as he talked now, and the firelight played fanciful lights and shades with the richness of his hair.

"Nobody loved me that I know of, unless it was my father. If he did, he never showed it. He was a silent man, and grieved about my mother's death. I was a homely little fellow, and they have always said I had the temper of my hair. My aunt used to say I was hard to manage. I think that was true. I must have had some love in my heart, but nothing but my mother ever called it forth. I went through school at war with all my teachers. I got through because I naturally liked books.

"Father wanted me to be a farmer, but I wanted to go to college; so he gave me a certain sum of money and sent me. I used the money as I pleased, sometimes wisely and sometimes unwisely. When I got out of money, I earned some more or went without it. Father was not the kind of man to be asked for more. I had a good time in college, though I can't say I ranked as well as I might have done. I studied what I pleased, and left other things alone. Father died before I graduated, and the aunt who kept house for him soon followed; and, when I was through college, I had no one to go to and no one to care where I went.

"Father had signed a note for a man a little before he died, with the usual result of such things, and there was very little remaining for him to leave to me. What there was I took and came to Florida, having a reckless longing to see a new part of the world, and make a spot for myself. I never had known what home was since I was a little fellow, and I believe I was homesick for a home and something to call my own. Land was cheap, and it was easy to work, I thought, and my head was filled with dreams of my future; but I soon saw that oranges did not grow in a day and produce fortunes.

"Life was an awfully empty thing. I used sometimes to lie awake at night and wonder what death would be, and if it wouldn't be as well to try it. But something in my mother's prayer for me when I was almost a baby always kept me from it. She used to pray, 'God make my little Chris a good man.'

"I began to get acquainted with a lot of other fellows in the same fix with myself after a while. They were all sick of life, — at least, the life down here, and hard work and interminable waiting. But they had found something pleasanter than death to make them forget.

"I went with them, and tried their way. They played cards. I played, too. I could play well. We would drink and drink, and play and drink again —"

A little moan escaped from the listener, and Christie looked up to find her eyes filled with tears and her fingers clutching the arms of the chair till the nails were pink against the finger-tips with the pressure.

"O, I am doing you more harm!" exclaimed Christie. "I will stop!"

"No, no," said Hazel. "Go on, please;" and she turned her face aside to brush away the tears that had gathered.

"I was always ashamed when it was over. It made me hate myself and life all the more. I often used to acknowledge to myself that I was doing about as much as I could to see that my mother's prayer didn't get answered. But still I went on just the same way every little while. There didn't seem to be anything else to do.

"Then the night before Christmas came. It wasn't anything to me more than any other day. It never had been since I was a mere baby. Mother used to fill my stocking with little things. I remember it just once.

"But this Christmas I felt particularly down. The orange-trees were not doing as well as I had hoped. I was depressed by the horror of the monotony of my life, behind and before. Then your things came, and a new world opened before me.

"I wasn't very glad of it at first. I am afraid I resented your kindness a little. Then I began to see the something homelike they had brought with them, and I could not help liking it. But your letter gave me a queer feeling. There seemed to be obligations I could not fulfil. I didn't like to keep the things, because you wanted a Sunday school. I was much more likely to conduct a saloon or a pool-room at that time than a Sunday school.

"Then I hung that picture up. You know what effect it had upon me. I have told you of my strange dream or vision or whatever it was. Yes, it was all true. I never deceived you about that or anything else except that I did not tell you I was not what you supposed. I thought it might embarrass you if I did so at first, and then it seemed but a joke to answer you as if I were a girl. I never dreamed it would go beyond that first letter when I wrote thanking you."

His honest eyes were on her face, and Hazel could not doubt him.

"And then, when the writing went on, and the time came when I ought to have told you, there was something else held me back. Forgive me for speaking of it, but I was trying to be perfectly true to-night. You remember in that second letter that you wrote me, where you told me that you were praying for me, and — you —" Christie caught his breath, and murmured the words low and reverently, "You said you loved me —"

"Oh!" gasped Hazel, clasping her white hands over her face, while the blood rushed up to her very high temples and surged around her little seashell ears.

Chapter 12

The Whim Completes Its Justification

"Forgive me!" he pleaded. "It need not hurt you. I knew that love was not really mine. It was given to the girl you thought I was. I knew without ever having seen you that you would sooner have cut out your tongue than write anything like that to a strange man. I ought to have seen at once that I was stealing something that did not belong to me in appropriating that love.

"Perhaps I would not have put it from me even if I had seen it. For that love was very dear to me. Remember I had never been loved in the whole of my life by any one but a mother who had been gone such years! Remember there was no one else to claim that love from you.

"And remember I thought that you would never need to know. I never dreamed that you would try to search me out. Your friendship was too dear to me for me to dare to try; and, too, I knew you would consider me far beneath you. I could never hope to have you for the most distant friend, even if you had known all about me from childhood.

"My hope for your help and comfort and friendship was in letting you suppose me a lonely old maid. Remember you said it yourself. I simply did not tell you what I was.

"But I do not take one bit of blame from myself. I see now that I ought to have been a good enough man to have told you at once. I should have missed a great deal, perhaps, as human vision sees it, have missed even heaven itself, unless the very giving up of heaven for right had gained heaven for me.

"I can see it was all wrong. The Father even then had spoken to my heart. He would have found me in some other way, perhaps; and it would have been your doing all the same, and I should have had the joy of thanking you even so for my salvation. But I did not, and now my punishment is that I have brought this suffering and disappointment and chagrin upon you. And if I could I would now be willing to wipe out of my life all the joy that has come to me through companionship with you by letters, if by so doing I might save you from this annoyance.

"For I have one more thing to tell you, and I will ask you to remember that I have never but once, in so many words, dared to tell you this in

73

writing, and then only in a hidden way, because I thought if you knew all about me you would wish me not to say it. But now I must tell it. The punishment to me is very great, not only that you suffer, but that I have merited your scorn — for I love you! I love you with every bit of unused love from all my childhood days, in addition to all the love that a man's heart has to give. I have loved you ever since the night I read from your letter that you loved me — a poor, forlorn, homely girl as you thought — and that you thought I loved you too; and I knew at once that it was so.

"I want you to know that since that night I have had it ever before me to be a person worthy of loving you. I never dared put it 'worthy of your love,' because I knew that could never be for me. But I have tried to make myself a man such as you would not be ashamed to have love you, even though you could never think of loving in return. And I have fallen short in your eyes, I know. But in what you did not know of my life I have been true.

"Can you, knowing all this, forgive me? Then I shall go out and try to live my life as you and God would have me do, and remember the joy which was not mine. But you gave me one joy that you cannot take away. Jesus Christ is my Friend.

"Now I have said all there is to say, and I must go away and let you rest. Can you find it in your heart to say you forgive me?"

Christie rested his elbow on the arm of the chair, and dropped his head on his hand, while the firelight flickered and glowed among the waves of ruddy hair again. He had said all there was to say, and he felt he had no hope. Now he must go forth. The strength seemed suddenly to have left him.

It was very still in the room for a moment. They could hear each other breathe. At last Hazel's little white hand fluttered timidly out toward him, and rested like a rose-leaf among the dark curls.

It was his benediction, he thought, his dream come true. It was her forgiveness. He held his breath, and dared not stir.

And then, more timidly still, Hazel herself slipped softly from her chair to her knees before him. The other hand shyly stole to his shoulder, and she whispered: "Christie, forgive ME. I — love — *you.*"

Then Hazel's courage gave way, and she hid her blushing face against his sleeve.

Christie's heart leaped forth in all its manhood. He arose and drew her to her feet tenderly, and, folding his arms about her as one might enfold an angel come for shelter, he bent his tall head over till his face touched her lily face, and he felt that all his desolation was healed.

There were steps along the hall that instant, lingering noisily about the door, and a hand rattling the door-knob, while Victoria's voice, unnecessarily loud from Ruth's point of view, called: "Is that you, Ruth? Are the others through dinner yet? Would you mind stepping back to the office and getting the evening paper for me? I want to look at something."

Then the door opened, and Victoria came smiling in. "Time's up," she said playfully. "The invalid must not talk another word to-night."

Indeed, Victoria was most relieved that the time was up, and she looked anxiously from Hazel to Christie to see whether she had done more harm than good; but Hazel leaned back smiling and flushed in her chair, and Christie, standing tall and grave with an uplifted look upon his face, reassured her.

She led him away by another hall than that the family would come up by and was in so much hurry to get him away without being seen that she scarcely said a word to him. However, he did not know it.

"Well, is it all right?" she laughed nervously as they reached the side doorway.

"It is all right," he said with a joyous ring in his voice.

Through the hall, out the door, and down the steps went Christie Bailey, his hat in his hand, his face exalted, the moonlight "laying on his head a kingly crown." He felt that he had been crowned that night, crowned with a woman's love.

"He looks as if he had seen a vision," thought Victoria as she sped back to "view the ruins," as she expressed it to herself.

But Christie went on, his hat in his hand, down the long white road, looking up to the stars among the pines, wondering at the greatness of the world and the graciousness of God, on to his little cabin no longer filled with loneliness, and knelt before the pictured Christ and cried, "O my Father, I thank Thee."

Quite early in the morning Hazel requested a private interview with her father.

Now it was a well-acknowledged fact that Judge Winship was completely under his daughter's thumb; and, as the interview was a prolonged one, it was regarded as quite possible by the rest of the family party that there might be almost anything, from the endowment of a college settlement to a trip to Africa, in process of preparation; and all awaited the result with some restlessness.

But after dinner there were no developments. Hazel seemed bright and ready to sit on the piazza and be read to. Judge Winship took his umbrella and sauntered out for a walk, having declined the company of the various members of his family. Mother Winship calmed her anxieties, and concluded to take a nap.

Christie had gone about his morning tasks joyously. Now and again his heart questioned what he had to hope for in the future, poor as he was; but he put this resolutely down. He would rejoice in the knowledge of Hazel's forgiveness and her love, even though it never brought him anything else than that joy of knowledge.

In this frame of mind he looked forward exultantly to the Sunday-school hour. The young men when they came in wondered what had come over him, and the scholars greeted their superintendent with furtive nods and smiles.

During the opening of the Sunday school there came in an elderly gentleman of fine presence with iron-gray hair and keen blue eyes that looked piercingly out from under black brows. Christie had been praying when he came in. Christie's prayers were an index to his life. During the singing of the next hymn the superintendent came back to the door to give a book to the stranger, and, pausing in hesitation a moment, asked half shyly, "Will you say a few words to us, or pray?"

"Go on with your regular lesson, young man. I'm not prepared to speak. I'll pray at the close if you wish me to," said the stranger; and Christie went back to his place, somewhat puzzled and embarrassed by the unexpected guest.

He lingered after all were gone, having asked that he might have a few words with Christie alone. Christie noticed that Mortimer had bowed to him in going out, and that he looked back curiously once or twice.

"My name is Winship," said the Judge brusquely. "I understand young man, that you have told my daughter that you love her."

The color softly rose in Christie's temples till it flooded his whole face, but a light of love and of daring came into his eyes as he answered the unexpected challenge gravely, "I do, sir."

"Am I to understand, sir, by that, that you wish to marry her?"

Christie caught his breath. Hope and pain came quickly to defy one another. He stood still, not knowing what to say. He realized his helplessness, his unfitness for the love of Hazel Winship.

"Because," went on the relentless Judge, "in my day it was considered a very dishonorable thing to tell a young woman you loved her unless you wished to marry her; and, if you do not, I wish to know at once."

Christie was white now and humiliated.

"Sir," he said sternly, "I mean nothing dishonorable. I honor and reverence your daughter, yes, and love her, next to Jesus Christ," and involuntarily his eyes met those of the picture on the wall, "whom she has taught me to love. But, as your daughter has told you of my love, she must have also made you acquainted with the circumstances under which I told it to her. Had I not been trying to clear myself from a charge of deceit in her eyes, I should never have let her know the deep love I have for her; for I have nothing to offer her but my love. Judge Winship, is this the kind of home to offer to your daughter? It is all I have."

There was something pathetic, almost tragic, in the wave of Christie's hand as he looked around the cabin.

"Well, young man, it's a more comfortable place than my daughter's father was born in. There were worse homes than this. But perhaps you are not aware that my daughter will have enough of her own for two."

Christie threw his head back proudly, his eyes flashing bravely, though his voice was sad: "Sir, I will never be supported by my wife. If she comes to me, she comes to the home I can offer her; and it would have to be here, now, until I can do better."

"As you please, young man," answered the Judge shortly; but there was a grim smile upon his lips, and his eyes twinkled as if he were pleased. "I like your spirit. From all I hear of you you are quite worthy of her. She thinks so, anyway, which is more to the point. Have you enough to keep her from starving if she did come?"

"O, yes," Christie almost laughed in his eagerness. "Do you think — O, it *can*not be — that she would come?"

"She will have to settle that question," said her father, rising. "You have my permission to talk with her about it. As far as I can judge, she seems to have a fondness for logs with the bark on them. Good afternoon, Mr. Bailey. I am glad to have met you. You had a good Sunday school, and I respect you."

Christie gripped his hand until the old man almost cried out with the pain; but he bore it, grimly smiling, and went on his way.

And Christie, left alone in his little, glorified room, knelt once more, and called joyously: "My Father! My Father!"

"This is perfectly ridiculous," said Ruth Summers looking dismally out of the fast-flying car-window at the vanishing oaks and pines. "The wedding guests going off on the bridal tour, and the bride and bridegroom staying behind. I can't think whatever has possessed Hazel. Married in white cashmere under a tree, and not a single thing belonging to a wedding, not even a wedding breakfast —"

"You forget the wedding march," said Victoria, a vision of the organist's fine head coming to her, "and the strawberries for breakfast."

"A wedding march on that old organ," sneered Ruth, "with a row of black children for audience, and white sand for a background. Well, Hazel was original, to say the least. I hope she'll settle down now, and do as other people do."

"She won't," said Victoria positively. "She'll keep on having a perfectly lovely time all her life. Do you remember how she once said she was going to take Christie Bailey to Europe? Well, I reminded her of it this morning, and she laughed, and said she had not forgotten it; it was one thing she married him for, and he looked down at her wonderingly and asked what was that. How he does worship her!"

"Yes, and she's perfectly infatuated with him. I'm sure one would have to be, to live in a shanty. I don't believe I could love any man enough for that," she said reflectively, studying the back of Tom Winship's well-trimmed head in the next seat.

"Then you'd better not get married," said Victoria. She looked dreamily out of the window at the hurrying palmettos and added: "One might — if one loved enough;" and then she was silent, thinking of a promise that had been made her, a promise of better things, signed by a true look from a pair of handsome, courageous eyes.

Christie and Hazel watched the fast-flying train as it vanished from their sight, and then turned slowly toward their home.

"It is a palace to me now that you are in it, my wife!" Christie pronounced the words with wonder and awe.

"You dear old organ, it was you that did it all," said Hazel, touching the keys tenderly, and turning to Christie with tears of joy standing in her eyes she put her hands in his and said, "My husband."

Then as if by common consent they knelt together, hand in hand, beneath the picture of the Christ, and Christie prayed; and now his prayer began, "Our Father."